Reorganizing the Rust Belt

Reorganizing the Rust Belt

An Inside Study of the American Labor Movement

Steven Henry Lopez

UNIVERSITY OF CALIFORNIA PRESS

Berkeley   Los Angeles   London

University of California Press
Berkeley and Los Angeles, California

University of California Press, Ltd.
London, England

© 2004 by the Regents of the University of California

Library of Congress Cataloging-in-Publication Data
Lopez, Steven Henry, 1968–
    Reorganizing the Rust Belt : an inside study of the
American labor movement / Steven Henry Lopez.
        p.   cm.
    Includes bibliographical references and index.
    ISBN 0-520-23280-1 (cloth : alk. paper)
— ISBN 0-520-23565-7 (pbk. : alk. paper)
        1. Service industries workers—Labor unions—
Pennsylvania—Pittsburgh—Case studies.   2. Labor move-
ment—Pennsylvania—Pittsburgh.   3. Service Employees
International Union.   I. Title.
HD6515.S45 L67   2004
331.88'11'000974886—dc21   2003014236

Manufactured in the United States of America
12   11   10   09   08   07   06   05   04
10   9   8   7   6   5   4   3   2   1

The paper used in this publication meets the minimum
requirements of ANSI/NISO Z39.48–1992 (R 1997)
(Permanence of Paper). ⊚

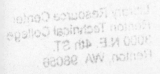

In Memory of Vincent Hearn Lopez

CONTENTS

Postindustrial Pittsburgh

*Low-Wage Work
and the Challenge for American Labor*

In the summer of 1976, as an eight-year-old boy, I took a train trip with my family from New York to St. Louis. One of my most distinct memories from that trip is of waking up in the early morning hours to find the train stopped in a station. Outside was a gray vista of dirty brick buildings. The faint smell of sulfur penetrated the train. It was raining. "Where are we?" I asked.

"We're in Pittsburgh," my father replied.

"What kind of a place is Pittsburgh?" I wanted to know.

"It's an ugly city," my dad said. "They make steel here. That's why it's so polluted. Just look at the soot on those buildings."

My father had no way of knowing that he was to be among the very last of a long line of visitors to register such impressions. Visitors to Pittsburgh had been remarking on its squalor and pollution and the hellish sight of its mills for nearly 100 years. In the 1880s, William Glazier wrote that upon arriving in Pittsburgh he felt as if he had "reached the outer edge of the infernal regions." In 1909, the *American Magazine* referred to the city as an "inferno." In 1931, Lincoln Steffens said that Pittsburgh "looked like hell, literally."[1] Anyone who views photographs of the city taken from the late 1800s to the 1940s can understand this reaction. Aerial views and pictures taken from the heights of the south-side hills show more smoke than city, while pictures of the mills them-selves show great spouts of flame and smoke shooting up into the sky, obscuring the sun by day and providing an eerie incandescence at night, when the flaming furnaces' light reflected off the low ceiling of smoky cloud. In 1976 my father could not suspect that all of this was about to end — but by the time I next returned to Pittsburgh as a 28-year-old doc-toral student, the Pittsburgh my father had described had become a city of memory. Of the dozens of steel mills that had still existed in south-western Pennsylvania 20 years before, only one remained. The Edgar Thomson Works, the first integrated steel mill in the region when it was built in 1875, was now also the last. The fires of the region's steel indus-tries, after burning for 100 years, had been almost entirely quenched; the skies were now clear. They don't make steel in Pittsburgh anymore.

Big steel and big labor were both born in Pittsburgh (both the Ameri-can Federation of Labor [AFL] and the Congress of Industrial Organi-zations [CIO] were founded here), and both died here as well, as pattern bargaining and the high-wage industrial economy collapsed together. Between 1974 and 1993, the Pittsburgh region lost 157,000 high-wage manufacturing jobs — just over 18 percent of the region's total employ-ment.[2] Others have ably told this story and chronicled its immediate human impact;[3] it is not my purpose to duplicate their efforts. Instead, rather than viewing the deindustrialization of Pittsburgh as an ending, I take this history as my starting point. How are we to understand Pitts-burgh a decade after deindustrialization, and does the answer to this question have any larger significance?

We can understand a great deal about Pittsburgh in the poststeel era by looking briefly at what happened in the 1990s in Homestead, just across the river from Pittsburgh. Here once stood the U.S. Steel Home-stead Works and the Mesta Machine company, both world-famous sym-bols of American manufacturing might. The Homestead works, which contained the largest plate steel mill in the world, made the armor for battleships and aircraft carriers that helped defeat fascism in World War

II and made steel for the great bridges of San Francisco and for many of the skyscrapers that came to dominate the skylines of American cities. Mesta Machine was a tool-and-die company that sent parts to the Soviet Union under lend-lease during the war. Nikita Khrushchev, who was a factory worker during the war, was so impressed with the Mesta Machine parts he used during that time that when he visited the United States in 1959, he insisted on coming to Pittsburgh to see Mesta Machine for himself.[4]

If you drive today over the Homestead High-Level Bridge from the Pittsburgh side of the Mon River, as you approach the southern bank you see the site of these former industrial behemoths stretching out for several miles in both directions on either side of the bridge. For more than 10 years, these sites were just brown, flat places along the river. Now, however, you see something new: the sites have been reclaimed for commerce. On the right, a 22-theater multiplex; on the left, a large shopping complex. Where Mesta Machine once stood, now there is a new water park. The old Pittsburgh economy employed at one time nearly 30,000 people on these sites; they were unionized workers who did difficult and often dangerous work, but they were very highly paid. (One former steelworker who worked at Homestead told me that in 1979, the year he was laid off, he made $70,000 in wages and overtime pay. In 2000 dollars that would be equal to about $160,000.)

The new shopping, recreation, and entertainment complex, on the other hand, will employ about 5,000 workers when it is fully completed. Construction is being done with nonunion labor, and almost all of the service employees here earn wages at or only slightly above the legal minimum wage of $5.15 per hour, or $10,300 for a full-time worker. This, then, is the face of postindustrial Pittsburgh. The new economy has created, not the "jobless future" or "end of work" painted by some writers,[5] but new jobs — so much so that the collapse of industrial employment in Pittsburgh has been neatly balanced by the rise of new jobs in the service occupations. In fact, so many new service jobs have been created that, despite the exodus of more than 150,000 industrial jobs between 1974 and 1993, total employment in the Pittsburgh metro area held steady (at 863,000) between 1974 and 1984 and then actually *grew* by 105,000 jobs by 1993.[6] With the worst of the plant closings over, in the second half of the 1990s, the Pittsburgh region's total employment continued to grow, reaching just under 1.1 million jobs in the first quarter of 2000.[7] Since the population of the Pittsburgh metro area was slowly declining throughout this period (by just over 2 percent in the 1990s), this job growth had pushed local unemployment under 5 percent by the first quarter of 2000.[8] The recession of 2001–2003 pushed Pittsburgh's unemployment rate back up to 7 percent by early 2003, but total employment in the metro area continued to rise slowly in 2001 and 2002 before falling back to just over 1.1 million in the first quarter of 2003.[9]

The problem facing postindustrial Pittsburgh, therefore, is not so much a dearth of jobs but rather the fact that the new jobs do not pay a living wage. What the region's growing legions of low-wage workers really need, in other words, is jobs that pay better. But most of Pittsburgh's new postindustrial employment is accounted for by the growth of low-wage jobs in retail, eating and drinking places, personal services, health care, and "business services" (which includes highly paid lawyers and financial analysts but also janitors, data entry clerks, copy shop employees, and so forth). Unlike the full-time, unionized, high-wage jobs of the industrial past, the new jobs are more likely to be part time, have fewer benefits, be nonunion, and pay poorly.

In some ways, then, Pittsburgh has come full circle. Before the 1930s, Pittsburgh's miners and metal workers earned poverty wages and lived in miserable, rat-infested slums. The passage of the Wagner Act and the unionization of steel and mining forced these industries to pay living wages, allowing these formerly downtrodden and poverty-stricken workers finally to join the ranks of the great American middle class. Today, the steelworkers and miners are gone, and rapidly vanishing with them is the very idea that working-class jobs ought to pay enough to raise a family, buy a house, take vacations, and put the kids through school. The new low-wage workers find themselves faced with the prospect of lifelong, working poverty. More than ever, they need a revitalized labor movement capable of forcing service employers to pay a fair day's wage for a fair day's work.

But what has become of the labor movement? What has happened to unions as a result of the collapse of southwestern Pennsylvania's industrial economy? To get a glimpse of this we must travel to another of Pittsburgh's old industrial suburbs on the north shore of the Allegheny River. Here another large steel mill was closed and torn down in the 1980s. In a working-class residential neighborhood that was once situated near the mill, the visitor to this neighborhood can observe a tidy, modern, two-story yellow-brick office building sitting incongruously in a narrow residential street. Inside, one can see on the walls a number of large, very old photographs. The photos are of steelworkers from the mill; the building was the offices of the mill's local of the United Steelworkers of America (USWA). The mill is gone; the USWA local is gone; all that remains of the old labor movement is the building and the pictures on the wall.

The pictures remain because the building now serves as the offices of Local A of the Service Employees International Union (SEIU). Here, in this building, we can see the old labor movement literally being superseded by the new: representing nearly 15,000 janitors, nursing home workers, school crossing guards, cafeteria workers, and clerks, Local A is now the second-largest union local in Pittsburgh. Local A began life in the 1960s as a truly marginal organization in the labor movement of southwestern Pennsylvania, representing a small number of janitors, clerks, and nursing home workers employed by Allegheny County. In the 1970s the union also began to organize and represent school district employees and employees of the other counties in the Pittsburgh area. In the 1980s, even as the industrial economy of Pittsburgh was crashing, the local began to organize nursing home workers in the private sector. By the end of the 1990s, Local A had organized about 3,000 nursing home workers, and the number continues to grow.

This study is about the inroads the SEIU is making into this new terrain of postindustrial work. In it, I explore the promise of this kind of organizing as well as the difficulties involved through an analysis of grassroots union campaigns involving Local A and its nursing home workers. The study is based on fieldwork I conducted in 1997 and 1998 as an organizing intern at Local A and on interviews and archival research conducted between 1997 and 1999. I entered the field with few preconceived notions about organizing, determined to find out whether I could discover in Local A's activities the key to the revitalization of labor.

But why should a study of new union organizing focus only on service workers? Why not follow the steel mills instead and study efforts by the steelworkers' union to organize the new mills of the American South? Such an undertaking would be fascinating and important, but I had two reasons for wanting to study service workers. First, while manufacturing is still important to the economy,[10] manufacturing *employment* is increasingly insignificant everywhere (not just in Pittsburgh or the Rust Belt) because of the tremendous increases in automation and the efficiency of manufacturing operations. The previously mentioned Edgar Thomson Works, the last integrated steel mill in southwestern Pennsylvania, provides a clear example to illustrate this point. Edgar Thomson produces as much steel today as it did 30 years ago — but the mill once employed more than 10,000 workers. Today, fully modernized with the latest computer-controlled oxygen furnaces and twin continuous casters, Edgar Thomson employs about 600 people. The story is the same in nearly all sectors of manufacturing. Making things is no longer a mass-employment proposition. Whether labor succeeds or fails in manufacturing is of declining significance to the fate of the union movement and to the working class as a whole.

Second, manufacturing workers increasingly must compete in a global labor market with poorly paid, yet highly efficient, export workers in places like Mexico, Brazil, Thailand, Singapore, and India.[11] Thus workers in the textile and garment industries, for example, find that when they unionize, firms simply move production offshore.[12] Indeed, the emerging global labor market may not be limited to manufacturing but may include certain kinds of services such as airline maintenance facilities and data entry services, which do not necessarily need to be located in a particular place. Under the current legal framework and given the increasing ease with which production in such industries can be relocated, workers and unions in these industries may truly face an untenable situation at present.

Conversely, not only do workers in nonmobile sectors have more potential leverage over employers than their counterparts in more foot-loose industries can muster, but the struggles of place-specific service workers have important implications for workers in industries directly subject to capital mobility. The only way to change the situation faced by workers in mobile sectors — at home and abroad — is by passing labor law reform and by forcing the U.S. government to make labor and environmental standards an integral part of American trade policy. But at present the movement is much too weak politically to push through a fundamental redefinition of labor law or trade policy. Such battles will have to be fought after — and if — the movement can succeed in retaking the parts of the U.S. economy that are not directly threatened by globalized production, that are among the fastest-growing low-wage sectors, and in which unions can do the most good in the short run: health care, retail, building services, and the hotel and restaurant industries. Until the labor movement solidifies and anchors its base in these sectors, it will not have the ability to radically change the context for organizing in manufacturing. This is why service sector organizing is so important and why, in my view, studying unions' efforts to organize service workers can tell us much about the prospects for the labor movement as a whole.

The nursing home industry is a good subject for such a study because it provides in many ways a prototypical example of the kind of low-wage, postindustrial service employment that is coming to typify Pittsburgh's economy. The private nursing home industry — which essentially did not exist before Medicare and Medicaid were passed in 1965 — is one of the fastest-growing industries in America.[13] Nurses'

aides, who constitute 85 percent of nursing home employees and perform nearly all of the hands-on care, earned an average wage of $6.06
nationally in 1996.[14] Low wages, backbreaking work, emotional strain,
and inadequate training combine to produce astronomical rates of employee turnover — more than 100 percent annually for the industry as a
whole.[15] Nurses' aides also suffer from extremely high rates of occupational injury.[16] Unless unions can somehow improve these workers' conditions on the job as well as their material standards of living, nursing
home work will never provide most nurses' aides with on-the-job dignity
and safety or a ladder out of poverty.

But if the story of Pittsburgh's uneven transition from the City of
Steel to a postindustrial economy leads to questions about unions' ability to organize postindustrial occupations like nursing home workers,
another question could well be asked: Why should we care about
Pittsburgh in the first place? Why come to Pittsburgh to study contemporary union organizing, when as a graduate student at Berkeley I could
just as easily have studied the efforts of the SEIU, Hotel Employees and
Restaurant Employees (HERE), and other unions to organize low-wage
service workers — nursing home workers, even — in my own backyard,
the Bay Area? Indeed, people do not typically come to Pittsburgh to
study new things! Instead, studies of such places typically focus on the
destruction of the old and the impact of that destruction.[17] Some writers have even suggested that new research on union organizing should
concentrate not on Rust Belt cities but on the fast-growing cities of the
Sunbelt — like Las Vegas, which John Sweeney has called the hottest
union city in the country.[18]

One reason to be interested in Pittsburgh is that while there is certainly much to be learned by studying organizing in the new cities of the
Southwest, old places do not go away. They continue to change, and it
is important to study what happens to them. In my view, to imagine that
places like Pittsburgh are no longer interesting because, we think, history has passed them by is to ape the way our economy uses up people
and places and then throws them away.

But I also had a more important reason in mind: I was interested in the *transition* between the old labor movement and the new, and I felt that studying union organizing in the Sunbelt would emphasize only the new. The places are new, the industries are new, the unions are new, and many of the workers are new immigrants. Pittsburgh, the prototypical Rust Belt city, was, I felt, the ideal locale for my study because it is in places like this that the new labor movement must really confront the legacies of the old. I wanted to explore how the local context of industrial unionism, its rise and its collapse, affected the contemporary efforts to organize service workers in the new economy. Hence the central questions of this study: If Pittsburgh has come, in a sense, full circle, does that mean that unions' problems today are the same as in the 1920s? Or has a half-century of a certain kind of industrial unionism left legacies that can be discerned most clearly in places like Pittsburgh? What are the dilemmas that unions like Local A must face as they attempt to build a new labor movement on the rubble of the old, and to what extent are they related to the history of the movement itself?

In defining the study this way, I have made choices, and choices always have consequences. My decision to study service sector organizing means that what I have to say in this study may not be very relevant to the experiences of unions attempting to organize in sectors directly affected by capital mobility. Likewise, just as the decision to study organizing immigrants in California leads Ruth Milkman and her contributors[19] to emphasize problems and opportunities that may not be critically important elsewhere, my study of nursing home organizing in Pittsburgh may emphasize some dilemmas that are less important in parts of the country where many low-wage workers are new immigrants or where the labor movement does not have a deeply rooted local history. On the other hand, the ability of the labor movement to reorganize old industrial areas is crucial in its own right — both for the future of the movement itself and for the American ideal of shared prosperity.

ACKNOWLEDGMENTS

I would like to thank the many members and officials of the Service Employees International Union who made this research possible by allowing me to study their union. I would also particularly like to thank Local A's staff director, referred to here as "Joe Reilly," for reading and commenting on drafts of my work. This research was completed with funding from the Sociology Department of the University of California at Berkeley, the Institute of International Studies at Berkeley, and Berkeley's Institute of Industrial Relations. I would like to thank all of these departments and organizations. Thanks also to Naomi Schneider of the University of California Press for her enthusiasm for the project, to production editor Kate Warne, and to copyeditor Elisabeth Magnus for her careful work and attention to detail. I would also like to thank photographer and friend Joe Blum for permission to use one of his pictures on the cover of this book. I am grateful to Eddy U, Kim Voss, Peter Evans, Ian Robinson, Rachel Sherman, Dan Clawson, Ruth Milkman, Sean O'Riain, and Dan Kovalik, each of whom read and commented on all or part of the manuscript or gave other assistance. I could never have completed this project without the unflagging support of Michael Burawoy, who always seemed convinced that I had it in me, even when I was sure he was mistaken. For his countless hours spent reading my work, commenting on drafts, and encouraging me to continue, I owe a debt of gratitude that is hard to put into words. Most of all, I want to say thank you to my wife, Kim Lopez. Kim read and commented on various pieces of the manuscript, tirelessly discussed the project with me, and through it all remained optimistic.

ONE

Introduction

From Business Unionism
to Social Movement Unionism

In the 1950s, the heyday of "Big Labor" in the United States, sociologists like Daniel Bell and Seymour Martin Lipset — representing the dominant liberal consensus of the day — defended the peculiarly American idea of business unionism against all critics. To those on the right who still saw trade unions as evidence of "creeping socialism," liberal sociologists argued that an increasingly "responsible" and "mature" American trade union movement had properly jettisoned dangerous ideas about class struggle, and they noted approvingly that unions had abandoned ideology and social criticism in favor of a more narrow conception of their role: to provide representation services on the shop floor and in collective bargaining over hours, wages, and conditions of work. To those on the left who criticized business unionism precisely for its top-down forms of organization, low participation rates, and self-aggrandizing leaders, liberal sociologists replied that while business unions might be undemocratic internally, by and large they still gave workers a voice on the shop floor, delivered a steadily rising standard of living, and served the purposes of democracy by helping to give workers an organized (though moderate) voice in national politics.

Anyone who spends a day at a major academic library reading books about unions written in the 1950s can find dozens of works representing variations on these three perspectives. There were vigorous debates during that decade about whether unions were good or bad for the economy and for society, what unions ought to look like, and how they ought to behave. The interesting thing about these 45-year-old debates, however, is not what people argued about but rather what everyone accepted: that trade unions were a permanent feature of industrial relations in advanced capitalist countries such as the United States.

For the modern reader, that naive assumption marks these musty texts immediately as belonging to another era. In today's world, by contrast, trade unions seem almost completely irrelevant, both to politics and to the economy. Unions represent less than 10 percent of private sector employees, down from a postwar peak of 35 percent. Indeed, the contemporary figure is about the same as it was in 1935, before the Wagner Act was passed.[1] And numerical decline is reflected in decreased political influence. In the early 1960s the AFL-CIO could still mobilize support for major social legislation, driving passage of Medicare and Medicaid. By the late 1970s the AFL-CIO could not pass a modest package of labor law reform, even under a liberal Democratic president and a Democratic Congress. Since then, no significant social legislation championed by labor has been passed — unless one counts the recent Family and Medical Leave Act, which allows workers to take limited *unpaid* leave to deal with family or health emergencies.

In retrospect, we can see that the heyday of Big Labor did not signify the permanent acquiescence of capital to collective bargaining. Unions never penetrated the "right-to-work" South (where union shops were outlawed), nor did they represent many workers outside construction, manufacturing, mining, transportation, utilities, and communications. Throughout the postwar period, the changing industrial composition of the economy steadily eroded organized labor's industrial base. As union density declined, employer offensives against unions steadily grew more sophisticated and bolder, and U.S. labor law and its administration gradually shifted more and more in employers' favor.[2] And while the growth of union representation in the public sector helped mask, for a time, the overall decline, by the 1990s even public sector workers were coming under attack from privatization, contracting out, shrinking public budgets, and union busting.[3] For the contemporary labor movement, then, the overriding questions are whether it can survive at all and whether it has any important role to play.

ALTERNATIVES FOR LABOR REVITALIZATION

In 1972, AFL-CIO president George Meany was asked why union membership was declining as a percentage of the labor force. "I don't know, and I don't care," he responded. "I used to worry about the . . . size of the membership," Meany went on. "I stopped worrying because to me it doesn't make any difference."[4] This sort of arrogance was beginning to seem foolhardy by the time Lane Kirkland replaced Meany as AFL-CIO president in 1979. By then, it was becoming clear that organized labor needed a survival strategy. Lane Kirkland's administration, taking the decline in labor's membership and influence quite seriously, attempted to design such a strategy.

The problem, as Kirkland saw it, was that labor unions could not recover their strength through organizing without labor law reform. Kirkland's view that the law was a barrier to organizing is still viewed as accurate by academic observers. American labor law lacks meaningful sanctions and penalties for labor law violators, thus providing employers with incentives to routinely use illegal tactics to avoid unionization.[5] The law allows employers to run lengthy antiunion campaigns during which they can force their employees to listen to antiunion speakers and presentations. And even when workers win certification elections, management can often break the new union by stonewalling at the bargaining table; as a result, only about two-thirds of union certification election victories ever lead to a first contract.[6] Current U.S. labor law also does little to protect the rising tide of contingent workers; temporary workers and "casual workers" do not get to vote in National Labor Relations

Board (NLRB) elections. The rise of contracting-out arrangements is also hard to deal with, given existing bans on secondary strikes and boycotts. And the law's rigid distinction between workers and supervisors creates a gap in coverage that is growing with the rise of professional and white-collar work: "workers" have collective bargaining rights, but "supervisors" do not.[7]

When Lane Kirkland took office in 1979, the prospects for legal reform seemed remote. Business opposition had just defeated a very modest labor law reform package in a Democratic Congress under a Democratic president. So although the need for reform was increasingly desperate, there seemed to be no hope for help on the legal front unless labor unions could persuade business to support reform. But in the late 1970s and early 1980s, big business was engaging in an all-out attack on organized labor. How could capital's new, overt hostility toward labor be turned back into acceptance? The argument advanced in the 1980s by the AFL-CIO under Lane Kirkland's leadership was that the best way for labor to blunt the business attack on unions and workers was to adopt a more conciliatory stance. As Ian Robinson sums up the strategy, "[U]nions would downplay their adversarial traditions and become partners in the intensifying international competitive struggle. Labor's contribution to this partnership would be greater flexibility in workplace organization, and more positively, the encouragement of productivity-enhancing employee voice."[8] This conciliatory turn was supposed to accomplish two things. First, it would reintegrate labor unions into the economy by helping employers see that increased productivity and quality could best be attained with unionized workforces in the context of cooperative labor-management relations. And second, a new era of labor-management cooperation would reduce employers' opposition to labor law reform.

The Kirkland strategy failed miserably. It quickly became clear that employers preferred union busting or avoidance to labor-management cooperation. Cooperation appealed only to employers in the shrinking sectors and industries where employers were still forced to deal with unions.[9] Even in highly unionized industries like automobile manufacturing, employers chose to avoid unions, rather than cooperate with them, when they could. And organized labor's contention that cooperative labor relations could help firms achieve higher quality and productivity was fatally undercut by the success of nonunion Honda and Nissan assembly plants in Ohio and Tennessee, which demonstrated that quality and increased productivity in manufacturing were possible *without* unions.

In the 1990s, to be sure, sophisticated advocates of labor-management cooperation and employee involvement continued to argue that, if done right, employee involvement could benefit unions, workers, and firms.[10] But the argument that the benefits of a unionized employee involvement approach should outweigh the bottom-line appeal of sweating workers or pursuing employee involvement without unions has continued to fall on deaf corporate ears. The experience of the 1980s and 1990s demonstrated that most employers simply aren't interested in cooperating with unions and that most unions aren't strong enough to make them.

The failure of labor-management cooperation to achieve widespread acceptance as an alternative to nonunion operation guaranteed that it would fail to persuade employers to take a more friendly attitude toward labor law reform. After the Democratic Party regained control of the presidency and both houses of Congress in 1992, President Clinton created the Dunlop Commission to explore the possibility for a business-labor compromise on labor law reform. Few employers were interested, and the idea of labor law reform died a quiet death.[11] Labor academics, legal scholars, and union officials continue to advocate wide-ranging reforms in U.S. labor law, including card-check certification to ease organizing; first-contract arbitration to prevent management from dragging its feet at the bargaining table; and an end to the ban on secondary strikes and boycotts to make it easier for unions to organize industries in which subcontracting is common.[12] But whatever the merits of labor law reform for unions and workers, it is off the political agenda for the foreseeable future. Like widespread labor-management cooperation, labor law reform will not happen until *after* labor unions find a way to recover their numerical and political strength.

Recognizing that labor law reform is not in the offing, some students of the labor movement have proposed what might be termed "full-service" unionism as an alternative survival strategy. According to this view, unions should seek to attract members on an occupational and/or geographic basis rather than organizing work site by work site. One idea is that by providing training and job placement services, unions could gradually up-skill and professionalize low-wage service occupations characterized by high turnover and "job-hopping."[13] This approach may appeal to some employers (particularly when labor markets are tight) in market segments for which delivering quality services is difficult to achieve with a high-turnover workforce. Unfortunately, in many low-wage services, a significant segment of employers are indifferent to the impact of employee turnover on quality. In the nursing home industry, for example, state and federal reimbursement rules, combined with inadequate quality and staffing standards and enforcement, mean that employers have no real financial incentives to reduce turnover and/or improve the quality of care.[14] In some ways, therefore, this idea resembles proposals for more union-management cooperation: it requires that management be more interested in cooperation than in union busting.[15] Clearly, another alternative is needed.

SOCIAL MOVEMENT UNIONISM:
A VIABLE SURVIVAL STRATEGY FOR LABOR?

In October 1995, John Sweeney's "New Voice" slate defeated Lane Kirkland's handpicked successor in the first contested election for president that the AFL-CIO had ever had. About his candidacy, Sweeney said, "I decided to run for president of the AFL-CIO because organized labor is the only voice of American workers and their families, and because the silence was deafening."[16] Sweeney, the first AFL-CIO president to come from the ranks of a "post-industrial" union, is a former president of the Service Employees International Union (SEIU), which in 1995 was the third-largest union in the country, with 1.3 million members. Unlike most of organized labor, the SEIU was growing, reaching 1.5 million members in the year 2000, when it became the largest U.S. union.

Sweeney's AFL-CIO represents a marked departure from the thinking of the AFL-CIO under Lane Kirkland. Against Kirkland's conciliatory approach, Sweeney has called for a more activist labor movement, one that could begin to challenge the supremacy of corporate rule. Sweeney has promised to reinvent organized labor, to transform it from a collection of sclerotic special interest groups into a once again broad-based social movement. In its first five years, Sweeney's administration moved the AFL-CIO toward this goal by becoming both more critical of capital (and the emerging new global order) and more inclusive.[17] The labor federation under Sweeney has become more critical of the status quo in at least three respects. First, it has moved away from viewing U.S. corporations as partners in competition with foreign firms and workers, developing instead "a discourse that targets transnational corporations as the principal architects of the neoliberal agenda."[18] Second, for the first time the AFL-CIO has begun to cooperate with labor movements in other countries — as well as with environmental and human rights movements — to try to articulate alternatives to neoliberal globalization and to oppose the World Trade Organization (WTO) and neoliberal trade agreements like the North American Free Trade Agreement (NAFTA) and the General Agreement on Tariffs and Trade (GATT). In this respect, the anti-WTO protests in Seattle in November 1999 were truly historic: tens of thousands of AFL-CIO union members marched alongside environmental and human rights groups, signaling the unprecedented possibility that a labor/environment/human rights coalition could emerge as a potent political force. And third, the AFL-CIO has begun to increase the proportion of its political spending devoted to member education and getting out the vote and to decrease the proportion devoted to political contributions to the Democratic Party.

The AFL-CIO has also become more inclusive, rapidly increasing the representation of women and minorities on its executive board. It has fought hard and visibly for increases in the minimum wage, which would benefit low-wage nonunion workers and union members alike. The AFL-CIO under Sweeney has reversed a long tradition of hostility to immigration by calling for blanket amnesty for illegal immigrants and an end to criminal sanctions against employers of illegal immigrants. The labor movement has recently "increased outreach to students, university faculty, clergy, and social movement organizations with whom the AFL-CIO shares — and seeks to expand — common ground on domestic and international policies."[19] And most important, instead of assuming that unions cannot organize successfully without labor law reform, Sweeney has argued from the start that labor *can* and *must* organize to save itself. Under Sweeney, the AFL-CIO has made substantial increases in its expenditures on the Organizing Institute, which trains union organizers, who then take jobs with unions around the country. It has promoted new organizing strategies, launched innovative programs like Union Summer, and pressured often-moribund local labor councils to play an active role in supporting the organizing and efforts of their member locals.

By itself, of course, change within the AFL-CIO does not signal revitalization for the movement as a whole: as a national labor federation, the AFL-CIO does not directly represent or organize union members. That task falls to its member unions and their local affiliates, over which the AFL-CIO leadership has no real control. That said, however, Sweeney's rise within the ranks of the labor movement and the AFL's new posture do reflect a real shift within the labor movement. Sweeney's election signaled the growing recognition that the old ways were not working and that it might be time for the labor movement as a whole to adopt the new approaches being pioneered by Sweeney's union, the SEIU. During the last two decades, while organized labor in general suffered defeat after defeat, the SEIU's organizing successes were substantial. Dating to the mid-1980s, the SEIU's Justice for Janitors campaigns in Washington, D.C., Los Angeles, New York, Las Vegas, Denver, and other cities have successfully organized tens of thousands of low-wage building service workers, while its national nursing home organizing campaign has organized more than 10 percent of the rapidly growing nursing home industry since the mid-1980s. The SEIU also achieved a historic victory in February 1999 by organizing a single unit of 74,000 minimum-wage home care workers in southern California — the largest successful unionization drive in the United States since 112,000 General Motors workers joined the United Auto Workers (UAW) in 1937.[20] Between 1996 and 2002, the SEIU organized 535,000 new members, making it the fastest-growing union as well as the largest.[21]

Organizing success in the SEIU is rooted not only in the union's willingness to devote real resources to organizing (the SEIU international claims that 45 percent of its budget goes to organizing) but also in its use of innovative organizing strategies and tactics at the local level. The common thread running through the SEIU's organizing success stories is that they combine grassroots mobilization, face-to-face interaction, rank-and-file leadership, and a strong social justice orientation in an explicit rejection of traditional U.S. business unionism. Rather than "selling" unions as a representational service that will benefit those who decide to purchase representation, these organizing campaigns have focused instead on building workers' solidarity. Rather than viewing bureaucratic election or grievance-handling procedures as the source of unions' strength, these campaigns have viewed solidarity and workers' links with local communities as the source of collective power. As a result, whether unions make use of NLRB procedures or bypass them altogether in their struggles for union recognition and new contracts, these campaigns' common denominator is reliance on creative pressure strategies including, but not limited to, direct action, community alliances, and political intervention.

These ideas are not really new, but until the early 1990s, the SEIU was the only large national union making organizing the centerpiece of its program and to adopt such innovative organizing approaches. During the last decade, however, other unions have begun to follow suit. Locals of the Communication Workers of America (CWA) have used grassroots organizing strategies to successfully organize large units of airline ticket takers. Hotel Employees and Restaurant Employees (HERE) locals have been aggressively organizing hotel and casino workers in Las Vegas and other cities, with promising results. And the Union of Needletrades, Industrial and Textile Employees (UNITE) has engaged in innovative cross-border organizing linking U.S. and Mexican textile workers.[22]

These developments, taken together, have caused considerable excitement among academic students of the U.S. labor movement and are spawning a new wave of scholarship on new forms of union struggle and the adoption of participatory, disruptive, and confrontational tactics. Indeed, students of labor have begun to talk about the emergence of "social movement unionism" in the United States.[23] Although not everyone uses the term, the idea that innovative and successful local unions are adopting (or should adopt) the strategies, tactics, and identity of a social movement is now appearing throughout the literature. The new labor scholarship identifies in these unions a number of common features.

First, social movement unions make use of what Bronfenbrenner and Juravich have called "rank-and-file intensive" grassroots approaches to organizing.[24] Rather than relying on traditional organizing techniques like mass mailings and distribution of union cards, movement unions engage workers face to face and utilize the talents of rank-and-file member volunteers to connect one on one with potential new union members.[25] Second, movement unions go beyond the strike, labor's traditional and routinized form of mobilization, to organize collective action campaigns emphasizing public protest and disruptive tactics in order to build workers' confidence and sense of collective power.[26] Third, social movement unions seek to build genuine labor-community coalitions in order to mobilize communities alongside union members.[27] Fourth,

Paul Johnston emphasizes that movement unions frame their demands *politically* rather than in terms of narrow labor market goals.[28] This is true not only in the public sector, where demands have always been framed as good public policy, but also increasingly in the private sector, where unions are now framing demands as claims to universal civil rights or justice in order to facilitate community alliances, to help bring political pressure to bear on private employers, and to attack neoliberal global restructuring.

Writers who have examined the turn toward social movement unionism in the United States have argued that movement unionism represents at least a potentially viable survival strategy for labor. Bronfenbrenner and Juravich's work was the first to provide statistical evidence for this proposition.[29] On the basis of their analysis of NLRB election data and surveys of union organizers, they found that although unions overall won only 42 percent of the certification elections that were held in 1994, when unions used more than five rank-and-file–intensive tactics (such as building a rank-and-file organizing committee, conducting house calls, running regular small group meetings, using rank-and-file volunteers from already organized units, and holding job actions, rallies, or solidarity days) the win rate rose to 67 percent. Each additional rank-and-file tactic, Bronfenbrenner and Juravich estimated, increased the union's chance of winning by 9 percent. Employer tactics also mattered — but each additional antiunion tactic used by employers decreased the chances of a union victory by only 6 percent, leading Bronfenbrenner and Juravich to conclude that union tactics matter more than employer tactics and that a comprehensive grassroots strategy is most likely to produce union wins.[30]

THE DILEMMAS OF SOCIAL MOVEMENT UNIONISM

Quantitative studies like those of Bronfenbrenner and Juravich are extremely valuable because they tell us that, statistically, movement approaches are more likely to succeed than traditional organizing approaches. But this research has two important limitations. First, it focuses on only one phase of struggle: the certification election and the first contract. It reveals little about the ability of movement unions to extend and defend their initial victories against the inevitable corporate counterattacks. And second, this sort of research cannot tell us *how* or *why* movement unionism succeeds. In particular, it cannot tell us what problems and obstacles movement unionism must overcome to achieve success or how these obstacles can be surmounted. Social movement unionism is not simply a laundry list of tactics, it is a process of change within the labor movement itself, and to know whether it can succeed over the long run we need to understand what its dilemmas are and how it might be able to deal with them. These questions are best answered not by macro-level statistical comparisons but rather by comparative case studies.

Unfortunately, however, existing case studies suffer from a tendency to tell success stories — ascendant narratives romanticizing workers' solidarity and downplaying internal obstacles, struggles, and difficulties. This kind of writing is not as useful as it could be because in it, militancy and working-class solidarity always triumph. In the real world, of course, militancy and working-class solidarity are usually difficult to achieve, and they do not always triumph. The point is not that we need more studies of failed campaigns — although failures are at least as instructive as successes — but rather that the task of the sociologist sympathetic to labor unions is to try to understand *how* successes are achieved. Case studies are an important tool for the sociologist, but they must be more analytical, more comparative, and less narrative.[31]

The failure of the existing case study literature to systematically examine how local unions struggle with specific dilemmas, obstacles, and problems connected to movement unionism is surprising because observers *have* identified a number of crucially important problems that social movement unionism must confront. *First, workers themselves often resist unions' efforts to organize or mobilize them.* Unions are often portrayed by employers, and perceived by workers, as narrow special interests, an unwelcome "third party" to the employment relation. Survey research on workers' attitudes toward unions has consistently reported that roughly one-third of unorganized workers desire union representation — which means that a majority of workers are initially either undecided, indifferent, or ideologically hostile. Somehow, movement unionism must overcome substantial working-class antiunionism to create new collective solidarities oriented toward collective action. *Second, adopting movement-style tactics requires a difficult process of organizational transformation.* Most local unions, even in the SEIU, are organizationally oriented toward the routine processing of grievances and arbitrations — the bread and butter of bureaucratic-servicing unionism. These organizational arrangements are not easily deployed in the service of rank-and-file mobilization, and (partially because they are legally enshrined in the labor relations framework) they have a solidity that resists change. *And third, movement unionism must directly confront the power of employers to intimidate, threaten, and punish their employees.* This power is based not only on the economic reach of employers but also on the way the existing legal framework for organizing and collective bargaining stacks the deck in capital's favor, giving employers an extensive legal and extralegal tool kit of devastating union-avoidance and union-busting strategies.

How unions can deal with these three main problems is the central question of this book. Unlike many existing studies of the new movement unionism, this book does not rely on statistical analyses of election data, nor does it describe unconnected success stories. Instead, the book is organized around a series of systematic comparisons of organizing and contract campaigns undertaken by a single SEIU local — referred to here as Local A — between 1995 and 1998. To study these campaigns, I conducted fieldwork as an organizing intern at Local A in 1997 and 1998, and I conducted interviews and archival research between 1997 and 1999. The president of the local, Janet Zimmerman,[32] allowed me to join the union as an intern in order to facilitate my study of union organizing, and my role as a participant observer was public knowledge at the union. (Readers interested in a detailed discussion of the research methods employed in this study, how these methods evolved in the course of the study, and the benefits and limitations of the methods used, can turn to the Appendix.)

The campaigns I studied include two attempts to win a certification election at a single nursing home (Part I); a multi–work site campaign against the privatization of county nursing homes and a related county-wide contract campaign (Part II); and a two-year statewide battle, also involving two other SEIU locals, to resist being broken by the world's largest nursing-home chain (Part III). These campaigns thus range in scope from the smallest to the largest campaigns in which a local union is likely to be involved. Studying the same union as it undertakes campaigns of different scope, over a period of four years, allowed me to explore how the requirements of success change as movement unionism ventures beyond the organizing drive centered on individual work sites. Moreover, the comparisons of campaigns over time at each level of struggle allowed me to examine how success and failure are dynamically intertwined at each level of struggle. By comparing campaigns that are actually linked in time, I could unravel the relationships between earlier and later campaigns. This approach allowed me to tease out how initial failures are turned into later successes; how successes of one kind can be turned into successes of another kind; and how apparent disasters can contain the seeds of success.

But if this study of social movement unionism represents a departure from previous examinations of recent events in the labor movement, its approach to analyzing collective action is also quite different from that employed by most contemporary analysts of social movements, who have generally been interested in explaining the *causes* of movements with reference to structural factors. Given my central interest in how local unions deal with the obstacles outlined above, I was concerned not so much with the external causes of collective action as with the processes through which unions and workers achieve collective action despite the obstacles. I view collective action, therefore, not as an effect of structural factors but as an accomplishment of self-conscious actors who struggle against the barriers to solidarity, effective organization, and strategic and tactical success. In this, my approach has more in common with the work of social constructionist theorists of social movements like Alberto Melucci than with the work of American scholars in the resource mobilization and political process traditions. Unlike many social constructionists, however, I do not believe that collective action is only a *discursive* accomplishment. This book's analysis of social movement unionism in terms of attempts to overcome a series of discursive, organizational, and strategic obstacles rooted in movement history and local context represents, I believe, a novel and useful way of analyzing social movements, a subject to which I return in the conclusion of the book.

PART I: CONFRONTING WORKING-CLASS ANTIUNIONISM

A number of scholars have observed that resistance to new forms of union struggle often comes from workers, whose expectations about what unions ought to do for them (and how) are rooted in their experience of business unionism. Although the problem has been identified, however, the literature on new union organizing has surprisingly little to say about how social movement union organizing overcomes worker resistance. Lowell Turner hints at the problem in passing, noting that in a United Mine Workers of America (UMWA) campaign the union's failure to develop trust and close relationships with workers prevented organizers from being able to counteract its reputation for violence, which management capitalized on by showing old films of picket-line violence by the Mine Workers.[33]

Kim Voss and Rachel Sherman raise the problem more directly in the context of a discussion of resistance by existing members to organizational transformation.[34] They present interesting evidence that union members' ingrained expectations about servicing often lead them to resist the union's efforts to encourage them to become more active in the union. Similarly, Bill Fletcher and Richard Hurd speak of the "servicing magnet" that constantly pulls local unions back to traditional representational practices to the extent that they are responsive to members' demands for service.[35] None of these writers, however, discuss the implications of workers' expectations about servicing for mobilizing in *new* organizing campaigns, nor do they devote much attention to the processes with which unions might deal with these lived experiences in that context. Voss and Sherman do mention some of the methods reported by their most successful locals to deal with the dilemma of member resistance to mobilization (education, training), but they do not directly examine how and why, or how well, these methods work.

Some recent work on organizing immigrants in the southwestern United States has considered a different, but related issue: how immigrant workers' previous union experiences affect new organizing campaigns. Roger Waldinger and Claudia Der-Martirosian, for example, note that immigrants from former East Bloc countries may be ideologically hostile to unions, while Mexican immigrants are often strongly prounion to begin with.[36] Miriam Wells, drawing on interviews with union organizers, discusses a variety of immigrant experiences, commenting of Chinese immigrant workers, for example, that because of their experience in China, "they think of unions as outside forces, arms of the government, rather than organizations formed by and for workers."[37] Organizers interviewed by Wells also commented on their experiences in organizing white workers that "young white workers tend to think that unions are anachronistic and that their leaders are 'old, fat white guys.' Older white workers tended to think that unions are good but weak."[38] These observations do not really represent what I have in mind when I speak of studying whether and how workers' lived experiences of business unionism pose obstacles to organizing and how unions deal with the problem. They present workers' experience as a set of group propensities noticed by organizers. Asians "vary in receptivity"; Latinos are "especially receptive"; African Americans "tend to be militantly pro-union."[39]

There is, of course, a huge literature on attitudes toward unions, including group attitudes.[40] The problem with surveying the union attitudes of various groups, as Eva Weinbaum and Rick Fantasia have pointed out in different contexts, is that such research doesn't reveal much, if anything, about how workers' "conflicting and contradictory views and questions"[41] can be suddenly transformed via organizing or episodes of collective action. What workers think is totally abstracted from actual social relationships and processes. On this point, Rick Fantasia relates a wonderful story about a survey research study at an English auto plant that concluded that "class consciousness was practically nonexistent." While the study was at the printer, the workers got hold of a copy, along with a report of company profits. A two-day "eruption" of "wild rioting" ensued.[42]

Fantasia's work itself perhaps goes furthest in examining the role of workers' lived experience in the context of an actual organizing campaign. In his study of a hospital organizing effort, Fantasia emphasizes that workers brought a variety of union experiences (or lack of experience) to the table and discusses some aspects of how rank-and-file activists dealt with the problematic aspects of lived experience. How lived experience of old-style unionism becomes an obstacle is not the major focus of his analysis, but Fantasia's understanding of organizing *as a process* represents the sort of research approach capable of understanding how this dilemma arises and is confronted by social movement unionism.

Part I of this book examines the question of worker resistance to unionization by comparing two organizing campaigns in which I was directly involved in 1997 and 1998 in my capacity as an intern at Local A. They took place a year apart at a nursing home I call Rosemont Pavilion. In the first of these two campaigns, the union lost a close certification election. The following year, the union returned with a different strategy and won a resounding victory. This comparison first reveals in Chapter 2 how and why workers' negative experiences and images of business unionism can lead them to reject unions — even when grievances are bitterly held and when management does not mount a vigorous antiunion campaign. I argue here that workers' perceptions that unions played a key role in Pittsburgh's deindustrialization, their association of unions with corruption, intimidation, and even violence, and their experiences of "do-nothing unionism" led them to be skeptical of, and even hostile to, union organizing campaigns. Chapter 3 goes on to introduce a new argument about the underlying reasons for the success of movement union organizing strategies: it is not just that face-to-face organizing techniques are generally superior to traditional union organizing tactics. Rather, social movement organizing allows the union to create a new vision of participatory, powerful unionism that is understood — by workers — to be *different* from the old-style business unionism of experience and cultural memory. The reinterpretation of negative experiences and images of unions as belonging to an outmoded form of unionism clears the way for workers to support the organizing effort.

PART II: DEALING WITH ORGANIZATIONAL LEGACIES

Writing on the new unionism is full of calls for organizational change, particularly for democratization.[43] This is interesting given the empirical findings of several studies showing that union members demand servicing, not mobilization or new organizing.[44] These findings support Dan Clawson's suggestion that by itself more democracy may lead, not to revitalization, but only to more servicing.[45] Kim Voss and Rachel Sherman, for example, studied a group of 14 union locals in the San Francisco Bay Area. Of the locals they studied, the ones that were the most innovative were locals that confronted crisis with visionary, top-down leadership and experienced substantial intervention from the centralized authority of the international union. Several of the most innovative locals owed their innovative character in part to their having been placed in trusteeship by the international union.[46]

In general, local unions *do* need to undergo organizational transformation to make use of social movement tactics in a comprehensive way.[47] Bureaucratic representational structures geared toward servicing existing members are not suitable either for massive new organizing or for mobilization of existing members. But changing local union organizations away from servicing is hard because resistance to organizational change from members is reinforced by resistance from union staff.[48] As Bill Fletcher and Richard Hurd conclude, union staff fear change because it may mean losing a role they are comfortable with, because they feel that training rank-and-file workers threatens their own jobs, or because it is easier to solve problems for workers than to teach them how to solve them on their own.[49] Indeed, moving from a servicing approach to an "organizing model" means more work for union staff.[50]

This research is extremely valuable, but so far it hasn't studied processes of organizational change directly. Instead, existing studies compare a small group of locals that have solved the most difficult organizational problems with a larger group of locals that have not. The value of the approach is that it allows researchers to ask what makes fully revitalized locals different from those with partially transformed organizations. The limitation of the approach is that it freezes time, making it difficult to understand processes of change *within* the all-important group of partially revitalized locals. To shed more light on how partially revitalized local unions deal with the organizational legacies of business unionism, we need studies that examine how such locals deal with their organizational difficulties over time.

Part II attempts to fill this gap by comparing the organizational dynamics of two interconnected union campaigns — the first a fight against the privatization of four public sector nursing homes that took place in Pittsburgh in 1996; the second a follow-up struggle in the spring and summer of 1997 over new contracts for the public nursing home workers and other county employees. I worked as a union intern on this second campaign, but I found that to understand it I was forced to trace its roots back to the first, using a strategy of interviews and documentary analysis. The analysis of the antiprivatization campaign in Chapter 4 shows that when the union possesses (or can construct) a *social justice* issue that appears to be more than "just" a union matter, the union may be able to bypass both internal organizational limitations and the servicing expectations of rank-and-file members. On the other hand, as the analysis of the contract campaign in Chapter 5 demonstrates, when workers (and others) perceive the subject of struggle as a "union" issue, workers accustomed to servicing are harder to mobilize (and allies less eager to lend their support). In this case, internal organizational problems must be dealt with — but as Chapter 5 also shows, local unions may mount short-term mobilizations via a series of temporary solutions to organizational problems. The Epilogue to Part II suggests, however, that even sporadic, short-term mobilizations based on temporary, ad hoc solutions to organizational problems can ultimately lead to significant organizational change in the longer term.

PART III: SOCIAL MOVEMENT UNIONISM: CHALLENGING THE POWER OF CAPITAL

As mentioned earlier, many writers have observed that U.S. labor law provides inadequate protections to unions and workers. Typically, this observation is given as an explanation for why unions have done so poorly at organizing new workers, or as part of a call for labor law reform.[51] It has been quite rare for studies to investigate how organizing unions actually attempt to deal with corporate power despite the obstacles posed by the legal framework.

When the Wagner Act was passed in 1935, the law was conceived quite explicitly as an aid to new organizing.[52] It guaranteed most workers' rights to self-organize, to collectively bargain, and to strike. However, the Wagner Act was silent on the question of whether employers were permitted to hire replacement workers to maintain their operations during a strike. In the 1938 *Mackay Radio* case, the U.S. Supreme Court decided not only that hiring replacement workers was legal but also that the legal right to strike without fear of employer sanction was not violated by permanent replacement of striking workers. *Mackay* thus deeply undermined Wagner's guarantee of a right to strike by giving employers an attractive strikebreaking weapon. Then, after World War II, the Taft-Hartley Act of 1947 scaled back labor's rights still further by outlawing secondary strikes and boycotts, outlawing the union shop, and allowing states to outlaw the closed shop. It is worth noting that under Taft-Hartley the general strikes of the late 1930s (which unionized much of American heavy industry) and the famous Flint sit-down strike (which unionized General Motors) would have been illegal. Hence the often seen argument that labor now finds itself back where it started in the 1930s ignores the fact that labor enjoyed legal protections between 1935 and 1938 that it has not enjoyed since.

The current legal framework is an obstacle to new organizing, since the failure of the law to provide for any punitive damages encourages firms to illegally intimidate and fire workers when they attempt to organize. But as the new unionism literature has found, grassroots organizing strategies have proven quite effective in this area. The key point to be kept in mind is that if workers really want to form and vote for a union, the employer ultimately cannot prevent them from doing so. The employer can intimidate, threaten, cajole, punish, and so on, but at the end of the day the law allows workers a secret ballot election. Thus questions about organizing new units in the first instance ultimately boil down to questions about how to build enough solidarity in the face of employer resistance and workers' own lived experiences. It seems that social movement unionism is effective in doing this, although, as I argue above, we don't know enough about how and why this is so.

When it comes to actually negotiating contracts, however, the situation is different. Now solidarity alone is not enough, because employers' consent must also be obtained. Workers can form unions without the agreement of their employer, but they cannot enjoy the protection of a collective bargaining contract without forcing their employer to agree to it and to abide by it. Companies have been able to make effective use of permanent replacement workers to get rid of unions they do not want to deal with. The standard union-busting approach to negotiations begins with the company making an "offer" it knows the union cannot accept, such as a drastic pay cut or the elimination of health benefits. In effect, the company dares the union to go on strike. If it does, the strikers are permanently replaced, a new, nonunion workforce is hired, and the union is broken. The only way a union can hope to win a strike of this kind is to effectively shut down the company — something few unions are able to do in an age of global firms and local unions.

There has been relatively little work examining how unions might deal with this sort of union busting. A number of studies deal with high-profile union defeats, chronicling the union-busting strategies outlined above.[53] Edna Bonacich has examined both the legal and tactical obstacles to sustained success in the garment and textile industries, as well as how UNITE has attempted to deal with these obstacles.[54] Her conclusions, as mentioned earlier, are quite pessimistic. Catherine Fisk and her coauthors have written about the economic and legal challenges in sustaining and expanding success in Justice for Janitors (JfJ) in Los Angeles, paying processual attention to how the union is trying to deal with these problems.[55] In particular, they discuss the problem posed by the legal restrictions on secondary boycotts in industries where contracting out is widespread. Finally, Tom Juravich and Kate Bronfenbrenner highlight the role of the "coordinated campaign" in their analysis of the victory of the United Steelworkers of America (USWA) victory against the Ravenswood Aluminum Corporation in the early 1990s.[56] According to Juravich and Bronfenbrenner, the Ravenswood campaign succeeded not only because it relied on a combination of multiple grassroots pressure tactics but also because it contained a crucial element absent in labor's high-profile defeats: at Ravenswood, USWA attorneys successfully convinced the courts that the strike was over unfair labor practices rather than economic issues. This rendered illegal the company's decision to replace striking workers and created liabilities for back pay that ultimately forced the company back to the table. These studies are a beginning, but much more attention is needed to questions about social movement unionism's ability to deal with corporate power and an uneven playing field. Was the USWA's Ravenswood victory an aberration — or does social movement unionism have a future?

Part III takes up this question by investigating two phases of a statewide struggle pitting Local A and two other Pennsylvania SEIU locals against Megacorp Enterprises, a giant for-profit nursing home company. The SEIU's relentless attempts to organize the nursing home industry had provoked Megacorp into a union-busting attempt. This struggle took place in 1995 and 1996, before I arrived on the scene in Pittsburgh, so my analysis of it is based on interviews and documentary evidence conducted and collected in 1997 and 1999. Part III thus examines the ability of unions to institutionalize their organizing successes in the private sector. Here the focus is on the extent to which social movement unionism is capable of withstanding a union-busting attack from an aggressive private sector employer willing to use all available legal (and extralegal) means to reverse 10 years of organizing successes. Chapter 6 demonstrates the crucial importance of the legally protected unfair labor practice strike and shows how grassroots worker mobilization can be used to provoke unfair labor practices that lay the groundwork for legally protected strikes. Chapter 7 then shows, however, that even when unions do pull off legally protected strikes, achieving settlements can still require months or years of enormous organizing effort. Moreover, such settlements do not permanently institutionalize the union's presence in an industry but rather represent truces — perhaps temporary — between labor and capital. I conclude therefore that victory over union busting through social movement struggle is possible but always tenuous.

CONCLUSION

Each of the three sets of comparative case studies in this book highlights a specific historically rooted obstacle that social movement unionism must overcome as it ascends from the shop floor to take on larger struggles over the future of an industry. However, as will be clear throughout the analyses presented in this book, this does not mean that the dilemmas of worker resistance, organizational legacies, and corporate power can each be identified with a specific level of struggle. Instead, this book shows how all three problems intertwine, growing ever more challenging as struggle moves outward and upward from the shop floor. As the analysis moves from organizing at the Rosemont nursing home in Part I, through the multi–work site campaigns of Allegheny County in Part II, to the statewide mobilization of Megacorp nursing home workers in Part III, we will see how increasing the *scope* of struggle means having to deal simultaneously with multiple dilemmas and obstacles that accumulate in additive fashion.

Thus the organization of the book parallels the organization of social movement unionism itself. Each step it takes must be built on solving the problems of the previous step and incorporating these solutions into new solutions to the ever more complex problems of a widening struggle. Social movement unionism cannot ordinarily bypass the shop floor to organize large numbers of workers all at once but must be built on a solid foundation of shop floor organization capable of withstanding counterattacks and linking up across work sites in larger struggles.[57] The comparative case studies presented in this book demonstrate that movement unionism *is* capable of doing just that in the nursing home industry, showing how a program of strategic nursing home organizing culminated in the creation of a genuine nursing home workers' movement in Pennsylvania.

On the other hand, the analyses presented here show equally that this process of movement building does not happen overnight but entails an arduous process of grassroots organization building, internal struggle and reform, and gradually escalating contests with capital. In Pennsylvania, as we will see, it took more than a decade of continuous organizing and struggle for the SEIU to progress from its first attempts to organize private sector nursing homes like Rosemont to the level of organizational and ideological readiness required to defeat Megacorp in the statewide battle chronicled in Part III. Thus, while the book does show how social movement unionism is able to deal successfully with the dilemmas of worker resistance, organizational legacies, and the power of capital, it also shows why movement unionism does not represent a quick fix for labor: it is not just that the diffusion of movement approaches throughout organized labor is slow but rather that rebuilding a workers' movement in the United States itself entails a difficult, long-term process whose outcome cannot yet be foreseen.[58]

PART ONE

Confronting Working-Class Antiunionism

Rosemont Pavilion

Rosemont Pavilion (the name has been changed to protect the confidentiality of workers and residents) sits well back from the two-lane blacktop, on a gently sloping hill overlooking a farmer's field. The nursing home is a single-story red brick building shaped like a capital "H," with one side of the "H" facing the parking lot. Rows of identical windows above identical air conditioners mounted in the brick stretch out on either side of the main entrance. It is a modest but respectable-looking building in a modest but respectable industrial suburb of Pittsburgh. Rosemont's exterior presents a quiet, peaceful scene, only occasionally disturbed by the comings and goings of visitors.

Like most long-term nursing home residents, most of Rosemont's residents are on Medicaid, the federal program that pays for long-term care for the indigent.[1] Medicare, the federal health care program for the elderly, pays substantially more for nursing home care but does not cover long-term care. As a result, most nursing home residents have a downwardly mobile "career" that begins with relatively generous but short-term Medicare coverage.[2] When Medicare eligibility expires, residents are forced to "spend down" whatever resources and savings they possess. Thus many of Rosemont's residents once owned homes and possessed incomes and savings, but now either they have sold their homes and spent down their savings, or they are in the process of doing so. Most of these people, now approaching the ends of their lives, are former industrial workers — metal workers and coal miners — or the wives of such workers. The world they once lived in, worked in, and helped build exists only in their own memories.

At the town hall, red dots on a wall map show the location of more than 100 mines in and around the township. Only a handful are operational today. A few miles closer to Pittsburgh, the signs of that vanished world are more visible: the bizarre landscapes of rusting and twisted metal and broken glass that line the Monongahela River between Monessen and Homestead. These are now neglected and lonely places, but they are the places that Rosemont's residents come from.

The residents have a lot in common with these places. Once they were at the center of American industry, but now the decline of their bodies mirrors the decline of the empty, abandoned mills. Both have been cast aside by a world that has moved on. The mill towns have been victimized by an economic system that uses up places and people and abandons them when they are no longer "valuable"; Rosemont's residents are victimized by a society that first pauperizes elderly people who need long-term care and then fails to ensure that public dollars are used to purchase good-quality care. Like the mill towns themselves, Rosemont's residents are often neglected and lonely.

The residents at Rosemont are cared for mainly by women — some young, some middle-aged — who encounter in their working lives a different world from that once experienced by their charges. It is a poorer world, one in which the men in their lives do not earn as much as men once did. It is a world in which most are working not to supplement the income of their households but as primary breadwinners. Most have (or had) husbands and fathers who worked at the hard, dangerous mill and mine jobs. These men once earned living wages for their work. Now these women work at very hard, often dangerous, jobs in the nursing home, and like the new workers at Homestead they do not earn a living wage for their work. The starting wage for nurses' aides at Rosemont in 1997, before the SEIU's first attempt to organize the facility, was $6.40 per hour. Dietary and housekeeping workers made just $5.45 per hour. Since annual employee turnover at Rosemont was more than 50 percent, more than half the workforce was earning at or near the entry wage. These wages and turnover figures are not unusual in the private nursing home industry. The average nurses' aide wage nationally was $6.06 in 1996, and annual employee turnover in private sector nursing homes averages more than 100 percent.[3]

Rosemont's external serenity belies the chaos that often occurs within. That chaos was never more acute than in May 1997, when the facility was having difficulty passing its annual state inspection. Rosemont had often received citations over the years by state inspectors for violations of the state and federal regulations governing nursing homes, but this time was worse than usual. State investigators had found violations of such severity that they had decided to suspend all further admissions to Rosemont until the facility had come into compliance.

The biggest problem was staffing — a problem that plagues the nursing home industry nationally.[4] According to state investigators' analysis of Rosemont's records, Rosemont was not even meeting Pennsylvania's minimum staffing requirement of 2.3 hours of nursing care per resident in each 24-hour period. On day and evening shifts each nurses' aide was caring for an average of 15 residents, and sometimes more than 20, especially on weekends. On the night shift each aide was caring for between 20 and 30 residents. To grasp the significance of these numbers, one has to understand the level of dependency of Rosemont's residents. Of the 104 residents who lived at Rosemont in the spring of 1997 (the facility had 120 beds), more than 100 were "nonambulatory" and required assistance bathing and dressing; 61 needed help to eat; 81 were incontinent of bladder; 35 showed "signs and symptoms" of depression; and 21 suffered from dementia.[5] Because so many residents needed help with basic bodily functions, the staffing ratios uncovered by state inspectors meant that residents' basic needs were not being met.

Investigators found that because of the shortage of nursing staff, not all residents were receiving their showers on the day or afternoon shifts. Instead, nurses' aides were being ordered to rouse some residents from sleep, between midnight and 2:00 a.m., to shower them. The residents, who had not been consulted about this plan, were apparently not happy about it; several sustained minor injuries and abrasions struggling against restraining chairs on their way to the shower room or while being bathed.

Residents who spend most of their time in bed are required by law to be repositioned every two hours to prevent the development of pressure sores. At Rosemont, overworked nurses' aides were unable to consistently comply with this regulation, and, not surprisingly, state inspectors found that pressure sores were a problem in the facility. Even worse, they found that some residents were not receiving treatment for their pressure sores or other physical problems. In several cases, aides reported that residents had pressure sores — but the facility did not implement care plans to treat the sores, nor were family members notified (as required by law) about the problem. In other cases, bruises, skin tears, or other injuries to residents also went untreated after being reported by nurses' aides. Over a 12-month period, more than 200 injuries of unknown origin had gone uninvestigated by the facility. Several complaints by residents of mistreatment by staff were also not investigated, according to the state inspection report.

Finally, the inspectors cited the facility for failing to provide a safe environment and for failing to take action where hazards were found. In one case, ants were discovered in a resident's bed and inside her incontinent brief, along with evidence of insect bites. Although nurses' aides reported the problem, nothing was done for more than two days, when the resident was finally moved to another room. No pest control efforts were made. Accident hazards also did not receive proper corrective attention according to the investigators. Malfunctioning locks on the wheels of a bed, for example, caused a resident to fall when the bed she was bracing herself against rolled away from her. No effort had been made to correct the wheel lock problem, and inspectors found numerous inoperable wheel locks that still posed a safety problem.

Rosemont's response to the Department of Health's findings was not to seek the root of the problems but rather to engage in a wave of mass firings and declare the problems fixed. The facility's administrator,[6] the director of nursing, and several dozen other employees, including nurses' aides, were blamed and sacked. However, the wave of dismissals only made the staffing situation worse, making it even more difficult to comply with the corrective measures Rosemont had been ordered to implement to improve staffing to meet Pennsylvania's legal minimum. Because the wages it offered were so low, Rosemont was unable to hire enough new employees to satisfy the state regulators. Rather than raise wages to attract employees, the facility resorted to hiring temporary personnel supplied by a staffing agency.

Both the dismissals and the use of temps outraged Rosemont workers. From their perspective, understaffing and high turnover were at the root of most of the quality problems, and their low wages were at the root of understaffing and high turnover. Sacking large numbers of nurses' aides was no way to solve the care quality problems. Even more galling was that at the same time management insisted that it could not afford to raise wages in order to attract and keep staff, it was paying up to $15 per hour for temporary nurses' aides supplied by the staffing agency. Frustrated with Rosemont's failure to deal with its quality problems responsibly, a group of workers led by June McMurray approached the SEIU for help organizing a union.

The two chapters that follow analyze successive attempts by the SEIU to organize Rosemont during the summers of 1997 and 1998. As mentioned in Chapter 1, I was directly involved in both campaigns as an organizing intern. During the first campaign, the union relied primarily on two traditional tactics: union meetings and a few mass mailings. The union did not build a rank-and-file organizing committee or train rank-and-file volunteers to organize their co-workers. Instead the campaign relied heavily on input from just two workers — usually the only attendees at weekly organizing meetings. No house visits were conducted, so organizers ultimately had little face-to-face contact with the majority of the workforce. There were no solidarity-building events or actions. The campaign culminated in a certification election that the union lost in a close vote. Large numbers of Rosemont workers literally cheered when the union's defeat was announced.

The following summer, the union took a very different approach. This time organizers self-consciously implemented specific grassroots strategies that the international union promotes in its training materials. They conducted targeted house calling to recruit a strong organizing committee. They trained committee members to organize and assess their co-workers and to participate in house calling throughout the campaign. The organizing committee was built into a functioning structure that reached into every work area in the nursing home. Union organizers and organizing committee members house-visited nearly every member of the bargaining unit. And unlike the first campaign, the campaign in 1998 was organized around an escalating strategy of collective action aimed at building workers' solidarity. This time, the union won the election by a two-to-one margin — and many of the same workers who had cheered the union's defeat the year before now visibly supported the organizing drive.

Why did Rosemont workers decide not to participate in the labor movement in 1997, then overwhelmingly reverse this decision one year later? What role did the union's tactics play in the outcomes of the two campaigns? If the union's shift in tactics was an important reason for the reversal, how or why did the new tactics make a difference? These are the questions of Chapters 2 and 3.

These are also just the sort of questions often asked by students of social movements interested in explaining people's decisions about participating in movements. Theorists of movement participation argue that, in general, people participate in social movements when movement actors are able to convert grievances into action. Recruitment networks reach people susceptible to calls to action, and the social and organizational ties involved in these networks affect the likelihood of participation.[7] Activists also engage in persuasive communication to try to convince mobilizing targets that collective action is the right solution to the problem and that their participation is critical to achieve the movement's ends; Bert Klandermans refers to this as *action mobilization*, while theorists like David Snow and Robert Benford speak instead of *framing* processes.[8] The targets of mobilization evaluate the apparent costs and benefits of participation, the ratio of which are affected by various kinds of collective and selective incentives.[9] The propensity to participate can also be radically altered by the transformative effects of consciousness-raising during episodes of collective action.[10]

Theories of movement participation would lead us to expect, correctly, that Local A's second organizing drive at Rosemont should have been more successful than its first attempt — because the union's second campaign activated social networks, enabled organizers to engage in face-to-face issue framing, and organized collective actions that led to consciousness-raising, while the first did not. But does this observation constitute an adequate explanation of the divergent outcomes of the two campaigns? Clearly, it does not. The mere fact that the union made use of these tactics in its second campaign did not make success a foregone conclusion. Depending on the context, social networks may encourage participation or discourage it. Attempts at face-to-face organizing may succeed in framing the issues in ways that seem to demand a collective response, or it may succeed only in further alienating people. Collective action may lead, not to consciousness-raising, but to disillusionment with the movement. To construct a truly satisfying explanation of the outcomes of Local A's two campaigns at Rosemont nursing home, we must answer several more specific questions. Why were these workers so opposed to unionization initially? What sort of communication took place in the social networks of Local A's second campaign, and what difference did it make? What did people talk about in the second campaign's face-to-face organizing effort, and how did it change people's minds? And why and how did the collective actions organized by the union in its second campaign help convince Rosemont workers that forming a union was the right thing to do? In short, we must identify the obstacles to participation in the first instance in order to understand how the union later overcame those obstacles.

In the two chapters that follow, I develop such an analysis. I argue that the most important difference between these two campaigns was not simply the features of the union's campaign but rather how well or poorly each campaign dealt with workers' negative experiences and views of business unionism. Workers do not stand before the labor movement as unfilled containers — as generic "prospective movement participants." Rather, they have specific experiences, perceptions, and views of unions — and these are not all positive. As a result they bring to the table ambivalence, skepticism, even hostility toward unions. Local A's first campaign failed to elicit participation, I argue, not because workers were not sufficiently fed up with management, or because management intimidated workers into submission, but because the union campaign did not grapple with workers' negative experiences and images of the labor movement itself. Conversely, Local A's second campaign succeeded a year later — despite a much more intense antiunion effort from management — because this time the union was able to inspire workers with a new and empowering vision of participatory unionism that contrasted sharply with their notions of business unionism. In this effort, the union made good use of recruitment networks, framing activities, and consciousness-raising — but the importance of these processes, the measure of their success, had to do with, not their mere presence or absence, or their generic qualities, but the role they played in the union's effort to transform workers' lived experiences of business unionism.

TWO

"See You Next Year"

The Failure of Traditional Organizing Tactics

The year 1997 was not the first time that June McMurray had contacted the SEIU to ask for help organizing a union at Rosemont Pavilion. In 1996, the union had explored the possibility of organizing the facility in response to an inquiry from McMurray. The union was particularly interested in Rosemont because it already represented a number of other nursing homes in the same chain, the Hewitt Group. Hewitt owned 19 nursing homes, seven of which were located in southwestern Pennsylvania. SEIU Local A represented five of these homes. Thus Rosemont was important for the union's own strategic plan; the union hoped that organizing all seven of the chain's southwestern Pennsylvania nursing homes would give it more leverage in coordinated bargaining with the Hewitt Group.

In 1996, the union's lead organizer had decided that the timing for a campaign at Rosemont was not right. She held several union meetings and distributed union interest cards, but only 30 percent of the workers signed and returned them.[1] Thus it seemed unlikely that there would be enough support for the union to carry a certification election. Since the union was also embroiled in the Megacorp campaign at that time (discussed in Part III), the organizer decided to back off and wait for a more promising moment.

In early June 1997, that moment seemed to have arrived, for three reasons. First, the struggle with Megacorp had been brought to an essentially successful conclusion, meaning that organizing resources and staff time that had been tied up dealing with Megacorp could now be more easily committed to a new organizing drive at Rosemont. Second, the nursing home was now much "hotter" than it had been the year before. The way management was dealing with the quality-of-care difficulties under the oversight of the Pennsylvania Department of Health — scapegoating large numbers of individual aides rather than addressing the deeper sources of poor quality — had significantly changed the situation, transforming many workers' long-standing grievances into determination to act. An initial union meeting, held in a nearby hotel, was attended by nearly one-quarter of the 71 employees in the prospective bargaining unit, and when interest cards were circulated in mid-June, slightly more than 50 percent of employees signed them over the next two weeks. This was a marked improvement over the previous year — but still less than organizer Joan Hardy had hoped for; the rule of thumb in the SEIU is that it's unwise to file for an election when fewer than 70 percent of the workforce have signed interest cards. In this case, however, a third factor encouraged Hardy to proceed with the campaign.

During contract negotiations with the Hewitt Group in the intervening year, the union had successfully extracted an agreement that provided for expedited, non-NLRB election procedures at both remaining nonunion Hewitt homes in southwestern Pennsylvania. This agreement reflected a national strategy on the part of the SEIU international union — which in the 1990s began encouraging member locals to try to obtain such agreements in collective bargaining with nursing home chains in order to ease organizing at nonunion chain-owned facilities. A common tactic among management attorneys and "union-avoidance" consultants is to challenge the union's proposed bargaining unit and force extended hearings on the issue of which employees should be in or out of the unit.[2] In NLRB-supervised elections, the election is generally scheduled six to eight weeks after the union files, but by exercising their legal right to a hearing on the appropriateness of the proposed bargaining unit — which gives company lawyers the opportunity to call witnesses and read reams of paperwork into the record — employers can delay the election for weeks or months.[3] During the delay, management continues its strategy of intimidating, cajoling, and persuading employees not to vote for the union. The longer the delay, the more time for the company to exert pressure on its employees, demoralize them, and attempt to undermine their solidarity and determination.[4] Therefore, the SEIU believes, agreements providing for expedited election procedures should improve the union's chances of success.

Local A had negotiated its first such agreement with the Hewitt Group in 1996. Under the terms of the agreement, the company acceded to an expedited election procedure supervised by an independent arbitrator instead of the NLRB. An arbitrator-supervised election would be held within four weeks of the union's filing for election, and both sides agreed to accept the arbitrator's rulings and decisions as final (i.e., neither side would seek to overturn the arbitrator's decisions by appealing to the courts or the NLRB). The company agreed to release to the union an accurate list of employees (containing names, job titles, and addresses) within one week of the petition. Finally, the company promised not to begin any antiunion campaign before the union filed for election.

The other parts of the election agreement were also important. Getting an accurate list of employees would make building an organizing committee and conducting house visits easier. Stipulating that the company would not begin conducting an antiunion campaign until the union petitioned for election meant that the company would only have four weeks to campaign against the union instead of the usual three to four months.[5] Hardy thus gave two reasons for her decision to proceed with the election, even though the response on interest cards was less than she'd hoped for. First, she didn't want to back off from an election two years in a row for fear of alienating the core group of union supporters at Rosemont. "They all want to have an election, and they're wondering why the union won't let them have one," she said. "At this point, I'd rather take them to election and lose than back off again." And second, "with the election agreement, management is not going to be able to mount much of a campaign. We can use the next four weeks to build our support." The union therefore filed a petition for election with the independent arbitrator at the end of June. The election was scheduled for just two weeks later.

Hardy had been right that the quick election would not give management much time to erode workers' support significantly—but she had overestimated workers' support for the union. On the day of the election, Hardy believed the union had enough votes to win—but instead Rosemont workers decided, by two votes, not to form a union. Why was support for the union so weak? Why couldn't the union get a strong majority of Rosemont workers even to sign cards, even though there was a strong core of prounion workers and a ready-made set of issues for workers to be angry at management about? Why did even some of those who signed union cards ultimately decide to vote against the union? This chapter shows that support for the union was weak because the campaign failed to address its most important obstacle: workers' lived experiences of business unionism in southwestern Pennsylvania.

WORKERS' GRIEVANCES

Theories of movement participation have long recognized that there is no one-to-one correspondence between grievances and action, but certainly antagonistic collective action without grievances is unlikely. Therefore the first step in our argument is to demonstrate that the 1997 organizing drive at Rosemont did not fail because workers were insufficiently aggrieved. Some elements of the conditions under which Rosemont workers toiled have already been sketched, but it is important to convey the incredible array of issues about which workers were already angry when the campaign began. The following discussion is based on observations made at organizing meetings (especially the first three, which were well attended), and on interviews with 10 Rosemont workers.[6]

The most contentious issues were understaffing and the care quality problems stemming from it. At organizing meetings I attended (in my capacity as an organizing intern at Local A), much of the discussion revolved around the staffing shortages, particularly as they affected the nursing assistants. Understaffing stemmed from two problems. First, at least until the nursing home got into trouble with state inspectors, the schedule itself had been inadequate. As one day shift worker explained, "Before the state came in, we were told that the ratio was 12.5 residents for each [member of the] nursing staff. But that includes nurses and LPNs, and they don't do direct care. For us [nurses' aides], it was really more like 15 to 1. And you can't do everything when you're that rushed." Another worker agreed. "Even when nobody calls off, I don't have time to bathe [residents'] legs every day and check their heels daily for [skin] breakdowns. Not on all of them. And sometimes with these residents, if you miss a day, they can have a problem . . . especially if they're not eating well." But despite these problems, workers' complaints about the understaffing fell on deaf ears. "We told [the director of nursing] that we needed more staff. And she yelled at us and said that we were well above staffing requirements."

The second problem was that absenteeism usually reduced real-world staffing below the scheduled levels. On all shifts, but particularly on the weekends, "call-offs" were a frequent problem. "On weekends," one evening shift nurses' aide said, "We have a terrible time getting staff. There's usually 65 patients on my side — right now it's 59 — and usually there are four nursing assistants. Last night I had 12 residents and that was an easy night." There were several reasons for Rosemont's absenteeism problem. First, low wages and its concomitant, high turnover, meant that inexperienced workers who had never worked in a nursing home before always formed a substantial proportion of Rosemont aides. Even if these workers had mastered the physical demands of the job during their six-week state-required training course, they were generally unprepared for the emotional demands of trying to get the job done under the impossible conditions they found at Rosemont. Calling off thus often became a survival mechanism for inexperienced workers at the breaking point. It was not uncommon for new workers to begin calling off more and more frequently until they finally stopped coming to work at all. As one experienced worker who'd been at Rosemont for six years said,

> In school they make it seem like the job is going to be a certain way, but when you get in here, you go "Oh, shit!" because it's so much harder than you thought. They just throw you out there on the floor, you know, and you're really not ready to deal with it at all. Lots of the new girls just can't take it. So they start calling off, or they just quit.

Lacking any real program of on-the job training, management expected experienced workers to help new ones while doing their regular jobs.[7] This created tension between experienced workers and the constant parade of new workers coming through the facility: "When you're [training someone new] you have in your mind that this person is more than likely going to leave too. When you're pressed for time yourself, it's hard to do a thorough job training someone that will probably leave anyway. We usually figure a new person is going to last two weeks. Most of them don't make it past that."

Because Rosemont's wages were so low, management also had continual difficulty finding a steady stream of new workers to replace those who left. "I see the ad in the newspaper every week," one aide said. "Most weeks, nobody applies. Why would they? You can make $6.40 an hour in lots of better ways than this. They're not going to be able to keep people unless they pay better."

Desperate for staff, management often continued to schedule workers who frequently called off, or workers who had not turned up for scheduled work in days. This infuriated those who showed up faithfully and who often came in on their own days off to help ease staffing crises. "A lot of times you look on the schedule and you see names down there that you know are people who have quit, or haven't come to work in a while.

I guess [the director of nursing] feels like her ass is covered as long as she's got a name to put down for that slot — but you know that day you are going to be working short for sure."

In addition to the staffing problems, Rosemont workers were also particularly angry about what they perceived as management's indifference to the residents, the lack of respect for residents' dignity. One worker said:

Sometimes they make comments about the residents. Like the other day, some of the residents wanted to sit out in the hall, and the supervisor said to the aide who asked about it, "No, we can't have them cluttering up the place like firewood." And the residents could hear how they were being spoken about, you know. It just wasn't handled in a nice way, a caring way. That's the kind of stuff that really burns me.

Management's failure to deal promptly with documented care problems seemed to reflect this attitude. The incident described earlier, in which a resident suffered for days with an insect infestation in her bed before the DON would even agree to move her to another room, was typical of management's record, according to workers I spoke with. One nurses' aide outside the core group of union supporters actually called me at home one evening to recount the events of the preceding weeks as they related to one of her residents. Management — and the Pennsylvania Department of Health — had been completely unresponsive to her complaints and she just wanted to tell somebody. "Put it in your report," she said. "I want people to know how bad things are here."

Three weeks earlier, she had discovered an unusual, itchy, flaky rash on her patient, and had reported it to her supervisor. No action was taken to diagnose or treat the rash, and within a few days it had spread all over the resident's body. Each day the aide reported the condition of the rash — to the DON as well as to the immediate supervisor — but nothing was done. Ten days later the aide herself came down with the same kind of rash. She went to the doctor and discovered the rash was scabies. The next day she went in, armed with her diagnosis, and told the DON that she couldn't work on the floor because she'd contracted scabies from the resident and that they needed to get him treated. The DON scoffed, saying that if the aide did have scabies she'd probably gotten it outside the nursing home. Finally, more than four weeks after the initial report, a physician examined the resident and confirmed that the rash was scabies. The aide was livid. "Why didn't they have a doctor look at the rash right away when I first told them about it? There was no way [the resident] should have had to wait that long, as miserable as he was."

Every aide I talked to had her own angry stories about instances in which residents who clearly needed medical attention or a modified care plan were ignored by management, sometimes for weeks. I heard about residents falling out of broken chairs; I heard from the aides who had been ordered to roust residents in the middle of the night for showers; and I heard about management's indifference to aides' reports of resident injuries. "If you find a broken bone, or a skin tear, or a bruise," said one aide, "and you tell management about it, a lot of times they don't do anything right away. They don't like calling the doctor in too often, because it costs money. And they never investigate injuries like they're supposed to.[8] A lot of times they'll just blame it on you."

Workers also felt that management's indifference to patients' needs was reflected in its attitude toward maintaining the nursing home's physical plant, equipment, and supplies.

> A lot of times the equipment is faulty. It can be little things, like no batteries for the blood pressure cuff. You tell your charge nurse about it and basically it just goes on deaf ears. . . . It pisses me off. We're there to care for these residents and if we don't have the necessary equipment then how can you do your job? I can buy batteries myself but that's not the point.

According to another worker, "We've gone without supplies because they didn't pay the bills and companies wouldn't deliver. The diapers that we use, we were completely out of them for a couple of days. Finally they got a different company to deliver. They had the money, they just didn't pay the bill, so we went without."

Workers were also angry about the condition of the building:

> The ceiling fell in about a year ago. It was raining and the roof was leaking and a whole section of plasterboard just came down. We've had a leaky roof for a whole year, and they're just now putting a new roof on. For a year we had buckets in the halls and in some of the rooms when it rained. There's times in the winter when they didn't pay the guy and we couldn't get the driveway plowed. If somebody slips and falls on the ice and sues them it's going to cost them a lot more than paying for the snowplow. But that's the kind of outfit they are.

Another worker complained about management's failure to provide a properly functioning "airborne isolation" ward for residents with infectious diseases.

> In our airborne isolation room, there's no negative airflow and the doors are always open. When the state comes in it's a miracle how these people are cleared out of there. They're not on isolation for the state to see because we can't do it properly. And if [the residents] are really bad, they find ways of sending them to hospital so they're not there when the state is in. The things they try to get away with, it's sickening. And the bad thing is they do get away with most of it.

Workers were also angry about management's indifference to their own safety. They complained that they were rarely informed about patient's medical conditions, even when a patient had an infectious disease.

> There are times where we'll be doing PM care on residents and then a week later we'll find out that they have a disease that we should have known about — something infectious, either airborne or contact. Nobody tells us. Once we had a guy who had AIDS and we weren't told about it. He was combative and he would bite, and he would ejaculate and there would be semen we'd have to clean up. I

mean, yes we wear gloves and stuff, but in a case like that you might want to just be a bit more careful around the patient.

Some Rosemont workers complained that supervisors ordered them to perform tasks without due regard for the safety of the worker.

> My supervisor told me to shower a lady, to take vitals on her. I told her that the lady was very combative and that I needed some help but she made me do it anyway. I would have gotten written up for refusing. Well, I got beat up. I was down on the floor getting beaten up and they had to come running to help. . . . They just won't give us enough staff to have help when the residents get combative.

Finally, in addition to staffing, quality of care, and safety issues, all the workers I talked to were upset about the way management exercised arbitrary authority, targeting some workers for discipline (often unfairly or on unfounded charges) while letting others slide. Workers were most angry that management had fired large numbers of workers in response to the quality problems that were preventing the nursing home from passing its state inspection. "We lost so many people all at once," one said. "That didn't solve anything. In fact, the care is worse here now than it was before, because now we're even shorter on staff." Workers were also angry about individual injustices they observed on a daily basis. Part-time workers were routinely scheduled to work just a few hours short of full time in each pay period so that they worked essentially full-time hours but received no benefits. Shifts and schedules often changed without any notice, without any allowance for workers to rearrange child care and transportation. But most offensive was workers' perception that management always "shot the messenger" if they spoke up about a problem, even a care problem. "Being a nonunion home, we're basically told to just shut up and do as we're told," said one worker. "People here are afraid to report things that they find, because they know that most likely they'll be the one who is blamed," said another.

MANAGEMENT'S NONCAMPAIGN

Theorists of social movements have understood the social control activities of authorities as raising the costs of participation.[9] In the case of union organizing campaigns, workers must first of all face the opposition and hostility of their bosses. Employers' use of aggressive antiunion tactics during organizing campaigns, such as use of union-avoidance consultants, the illegal discharge of union activists, and election delays and appeals, have increased sharply in the last several decades.[10] Between 1992 and 1995, employers in more than one-third of all NLRB certification elections illegally fired workers for their union activity — and more than half made illegal threats that unionization would lead to layoffs or shutdowns.[11] Such antiunion tactics have been found to be quite effective in discouraging workers from supporting unions.[12] Therefore, if the management at Rosemont engaged in strongly punitive antiunion measures, we might expect this to contribute to the union's defeat.

Interestingly, however, Rosemont largely lived up to its obligations under the election agreement. Management limited its antiunion campaign to the two-week period between the union's petition for election and the election itself, and its efforts were remarkably restrained. No workers were targeted or fired for their union activity, and no individual threats were made. There were rumors that some workers had been promised raises if they agreed to vote against the union, but the union was not able to pin these rumors down. The closest thing to a documented case of unlawful antiunion communication during this period was one incident in which Rosemont's administrator wrote a sarcastic note to June McMurray: "Union meeting today at [a local diner] — how come I'm not invited?"[13]

The nursing home did hold several mandatory antiunion meetings, with speakers and films aimed at convincing workers that a union wouldn't be in anyone's interest. These meetings focused on workers' right to vote no, emphasizing that even workers who had signed interest cards did not have to vote for the union. Management also dispensed misleading information about union dues and argued that if the workers voted for a union, the union could "take them out on strike" with no guarantee of getting anything for it. But while these mild forms of antiunion communication may have had some impact on how workers voted, by themselves they don't explain why so many workers, with so many grievances against management, would vote against the union. Indeed, as we shall see in the next chapter, management's campaign in the 1998 campaign — which the union won by a two-to-one margin — was much longer, more sustained, and more intense. In the remaining sections of this chapter, I show that the most important reason for the failure of the 1997 campaign at Rosemont had to do with, not how workers related to management, but how they related to the union.

LIVED EXPERIENCES OF BUSINESS UNIONISM

On the day the ballots were counted, I sat in a windowless room inside the nursing home with Joan Hardy, June McMurray, and several other rank-and-file workers who'd been behind the effort to unionize Rosemont. Also present were the nursing home's administrator and director of nursing. The atmosphere was tense as the independent arbitrator stood at a table at the front of the room and methodically pulled individual ballots from the box, held them up for all to see, and declared them as "yes" or "no" votes. The count was close throughout. Now the union was ahead, now the company took the lead. With five or six ballots left to count, the union was up by a couple of votes. But the count ended with a string of "no" votes, and then it was over: the union had lost. The administrator broke into a triumphant grin.

As soon as the count was concluded, we filed out of the room and toward Rosemont's main entrance. But even as we filed out, news of the outcome spread with lightning speed throughout the facility. And I began to hear a sound I never expected: I left the building with the cheers of Rosemont workers ringing in my ears. They were *cheering!* I was dumbfounded. I could not believe that the downtrodden, underpaid workers at Rosemont were *glad* that they would remain without griev-ance procedures, wage scales, and collective bargaining rights. I knew how bad the working conditions were at Rosemont; I knew how low the wages were and how random, arbitrary, and unfair the application of management discipline was. To me, it seemed obvious that if anyone, anywhere, was in need of a union, it was the employees at Rosemont. And not only had they said no, they were cheering about it, apparently spontaneously. I simply could not understand it.

Of course, none of the theories of movement participation outlined in the introduction to Part I really helps us to understand Rosemont workers' cheers either. To explain the union's defeat, these theories would point out variously that the campaign did not create or take advantage of social networks in or out of the workplace, that the union did not engage effectively in framing activities, and that the absence of collective action meant that consciousness-raising could not occur. And these are, to be sure, important observations. Consider, for example, the idea that social networks and mobilizing structures are important con-duits for information. It is true that the union's reliance on organizing meetings as the main source of communication with the workers left many workers in the dark about basic issues. Attendance at these meet-ings quickly dwindled to just a few workers, cutting the union off from the workers it was attempting to organize. As I would find out the fol-lowing year, many people had questions about issues like dues; the steps that would be involved in the organizing campaign itself; whether man-agement would know who voted for the union; the process of collective bargaining, and what rights they would have as individuals under a col-lective bargaining agreement. They did not receive answers from the union during the 1997 campaign.

This lack of basic communication certainly contributed to the union's defeat because when the election was held, many people did not have a clear idea of what they were voting for. "I don't know if I ever talked about the union with anyone," one nurses' aide said after the election. "There just wasn't any information. We were supposed to vote 'yes' or 'no,' but we didn't know enough about the union for a lot of people to vote 'yes.' What we had wasn't working, but it's hard to vote for something different unless you know what you're getting into." The union's inability to disseminate basic information also hurt its cause in other ways. According to June McMurray: "We had several people who never got the right information about the voting times. They were 'yes' votes but they showed up at 4:30, after the polls closed. So we lost a couple of votes right there." In addition, there was confusion about whether the ballots were secret or not. "A lot of people were afraid to vote yes because they thought management would know how they voted," McMurray added. "I talked to quite a few people after the election who thought management knew which way they voted. I said, "How are they going to know that? You didn't put your name on the ballot, you just checked off 'yes' or 'no.' But they still thought management would find out somehow."

And if the union did not establish enough links to the rank and file to transmit basic information, then it could not engage in the sort of meaningful framing activity that might have altered workers' views of unions in a positive direction, nor could it organize collective action that might enabled the sort of consciousness-raising experiences described by Rick Fantasia and Eric Hirsch.[14] On the basis of these considerations, it is fair to say that theories of social movement participation would have correctly predicted a low rate of participation in this particular campaign.

But while these theories do identify important weaknesses in the union's campaign that certainly contributed to its defeat, a satisfying explanation of the outcome so far eludes us because we still do not know *why* workers had such negative views of unions in the first place — views so strong that cheering would seem the appropriate response to news of the union's defeat. Workers' decisions to vote against the union, in other words, have a positive, meaningful content that is not captured by observations about the flaws in the union's campaign strategy. The story of the union's defeat is not only the story of what the union did or didn't do, it's also the story of why Rosemont workers were *against* the union. It's conceivable, for example, that workers might have been so eager to form a union that they could have decided to unionize *despite* the union's lackluster organizing effort. To explain the outcome we need to know not only what the union failed to do but also why the shortcomings in the union's organizing campaign mattered so much. In short, we need to understand what was behind the cheering of ecstatic nonunion workers.

Part of the problem is that movement participation theories generally assume that the question of participation applies only to those who already agree with the movement's goals and means. It would seem that people who don't support the movement, who cheer at its defeats, aren't likely to participate in it. Theories of movement participation would therefore write the cheering workers off as movement opponents. And yet, one year later, many of the same people who cheered the union's defeat in June 1997 *did* participate in the second unionization drive, not only by voting for unionization but also by participating in visible shows of support for the union. Somehow, then, we have to understand not only why so many Rosemont workers actively hoped for union defeat in 1997 but also why and how some of the same people could take a completely different position in 1998.

The nature and meaning of rank-and-file opposition to unionization at Rosemont did not begin to become clear to me until 1998, when the union returned for a second try with a more grassroots approach. In the summer of 1998, once again as an intern working on the campaign, I visited 36 of the workers in the proposed bargaining unit at their homes as part of the union's new organizing strategy. Even though these visits took place during the second campaign rather than the first, I draw on them here because it was only during these visits that I began to appreciate the real basis for workers' ambivalence and opposition. In my 1997 interviews, I had not thought to probe deeply about workers' experiences of unions, since I had assumed (wrongly) that the main issues explaining the outcome of the first campaign must lie with workers' relation to management. Unlike the interviews I had conducted in 1997, this time it was the workers who set the agenda for discussion. For the first time, I directly encountered the perceptions of, and experiences with, unions that lay behind workers' opposition to unionization. My discussions with workers during these 1998 visits revealed that three distinct sets of union experiences were functioning as a barrier to the SEIU's organizing efforts: *experiences of deindustrialization and job loss; experiences of union violence, intimidation, and corruption;* and *experiences and images of "do-nothing" unionism.* It is reasonable to assume that these issues did not suddenly arise in 1998; clearly, they had been salient in 1997 and had played an important role in the outcome of that campaign.

I want to emphasize too that the existence of these negative union experiences cannot be understood simply as an information problem — these were not simply misperceptions. Rather, they represented the legacies of half a century of business unionism in the Rust Belt. Workers brought with them sets of ideas about unions that they drew from their own experiences as union members, the experiences of family members, and their experiences of media messages about unions. At a minimum, these lived experiences reflected assumptions about what it meant to be a union member — and about the nature of the relationship between rank-and-file members and the union organization — which were antithetical to the SEIU's official ideal of a more grassroots, member-driven, movement-oriented model of unionism. And at worst, workers interpreted their own lived experiences of business unionism quite negatively, forming the source of strong antiunion sentiment and outright hostility to the organizing campaign.

Deindustrialization and the Fear of Job Loss

The decline of mining and manufacturing in the communities around Rosemont nursing home was sketched in the introduction to Part I. This decline was so complete that by 1990, there were no workers at all employed in the mining sector in the township in which Rosemont is located, although there were dozens of shut-down mines.[15] Similarly, in nearby McKeesport and Duquesne, industrial suburbs of Pittsburgh that had been the sites of large-scale steel manufacturing for a century, all of the mills were closed in the late 1980s.

These economic changes loomed large in the lives of workers at Rosemont. Many older workers had been directly affected. Men who lost industrial jobs in the 1980s rarely found new work at equivalent wages. Therefore, many of Rosemont's older female employees had gone to work in the 1980s or early 1990s to help cope with their families' sinking standard of living. Aside from minor differences in the details, the following older worker's story was almost identical to many others I heard:

> My husband and father both worked for Westinghouse. My husband
> was laid off from Westinghouse years ago when my daughter was lit-
> tle. Those were bad years. I worked two jobs, and one of them was
> sewing piecework. I hated that job, but I was there for the benefits —
> I needed hospitalization for two children and a husband. Finally
> he got a job at the prison. He still wasn't making great money but
> at least he had benefits. I quit the sewing job within a week of his
> benefits kicking in.

Older workers like this one, who had lived through the collapse of industrial unionism in the Monongahela valley, interpreted their experiences in a variety of ways. Some remained strongly prounion, blaming the companies for deindustrialization and viewing the decline in unions as a major reason that times had gotten so much harder than they used to be. Many of these women had husbands who felt the same way and who believed that their wives' job conditions would never get any better unless they organized a union. During organizing visits to a number of workers' homes, I met several strongly prounion men who welcomed me warmly and sat in on the discussion about Rosemont, chiming in with strongly worded comments about the need for a union there. Rosemont women with this kind of support were almost always prounion themselves and tended to interpret the economic disaster they were living through as something that had been perpetrated against the unions rather than something that the unions had caused.

However, this interpretation was far from universal. Equally common were workers who bitterly blamed the unions as much as the companies for what had happened to the industrial economy of the region. Several workers I spoke with were particularly angry about decisions their husbands' unions had made in the 1980s to go on strike even while management was planning or threatening to close or relocate their plants. "What were they thinking?" one woman said. "[Management] was just looking for an excuse to relocate the plant. And the union went out on strike just to get another dollar an hour. Hell, my husband was making $19 dollars an hour already. They didn't need that extra dollar an hour, not really. Management didn't care if they went on strike — they just closed the plant up for good. If the union hadn't gone on strike we might have kept the plant for a while longer, anyway."

This view was not limited to just a few workers. In one of the early organizing meetings I attended in June 1997, those present were talking about the views of their co-workers. One worker said, "If I hear one more time that so-and-so's husband lost their steel job because of the union, I'm gonna scream!" There was a chorus of agreement from the others, and Joan Hardy, the union organizer who was running the meeting, asked people to elaborate. "People say that the unions put the plants out of business because of the high wages," one said. "We hear that all the time."

Rosemont made good use of this issue during its brief antiunion campaign in 1997. The films workers were forced to watch juxtaposed footage of industrial strikes with footage of plant closings and deindustrialized areas. Management representatives told the workers in the mandatory meetings that the union wanted to make the nursing home uncompetitive. They argued that if they could afford to raise wages, they would, but that Medicaid reimbursement levels were so low that they couldn't raise wages or hire more staff and still make a profit. Management representatives were careful not to make explicit threats about shutting down the nursing home in response to unionization — but they did not need to be so explicit because this fear was already in the minds of Rosemont workers.

During my home visits the following summer, this issue was raised again and again by anxious workers, who were worried that forming a union might ultimately lead to the shutdown of the nursing home. How the union dealt with these questions in the 1998 campaign will be discussed in the next chapter, but the point here is that the union's arm's-length campaign tactics in 1997 had prevented it from dealing with the widespread view that unions were largely to blame for deindustrialization and that unionization might force the nursing home out of business.

Union Violence, Intimidation, and Corruption

Perhaps the most significant business union legacy was workers' association of unions with violence and intimidation. The stereotypical images of the corrupt union boss and the thick-necked labor goon have become standard types in movies and television shows,[16] but like most stereotypes they do contain a kernel of truth. Unions have always been less violent than their corporate opponents, especially if one defines violence to include forms of economic violence. However, the fact remains that some industrial unions have a reputation for using strong-arm tactics to intimidate bosses and to keep workers in line. Even worse, these tactics have sometimes been deployed by corrupt union officials against workers who have tried to democratize their unions. The cases are rare, but they tend to be famous. In one of the most widely known, the president of the United Mine Workers ordered the murder of the leader of a UMW reform movement in 1969.[17] In the mining country of southwestern Pennsylvania, older workers remember these events firsthand. Nothing makes contemporary organizing more difficult than these images of unions as not only corrupt but violent organizations.

At Rosemont nursing home, this view of unions was grounded in the experience of a core group of kitchen workers who had worked at the nursing home for nearly two decades. In 1980, the Teamsters union had organized the facility and won a certification election. However, the president of the Teamsters' Local apparently believed that strong-arm tactics were the best way to win a good contract. Instead of negotiating in good faith, the Teamsters' president began threatening the nursing home administrator with bodily harm if management would not accede to the Teamsters' demands. The nursing home refused, and the Teamsters escalated their attack. According to several workers I spoke with who had worked at Rosemont during this period, Teamsters came to the facility on several occasions and threw rocks through the windows, terrorizing the residents and angering the workers. On October 5, 1980, matters grew even graver: a homemade bomb was found underneath a car in the parking lot. According to press reports, the bomb, equivalent to three to five sticks of dynamite, failed to detonate only because the timing device was faulty. Police and FBI investigations failed to yield a suspect, but two months later, a similarly constructed device — this time filled with mud instead of explosive — was disguised as a gift and left under a Christmas tree inside the nursing home. The president of the Teamsters local that was organizing the facility made an anonymous telephone call to the management to warn them that there was a bomb in the building. His message was captured on tape and his voice identified by the FBI. He was eventually indicted and convicted on charges of making bomb threats, but no one was ever definitively connected to the October bomb.

As a result of this debacle, many workers at Rosemont remained staunchly antiunion for years afterwards. In 1997, a group of kitchen workers who had seen these events firsthand still vociferously opposed the union and went to great lengths to persuade their co-workers that forming a union could only lead to trouble. This group formed a vocal opposition to the small group of workers who were actually involved with the union in 1997, shouting down union supporters in break-room discussions. With encouragement from management, they formed a "just vote no" committee that held regular meetings, put up antiunion posters around the facility, and helped management distribute antiunion literature.

These antiunion workers formed social networks that militated *against* unionization and exerted social pressure on anyone who dared venture the opinion that a union might be a good idea, thus raising the costs of being prounion — especially in the kitchen, where the leaders of the antiunion group worked. In the summer of 1998, I visited two kitchen workers who had disagreed completely with the "just vote no" committee. However, the antiunion kitchen workers had intimidated both of them into silence. "I couldn't speak up," one said. "You don't understand what it's like in there. The kitchen is a closed environment. I have to deal with these people every day. They would have made my life miserable if I had said anything against them. I didn't agree with them, but I just kept my opinions to myself." The other prounion kitchen worker I talked to in 1998 felt the same way. She had been cautiously supportive of organizing a union but was terrified of her antiunion co-workers. "Please don't tell anyone that you visited me," she begged. "I believe in the union, but if they find out I was talking to you they'll all be after me."

Of course, the Teamsters' organizing campaign represents an extreme case. But the bitterness it left behind is not unique. Even campaigns that do not involve violence, intimidation, or corruption can leave an antiunion legacy in their wake. Linda Markowitz's[18] comparison of a top-down, business union United Food and Commercial Workers (UFCW) campaign with a more participatory, grassroots-oriented Amalgamated Clothing and Textile Workers Union (ACTWU) campaign shows that workers who initially support a union can emerge from successful organizing campaigns feeling very bitter, disappointed in the union, and even antiunion if the union does not live up to its promises or their expectations. Interestingly, Markowitz found that workers who had been involved in the ACTWU's grassroots, participatory, "workers are the union" campaign were even more bitter than their UFCW counterparts when the participatory ideals of their campaign were replaced by the realities of postcontract servicing. These findings highlight how crucial it is for union organizing campaigns to be honest and open with rank-and-file workers — and to follow through on promises. Campaigns that treat workers as votes, marginalize workers' concerns and issues, or fail to deliver on their promises can poison the well for years to come.

"Do-Nothing" Unionism

The fear of many workers, quite plainly, was that the union was only interested in their dues money — that if they voted for the union, the union would take their dues and not help them, leaving them perhaps worse off than before. These workers were intimately familiar with the workings of one organization — their employer — that exploited them and turned a deaf ear to their complaints, grievances, and problems. They feared that the union would not be different.

This fear was something I found myself encountering over and over again as I visited people at their homes. Their overriding concern was how much, and what kind of, representation they would get for their dues. Like wary and skeptical consumers, workers tried to figure out exactly what they were being asked to buy, how much it would cost them, and what guarantees they would have that they would actually get what they thought they were buying. How much were the dues? How did the union spend the dues? What if the union spent their dues money on things — like political candidates — that they didn't support? How much did the president of the local make? How could they be sure the union would fight for them? How could they be sure the union wouldn't "take my money and run" (as one worker put it)? "What kind of raises will we get if we vote the union in?" was a common question. The following worker's question was also typical: "They said that we could end up with no more than we have now, or less. What guarantee do we have that we'll get anything out of it?" Workers also worried about the possibility of a strike. "What if they don't agree to anything and the union calls us out on strike?" I was asked. "What will happen then? We can't just abandon these residents in here."

On one hand, these kinds of questions highlight something that theorists of movement participation have long emphasized: that people usually weigh the costs and benefits of participating — or at least, they weigh their *perceptions* of costs and benefits — before they commit themselves.[19] On the other hand, workers' assumption that they were being asked to purchase a service, as opposed to being asked to join in a collective effort to change their workplace, also reflected their experience with the norms and expectations of servicing-oriented business unionism. As numerous critics of business unionism have pointed out, the ideology of "servicing" discourages rank-and-file participation and creates dependence on professional union staff.[20] Workers were certainly right to be wary and careful in their decision making — but their assumption that the role of the union was to "fight for me" reflected a preexisting normative expectation, rooted in the ideology and reality of business unionism, that their role in the union would be a passive one.

Many workers I talked to had stories to tell about how they or people they knew had been "shafted" by their union. Either the union hadn't listened to their views, or the union had failed to represent them in some way. One woman I visited was particularly blunt. "Y'ins are buggers," she said. "You can make your promises, but they don't mean shit to me." She went on to complain about her experience as a member of a factory union in the 1970s. "That was an old-boy network," she said. "I was one of the only women there. They didn't listen to what I had to say because I was a woman. I didn't get the same raises [as the men], and when I had a grievance they didn't do anything with it. So as far as I'm concerned, your unions are just for the ones that run 'em." Sexism — and racism — is deeply rooted in the labor movement in southwestern Pennsylvania. The 1996 documentary film *Struggles in Steel*, by Tony Buba and Ray Henderson, documents how the USWA collaborated with metal-industry employers throughout the postwar period to keep African

Americans in the worst, lowest-paid positions and women out of the plants altogether. The USWA's discriminatory practices persisted well into the 1970s, when a lawsuit filed by a group of African American workers against both the union and the major steel companies finally resulted in a federal consent decree mandating affirmative action for minorities and women.

Other workers had different complaints. One woman's husband had been injured on the job, and he was fighting for his settlement when his plant closed. She was bitter because in her view the union hadn't done enough to get him a fair settlement. And some workers with direct experience in business union settings simply felt that the union had not been a significant factor in shaping the quality of their work life. Consider the case of a housekeeping worker, Gene, with whom I spoke early in the 1998 campaign. The union had learned from another worker that Gene, a quiet person who would not necessarily be influenced by others' loud opinions, was undecided about the union. He had told the union's informant that he didn't want to be visited at home but that he would like someone from the union to call him. When I spoke with him on the phone, he was pleasant but he made it clear that he was completely indifferent to the union. "I don't care whether it's voted in or not," he said. He explained that he had been working part time for a number of years at a local supermarket, where he was represented by the United Food and Commercial Workers (UFCW). "The union there doesn't mean a lot," he said. "Our wages there are not much more than minimum. The union makes no difference to my life there. So I don't see how it's really going to change much for me here either." Gene was respected by other workers in his department, and when he spoke up, his co-workers listened. Gene's views thus had hurt the 1997 campaign quite a lot, but the union hadn't known anything about him during that campaign.

Paradoxically, while many workers feared that the union would not do much, many of the same workers were concerned that one thing it might do was protect workers who did not do their jobs. A number of workers raised this as a primary objection to having a union. As one said,

"Don't unions make it harder to get rid of bad workers? How does it help me to have the union defending somebody who deserves to be fired?" Local A's 1997 organizing effort never proffered an answer to these questions.

CONCLUSION

As we have seen, Local A's first Rosemont campaign failed to incorporate features that social movements researchers have identified with high participation rates. The rushed, arm's-length nature of the campaign prevented organizers from engaging in sustained persuasive communication with more than a handful of workers, so no real attempt at framing was possible. The campaign did not mobilize the kinds of social ties and networks that sociologists have identified as important factors encouraging participation. Neither did it organize any participatory forms of collective action — thus negating the possibility that consciousness-raising might occur. But what I have tried to show in this chapter is that the *absence* of such facilitating factors as framing, networks, or collective action attempts cannot really form the basis of a satisfying explanation of the union's defeat. The notion of framing can help us understand aspects of the processes of persuasion that occur in effective organizing but not why workers should be so ambivalent toward unions in the first place. Theories emphasizing the role of social networks as an objective factor explaining participation miss the fact that it is not so much the existence of networks that leads people to participate (or not) but rather the *content* of the communication that these networks permit. To understand why Rosemont workers chose not to participate in the labor movement, in other words, we must understand the basis of their opposition from the inside, not as a set of factors but as a collection of concrete, contextualized, historicized meanings rooted in the lived experiences of the actors. It was only when I began to interrogate these lived experiences that I discovered the presence of business union experiences behind workers' ambivalence toward and distrust of the union.

Thus we see that in the contemporary context, anger at management is not enough to guarantee union victory: workers' concerns and anxieties about unions are drawn from their experiences of the labor movement, which, particularly in Rust Belt areas like Pittsburgh, can be quite negative. Campaigns relying on arm's-length organizing tactics like mailing lists or mass meetings are not able to deal effectively with workers' lived experiences of the movement itself. In the SEIU's first Rosemont campaign, the union failed not only because it was unable to convey basic information or counteract management claims but also because it was unable to defuse or refute antiunion sentiments among the workers themselves, let alone build collective solidarity by inspiring workers with a vision of an alternative form of participatory and powerful unionism.

In Chapter 3, we turn to the union's second attempt to organize Rosemont Pavilion. Here we will see how and why grassroots, face-to-face organizing techniques and escalating collective action succeeded: because, through them, the union's campaign enabled workers to reconstruct their lived experience of unions.

THREE

"It's a Union"

*Why Face-to-Face Organizing
and Collective Action Tactics Succeed*

When the final ballot was counted in July 1997, revealing that the union had lost the election, Joan Hardy walked up to Rosemont's administrator and said, "Congratulations, and see you next year. We'll be back." Then she met for a few minutes with June McMurray, who was just arriving for her afternoon shift, on the nursing home's front steps. McMurray was visibly shaken; she worried that she was going to be fired now that the election was lost. Hardy clearly felt terrible for McMurray. "Don't worry," she said. "We're going to do this again, and next time we're going to win." Because the election agreement between Local A and the Hewitt Group — like U.S. labor law — required the union to wait at least 12 months before filing a new election petition after losing an election, there could be no plans for an immediate second attempt. Therefore, all Hardy could do at that point was make arrangements to stay in close contact with McMurray over the winter. "We'll start organizing again in May or June," Hardy promised. "We're not going to give up, so hang in there."

Hardy proved as good as her word. But more important, she showed that she was capable of criticizing her own previous attempt to organize Rosemont. First, she recognized now that the union's strategy had been

63

flawed. The union had petitioned for an election without a strong majority on cards primarily to force the company to turn over an Excelsior list, an accurate list of employees and their addresses. "We knew they had to have the election within four weeks of our petition, but we thought they would try to push it back to give themselves more time to run their antiunion campaign. That's usually what the employer tries to do," Hardy explained. "We thought that once we got an accurate employee list, we could use those four weeks to build our support. But they were smart. They didn't think we had the votes, so they agreed to schedule the election right away [just two weeks after the petition]. And they were right — we didn't have the votes."

Hardy now felt that relying on the election agreement to get an accurate list of employees had been a mistake. Instead, the union should have done a better job of organizing and training a representative rank-and-file committee, whose members could have obtained the same information through their shop floor organizing efforts. There had been no serious attempt to train rank-and-file activists, either to organize their co-workers or to assess their level of support accurately. As mentioned in Chapter 2, Hardy had been relying almost exclusively on just two workers. Even in principle these two workers could not possibly organize 70 co-workers. Nor could these untrained volunteers accurately assess their co-workers' level of support for the union. Their assessments were not only devoid of concrete information but also unrealistically optimistic. At each meeting, during the discussion of the employee list, Hardy would ask about specific people. The rank-and-file workers would reply, "Oh, she's for the union" or "She's an anti." But these "assessments" were little more than guesses. As Hardy later admitted,

> June and Sharon, God bless 'em, they are hard workers and they will do anything you ask. But they were so eager to get the union in that they weren't listening to what people were really telling them. If they could think of a reason that someone should be pissed off at management, they would tell us the person was for the union. And

then we relied on their assessments way too much; we believed them when we shouldn't have.

The real problem, of course, did not lie with these worker volunteers but in the fact that the union hadn't given them any organizing training or done enough to build a viable rank-and-file organizing committee. Hardy recognized this as she prepared for the second campaign.

The union took a very different approach in the second campaign. This time, it based its campaign on the latest organizing manuals, pamphlets, and literature from the international union. Following the SEIU's grassroots organizing model, Local A now conducted targeted house calling in order to recruit a strong organizing committee and trained committee members to organize and assess their co-workers and to participate in house calling throughout the campaign. As it built the organizing committee into a functioning structure that reached into every work area in the nursing home, union organizers and organizing committee members also house-visited nearly every member of the bargaining unit. And in 1998 the union's campaign, unlike the first campaign, was organized around an escalating strategy of collective action aimed at building workers' solidarity. Using these tactics, the union was now able to get more than 70 percent of the workers to sign interest cards, to build workers' support for the union during the course of a more lengthy campaign, and to more accurately assess workers' real level of support. This time, the union won the election by a two-to-one margin, receiving only two fewer votes than it anticipated.

If Chapter 2 showed how workers' lived experiences of old-style unionism were at the root of the union's defeat in the first campaign, the question posed here is why and how the union was able to win such a decisive victory just one year later. Just as it is necessary to understand why the absence of social movement tactics leads to organizing failures, it is necessary to understand why and how adopting these tactics produces victories. This time we will see how the union's effort enabled it to deal with workers' negative business union experiences and replace them with a more positive view of a new kind of participatory, grassroots unionism. Building social networks and organization, building collective identity, and engaging in effective framing activities are all parts of the story — but these are significant only insofar as they enabled workers to view the movement in a new light. Before getting to these arguments, however, we must consider some alternative explanations for the union's success.

WORKER GRIEVANCES IN 1998

Changes in workers' grievances cannot explain the landslide victory in the second campaign. However, for two reasons, the level of workers' anger at management was probably higher in 1998 than it had been the year before. First, many workers felt that management had not lived up to promises it had made during the 1997 campaign. In 1997, Rosemont's administrator, who had just been hired in the spring of that year, had argued that workers should give him a chance to make changes. As one organizing committee member later recalled,

> He said it wasn't fair of us not to give him a chance. He promised
> that things were going to be different if we voted against the
> union, and if we voted the union in, he wouldn't be able to make
> the changes he wanted that would improve things. Now I've been
> here for eight years, you know, and I've seen dozens of administra-
> tors come and go. Nothing ever changes and they all come in telling
> us how different it's going to be. So I took that with a grain of salt.
> But a lot of the girls, the new ones, believed him, thought they
> should give him a chance.

By early June 1998, just 23 of the 71 workers who had been eligible to vote in the 1997 election, just 11 months earlier, were still employed at Rosemont. Several of the workers in this group were particularly angry that the promised changes had not materialized. "He promised that things would be different if we only gave him a chance," one worker said. "He said, how could we vote for the union when we didn't know what he was going to do for us? [Last year] I felt that he deserved a chance . . . but nothing changed. Things are as bad now as ever. If the union can help us, I guess I'm ready to try it."

The second new reason for workers' anger was that in the spring of 1998 the Hewitt Group posted notices at Rosemont explaining that "nonunion workers" in all of the chain's nursing homes would be losing some important health benefits. Until the change, Hewitt Group employees with five years of service earned paid hospitalization benefits for their family members. Now those in nonunion Hewitt homes would have to pay hundreds of dollars a month for health insurance for their dependent family members. In unionized Hewitt homes, of course, workers' health benefits were protected by their collective bargaining agreements. As much as the Hewitt Group would have liked to abrogate unionized workers' health benefits, they were bound by these collective agreements.

Hewitt made a serious blunder by posting these notices, which drove home the point that a union would have protected Rosemont workers from this benefit cut. Not all workers were equally outraged by the policy change, however. Some relied on spouses' health benefits and, as a result, felt that the change didn't affect them personally. For others, particularly new hires, five years seemed a long way off. As one new employee told me, "I'm not going to be here that long anyway. It's bad for the ones that need [the benefits], but it's not going to make much difference to me one way or the other." Still, for many workers, the benefits were an important issue.

Both the benefits issue and management's failed promises helped cast the union in a different light: the benefits issue highlighted the value of union organization, while management's failure to live up to its own promises made workers less likely to trust management's claims about unions. As a result, several workers I visited in 1998 said that although they had voted against the union in 1997, these issues had changed their minds. One of these workers actually joined the organizing committee in and played an active role in the second campaign. "If the only reason we're going to lose our health benefits is because we don't have a union, then maybe we do need one," this worker said. Thus, even if the union had not changed its campaign style, it might still have received more votes in 1998 than in 1997.

It is highly unlikely, however, that the union would have won the second election by a two-to-one margin using the same tactics it had employed in 1997. Recall that Chapter 2's discussion of how elements of workers' lived experience led them to be apprehensive, skeptical, or even antiunion was drawn from house visits I participated in during the summer of 1998 — *after* the two issues discussed above had made their impact on workers' views of the union. In other words, even though the health benefits issue and management's failed promises helped some workers reinterpret their experiences of unions, the union still encountered strong negative union experiences as an important obstacle in its 1998 campaign. For most workers I talked to in 1998, the benefits issue and management's failed promises were not, *by themselves*, enough to completely change their minds about unions or to solidify their support for the union. Instead, workers were now more likely to listen carefully to what the union had to say and to give the union a chance to persuade them. These issues may have given the union an important foot in the door (so to speak), but the union could easily have blown this opportunity by living down to workers' fears and apprehensions about unions. The union still faced the daunting tasks of channeling that anger into solid support and convincing the majority of still-undecided workers that forming a union represented a positive step toward a better work life.

MANAGEMENT'S ANTIUNION CAMPAIGN

If the intensity and duration of management's antiunion campaign could not explain the union's defeat in 1997, neither can it explain the union's success in 1998. In 1997, Rosemont had relied primarily on its strategy of scheduling a quick election to take advantage of the fact that, as it correctly perceived, the union had not built enough support to win. In 1998, however, Rosemont mounted a stronger antiunion campaign.

To be sure, many elements of Rosemont's antiunion campaign were the same in 1998 as they had been the previous year. Once again, management held mandatory meetings in which workers were subjected to antiunion movies and antiunion speeches from the administrator and corporate officers. Just as in the previous year, the emphasis of these meetings was not on intimidation but on persuasion. Rosemont once again tried to convince its workers that the union was only interested in them for their dues money; that the union would not be able to help them improve their jobs; and that they could end up with less through collective bargaining than they already had. And just as before, management's messages played on images of bureaucratic-servicing unionism: unions take your dues and do nothing for you except take you out on strikes that you can't win.

But there were also new elements. This time, unlike 1997 — despite the nursing home's formal agreement with the union not to begin any antiunion campaigning until after the union petitioned the arbitrator for an election — management began campaigning as soon as it became aware of the union's renewed organizing efforts in early July. Management's 1998 campaign lasted not just a few weeks but nearly three months — until the election was held in late September.

Rosemont's campaign was also more sophisticated than it had been the previous year. This time, workers were subjected to a barrage of antiunion literature designed by a union-avoidance consulting firm. Some of this literature took an educational tone, reminding workers to "remember your RIGHTS: you can vote 'NO' . . . even if you signed a union card" and that "you cannot be neutral. . . . If the union wins, it represents everyone, like it or not." Management also mailed "personal" letters from the administrator to each worker at his or her home. These letters were chatty and intimate, emphasizing the administrator's desire to solve the nursing home's problems without "interference" from a "third party." Other examples of antiunion literature, distributed at the mandatory meeting, were stronger in tone. "Collective Bargaining IS A GAMBLE," one handout warned. "No one knows what the outcome might be!" Next to the title was a picture of a roulette wheel labeled "union gamble." Slots in the wheel read "less," "more," and "same." The left side of the piece was decorated with pictures of poker chips, dice, cards, and a slot machine. The text emphasized the uncertainties associated with collective bargaining.

YOU COULD LOSE — The union could use your current wages and benefits as bargaining chips. After negotiations, you might end up with more, the same thing you have today (plus union dues), or less.

NO AGREEMENT IS REQUIRED — Whether or not a labor agreement would be successfully negotiated is a roll of the dice. The company doesn't have to agree to anything that is not in its best interest.

EVERYTHING IS NEGOTIABLE — If the union got in, even the benefits and work rules you like could be open to negotiation. You might have to live with whatever hand the union deals you.

NO GUARANTEE — What you actually get can be very different from what the union promises. The only "sure bet" is that a union contract will control your life on the job, whether you like it or not.
STAY SECURE & UNION-FREE — VOTE NO!

Another example of management's antiunion literature emphasized the disadvantages of the union itself. Captioned "Heads, the union wins. . . . Tails, you lose," and illustrated with pictures of quarters with heads or tails facing up, the handout listed ways in which the union would harm workers:

UNION INITIATION FEE — HEADS, THE UNION WINS. This is what it costs new employees to join the union.

MONTHLY UNION DUES — TAILS, YOU LOSE. Both the local and the international union would have their hands in your pockets every month.

SPECIAL ASSESSMENTS — HEADS, THE UNION WINS. You could be forced to pay additional money for a pet union project or to support a strike you never heard of.

UNION FINES — TAILS, YOU LOSE. If you disagreed with the union or broke a union rule, you could be fined, put on trial, and forced to pay.

STRIKES — TAILS, YOU LOSE AGAIN. First, you would lose your wages and benefits. You could not collect unemployment insurance. But your house payment, car payment, and other bills would continue.

SUPER SENIORITY — HEADS, THE UNION WINS. Stewards and other union officials would be the last to be laid off, even if they had less seniority than you.

INDIVIDUAL FREEDOMS — TAILS, YOU LOSE. You would lose the right to take complaints directly to the company or to make special requests.

TEAMWORK — TAILS, YOU LOSE. Unions are only good at putting up barriers, not tearing them down.
VOTE NO!

In addition to such literature, management also distributed antiunion cartoons. One cartoon portrayed union "promises" as baited fishhooks suspended from lines deployed by a fat, smug union official. Another cartoon — by far the most outrageous — portrayed a union fat cat (literally an obese, cigar-smoking cat wearing a suit) holding a "union authorization card" and saying "Go ahead, sign!" to a young, naive worker. In successive panels, as the cat says "It's just a piece of paper!" and "What have you got to lose?" the cat is gradually transformed into a hideous satanic figure, complete with horns, a tail, a forked tongue, and sharp, pointy teeth.

In addition to these tactics, management brought in more sophisticated and professional antiunion speakers than in 1997. Instead of hearing only from the administrator and corporate officers, this time workers were also subjected to lectures from professional antiunion speakers, including one who claimed to have been a union organizer himself. This speaker told stories about how he had "tricked" people into voting for unions by making promises on which the union could never deliver. He claimed that as an organizer he had been trained to lie and to manipulate workers into getting what the union wanted. "Damn, that guy was good," one organizing committee member said. "He even had me doubting a little bit, and I've been union all my life. I know he scared a lot of people in there today."

These examples of antiunion literature are in no way unique or unusual; instead, they represent exactly the sort of standard campaign literature produced by a professional union-avoidance consulting firm. When I showed Joe Reilly some of the literature early in the campaign, he laughed and said, "Same old stuff — dues and strikes." A few minutes later he returned with a folder full of management literature from past nursing home campaigns. Now I understood Reilly's reaction: it really was all the same. The letters used in one campaign could have been used in any of them — they all said the same things, in the same ways, using the same phrases. But however formulaic and unoriginal this literature (and the rhetoric of the antiunion speakers), the nursing home workers it was addressed to had never seen it before, so to them it seemed original and potent. I realized at that moment that simply showing workers this folder could have a powerful neutralizing effect. But to do this, the campaign would need to be based on face-to-face organizing.

FACE-TO-FACE ORGANIZING AND COLLECTIVE ACTION IN THE UNION'S SECOND CAMPAIGN

The union made use of two face-to-face organizing strategies in its 1998 campaign. The first was its effort to house-visit every worker in the proposed bargaining unit; the second was the one-on-one and small group work of the rank-and-file organizing committee, whose members talked to their co-workers in an organized way before and after shifts, in the break room, at lunch, and often on the phone.

Since Joan Hardy was the local's only full-time organizer, and because she was working hard on another organizing campaign at a nursing home two hours east of Pittsburgh, conducting a comprehensive house-calling effort meant expanding the local's organizing staff. The union therefore hired two organizing interns, of whom I was one, and a "member organizer," an experienced veteran of the Megacorp campaigns discussed in Part III. Carol Green had been a shop steward at a Megacorp nursing home for years and had gained valuable organizing experience during the union's two-year struggle with Megacorp in 1995 and 1996. Because of a work-related back injury, Green was available to help with the Rosemont campaign.

The union used Green not only on Rosemont but also on other campaigns as well, as part of its fledgling member organizer program. A number of labor intellectuals on the left have advocated that the labor movement make extensive use of member organizers in "member-to-member" organizing drives, arguing that rank-and-file members are more effective organizers because they show workers that the union belongs to the members rather than to a distant bureaucracy.[1] The SEIU has actively promoted this idea with its member locals; Local A created its program in response to this pressure from the international. However, Local member organizer program was not really a functioning entity. The local identified a number of rank-and-file members who were willing to act as volunteers, and it periodically provided training to these volunteers — typically in the form of a weekend retreat. But Local A did not make systematic use of them. Instead, they were deployed only on an ad hoc basis or for the (very) occasional special project or campaign. Green's active participation notwithstanding, most of the time the member organizer program existed more on paper than in reality. Still, Green did play a valuable role in the Rosemont campaign. Her tireless energy and, more important, her ability to relate to nurses' aides as a knowledgeable fellow-sufferer, were crucial ingredients in the success of the 1998 campaign.

Hardy prepared the inexperienced members of her organizing team — the interns — carefully. She and Joe Reilly, the local's staff director, also an experienced organizer, had the interns study SEIU organizing manuals, then trained us to conduct house visits. The training familiarized us with the issues we would encounter, taught us how to answer workers' questions about the union, and taught us how to employ the SEIU's numerical system for assessing workers' support for the union (workers who are strongly prounion and want to get involved in leading the campaign are assigned a "1"; workers who are prounion and willing to participate in activities that show their support publicly are assigned a "2"; undecided workers are assigned a "3"; and antiunion workers are assigned a "4"). We practiced these interactions in role-playing exercises, and as final preparation we were sent out into the field for two weeks to randomly house-visit workers at another nursing home.[2] We documented our assessments carefully and reported the results of each meeting to Joe Reilly.

Once Hardy and Reilly were satisfied that the interns were capable of conducting house visits, we were sent into the field again, this time for targeted house visits of Rosemont workers who the union believed might be good organizing committee material. Hardy could not take an active role in this effort, as she was working full time in central Pennsylvania on her other campaign. "OK, go find me a committee," she admonished. Armed with maps, the previous year's Excelsior list (now badly out of date), and a handful of names of workers the union thought might be willing to help form a real organizing committee, we began our search.

The union possessed some information about the workers it targeted for initial visits, and believed that they were union supporters, but did not know how strongly these workers felt about the union or whether they were good candidates for leadership roles. Therefore, our strategy was to ask workers how they felt about the idea of the union, what they saw as the most important issues at Rosemont, and whether they would be interested in helping with the campaign. If responses to these questions indicated strong support for the union and willingness to help, the goal of the visit was then to formally recruit the worker to the organizing committee. We were instructed to make it very clear to all recruits that as organizing committee members, they would be expected not only to make a specific commitment to attend weekly meetings for the duration of the campaign but also to do a great deal of work on their own time. We tried to give recruits a sense of why the committee was so important, what it needed to do if the organizing drive was going to be successful, and why they needed to get involved if they wanted to organize a union. We also emphasized the union's view that the weakness of the organizing committee had been a major reason for its defeat the previous year. We discussed the role a stronger, more representative organizing committee could play in the new campaign, and we stressed that forming a functioning organizing committee was also the first step in creating a functioning union structure in the workplace.

These targeted house visits proved to be a very successful committee-building strategy. We quickly found several day and evening shift nurses' aides whose peripheral involvement the year before stemmed mainly from the fact that no one had specifically recruited them or asked them to be part of an organizing effort. These workers were willing to get involved but had simply never been directly approached one on one. Having someone come to their home to invite them to get involved was an effective way to let them know that their input and participation in the organizing drive was genuinely wanted and needed. They, in turn, told us about new nurses' aides and helped us fill in new names, addresses, and phone numbers. Several of the new aides had told others at work that they wouldn't stay at the facility unless the union campaign succeeded. Armed with this information, we were able to visit these new workers and recruit them to the committee as well.

By early July, the union had assembled a committee representing nearly 15 percent of the workforce, with roughly equal representation from all three shifts in the nursing department. Not all of the workers we recruited to the organizing committee during this initial phase remained active throughout the entire campaign. Several decided to take a less active role as the tension began to mount, and one of the formerly antiunion workers on the committee suddenly changed sides midway through the summer. However, as the summer went on, ongoing house visits enabled the union to continually expand and deepen the committee by reaching out to more and more people.

Here we can see how, in contrast to the union's 1997 campaign, face-to-face organizing allowed the union to identify and activate the important minority of people who already viewed the union positively and who were willing to participate in a leadership role. This core group of workers was then organized into a new set of networks that helped the union reach out to the majority of workers who were much more ambivalent about the union. These activities began with a weekend house-calling "blitz," held July 10–11. For the first time, the union expanded its house visits from targeted potential committee members to all bargaining unit employees. The interns had helped recruit six member volunteers from other chapters of the local to attend a daylong training session on Friday, July 10, and then to spend the next day conducting house calls paired with more experienced organizers. The volunteers were Local A members who had expressed interest in joining the union's embryonic member organizer program during work site leader/steward training held several months earlier. The union reimbursed these workers for their lost wages for the Friday they would be taking off; they were then expected to volunteer their time on Saturday. In addition to the six member organizers from other chapters of the local, two Rosemont committee members were able to get Friday off and participate in the blitz. Joan Hardy did not want anyone to conduct house visits on Saturday who had not been trained on Friday; committee members who could not participate in the blitz would be trained later.

The eight teams house-called about 30 percent of Rosemont's workforce during the blitz. Of the 24 workers visited, 16 signed cards, and the union received detailed assessments of each visited worker, which proved to be quite accurate as the campaign went on. The success of the blitz led Hardy to decide that the remaining workers should be approached in much the same way. Rather than allowing the interest cards to circulate anonymously as they had in 1997, this time only staff organizers and members of the organizing committee were to "card" workers. All of the organizing committee members were trained to conduct "assessment interviews" of their co-workers. For each card returned signed, the committee member had to provide a detailed written assessment of the interview and of the signee's status with respect to the campaign. At the same time, interns and committee members would continue house calling until all the workers in the unit had been visited. From the blitz forward, both the house-calling strategy and the one-on-one work of the organizing committee were aimed primarily at the majority of workers who were undecided about the union. These workers all had their misgivings about, fears of, and issues with unions but were not strongly or firmly antiunion. These were the workers who could be influenced, whose negative experiences and images of unions could be dealt with through face-to-face organizing.

In addition to house calling, face-to-face organizing was also a function of the rank-and-file organizing committee. The organizing work of the rank-and-file committee itself was at least as important as house calling. Issues dealt with in house visits — discussed below — were reinforced in similar conversations between committee members and other rank-and-file workers in the break room, before and after shifts, in the parking lot, and on the phone. Unfortunately, as an organizing intern, I did not have access to these interactions in the first person. However, as an organizer I did keep abreast of the committee's work. Each committee member was responsible for a list of co-workers. Every week the committee kept the rest of the rank and file informed about the events of the week, and these contacts also allowed the committee to continuously adjust assessments as the campaign went along. Committee members were always available to answer questions and to talk about the union.

They also did a good job of neutralizing hard-line antiunion workers, both by helping to counter their influence with other workers and by persuading some of them not to vote in the election out of respect for the wishes of the majority. Since the union needed a simple majority of the voting workers, every antiunion worker who did not vote was one fewer vote needed by the union.

Committee members gave reports each week on events inside the facility, which helped the campaign respond to specific management attacks in a timely way and, more important, to take advantage of management blunders when people were unfairly disciplined or when there were care problems. Committee members also contributed articles appearing in the campaign's weekly newsletter, which helped raise their visibility as part of the campaign and added to the overall impression — already created by their everyday organizing activities inside the nursing home — that the campaign was being driven by rank-and-file leaders rather than by an external organization.

The committee's efforts were also crucial to the collective actions organized during the campaign. The campaign revolved around specific actions and activities, led by the organizing committee, that rank-and-file workers were encouraged to participate in. With guidance from Hardy, the committee organized button days and T-shirt days, informational picketing, leafleting of co-workers and residents' families as they drove in and out of the parking lot, several petitions and marches on the boss, and "impromptu" acts of resistance during mandatory antiunion meetings inside the facility. None of these actions could have been organized and carried out without the committee's efforts, and some of them were initiated by the committee. For example, a petition on behalf of workers in the kitchen and laundry departments was proposed by committee members during a brainstorming session on how to break down the barriers between those departments, which were weak, and nursing, where support for the union was strongest. Committee members knew that workers in laundry and dietary were suffering because they worked in closed-off areas without adequate ventilation. Particularly in the kitchen, temperatures often soared to well over 110 degrees. By petitioning for better conditions for these workers, union supporters in the nursing department could try to build some interdepartmental solidarity. The petition was ultimately signed by about two-thirds of the prospective bargaining unit; when all of the signatures had been collected, a delegation of 9 or 10 workers arranged to take their breaks all at the same time and go in to present the petitions to the administrator together.

The preceding discussion of the organizing committee's activities illustrates how, through their participation in house calling as well as their shop floor organizing activities, committee members formed the basis of new networks of communication and interaction that were crucial to the union's effort to mobilize workers who were themselves much more ambivalent than the core prounion group. These new networks served three purposes: dispersal of information, social pressure, and activation of solidarity.[3] Committee members' regular contact with an assigned list of co-workers enabled them to serve as sources of basic information about the campaign and about the union. Committee members were able to exercise social pressure by standing up to hard-line antiunion workers and asserting the right of prounion workers to express their views without being harassed. This helped to reduce the extent to which antiunion workers could create zones of intimidation within the nursing home. And the activities of the committee to organize collective actions like the petition on behalf of kitchen workers helped create new solidarities that strengthened the campaign.

But despite the centrality of these processes, by themselves they do not explain the ability of the campaign to convert initially ambivalent, distrustful, and skeptical workers into strong union supporters. The presence of networks is important, but, as I argued in the previous chapter, even more important is the specific content of the communication and interaction that these new networks facilitated. To understand how the union overcame workers' ambivalence and distrust, rooted in their specific experiences of business unionism, we need to understand in a specific way how the campaign overcame people's fear that unions caused job insecurity; how the union built credibility and trust; and how the union helped people begin to believe the possibility and value of a participatory, grassroots unionism. The construction of communication networks, framing, and consciousness-raising all played important roles in the union's effort to achieve these ends. But what is important is not simply *that* network building, framing, or consciousness-raising took place but rather *how*, through persuasive communication, social interaction, and collective action, the union campaign was able to deal with the negative perceptions and experiences of unions that workers brought to the table. The focus of this analysis is thus not on the union's framing activities or on consciousness-raising as such but rather on how the campaign interacted with workers' existing dispositions to produce a new set of positive union experiences capable of motivating participation in the campaign.

Overcoming Fears of Job Loss

The campaign eased workers' fears about job loss primarily through one-on-one discussion during house visits and via the work of committee members. During house visits, I found it was fairly common for workers to say, "They said we could all lose our jobs if the union gets in," and then wait to see what the response would be. Management had (illegally) suggested that if the workers at Rosemont formed a union, the company might be forced to close or sell the nursing home — a threat made by more than half of all employers facing organizing drives.[4] At Rosemont, the threat was a particularly effective one because it played on the association many workers made between unions and the deindustrialization and job loss that affected the region. However, the organizing campaign worked hard to dispel these fears in one-on-one discussions with workers.

House callers pointed out that management hadn't closed any of the five other Hewitt facilities where Local A represented workers and that

Hewitt was still making a profit at those facilities even though wages were higher and benefits better than at Rosemont. The house callers also brought with them copies of the facility's financial statement, a publicly available form that all nursing home operators are required to file with the Department of Health. This document showed that with an initial investment of $400,000, Hewitt's three partners had taken out a loan to buy Rosemont. Even after making their loan payments — and despite the fact that the state had suspended admissions for more than two months during the summer of 1997 — the partners had earned approximately $350,000 in profits at Rosemont during that year. This figure did not include money the company hid through the subterfuge of contracting the management of the facility out to a company that was actually owned by the Hewitt Group. The facility paid the management company several hundred thousand dollars for "management fees" over and above the costs of actually paying the salaries of the administrator and the management staff, thus allowing Hewitt to report lower profits.

Discussion of these issues convinced most workers that management's threats about job loss were bogus. This proved to be something workers were afraid of only until they understood the facts about the nursing home's profitability and the status of the other unionized homes in the chain. But in addition to the immediate fears about job loss, the union also had to deal with some bitterness on the part of workers who blamed unions (at least in part) for deindustrialization more generally and the decline in living standards that they had experienced. Like the other house callers, I spent a lot of time during house visits discussing such issues. When workers argued that unions' blind pursuit of higher wages had made the steel industry uncompetitive, at first I drew on what I had read about the decline of the steel industry in Pennsylvania, pointing out that the rapid growth of wages relative to productivity in steel after 1970 was an initiative of the companies, whose (mistaken) analysis of their competitive situation led them to believe that imports were gaining access to the US market only during periods of labor strife and work stoppages. Therefore, they reasoned, offering large wage increases in exchange for no-strike pledges would keep imports out by ensuring labor peace. The strategy failed, I argued, but it was a *management* strategy.

This argument did not seem to convince workers unless they were already sympathetic. I soon realized that skeptical workers were not going to take my word for it! If I was going to make any headway on this problem I needed to come at the issue in a way that resonated with elements of workers' experience. A better approach was to argue that the real reason "the mills went down" was that the companies did not modernize their facilities after the 1950s. This resonated much more strongly, as workers with any family connections to the mills had heard the same thing from relatives. Also, it helped to initiate discussion about the differences between nursing homes, steel mills and mines. Steel mills could be located somewhere else, and mines could be shut down while coal was bought from other places, but nursing homes have to serve the communities in which they are located. The idea of shutting a nursing home down and moving it to Korea always brought a chuckle.

Workers were also afraid that, as they had been told, the union would "take them out" against their will and end up getting them fired. This was the most difficult issue to discuss, since strikes are a scary subject for many workers, and yet the legal right to strike is an important one (even if it has been eroded by the increasing use of permanent replacement workers)[5] that the union did not want to downplay, renounce, or shy away from completely. On this issue, the house callers were trained to emphasize first of all that the SEIU did not recommend strikes lightly and viewed them as an absolute last resort. We said that Local A had never had to strike in any of the five other Hewitt homes it represented; it had always been able to reach contract agreements with Hewitt in the past without striking. We emphasized, too, that the SEIU understood that in health care occupations, workers had to always consider the needs of the residents. Hence the Megacorp strike (discussed in Part III) — which many Rosemont workers knew of and wanted to talk about — was only a three-day limited strike rather than an all-out strike (and we did not fail to point out *why* Megacorp workers had been forced to strike as well as the fact that they won). Finally, the most important point house callers tried to get across regarding strikes was that the decision to strike was made, not by the union hierarchy, but by the rank and file. "The decision would be up to you," I told workers. "You and your co-workers have the right to decide through a secret-ballot vote." My sense was that quite a few undecided workers I spoke with were never completely satisfied on the strike issue, but learning that they would have the right to decide by secret ballot whether to strike did ease some fears.

Building Trust: Combating the Image of Violence and Corruption

Workers who may have been worried about a repeat of the Teamster debacle were encouraged by the kinds of actions organized by the SEIU and by the growing camaraderie, excitement, and fun that workers were having, especially during impromptu meetings and rallies on the lawn just off Rosemont's property. Instead of intimidation or negativity, all of these actions emphasized nonviolence and positive themes. House calling also helped alleviate workers' fears about union violence and intimidation. House callers were carefully trained by the union to make the contact a positive one, even when encountering a hostile response. They were polite, they were respectful, and they listened carefully to what people had to say.

The house visits were a hot topic of conversation inside the facility according to members of the organizing committee. "Everybody knows who got visited the day before," one committee member said. "It's something different to talk about, that's for sure." Initially, some were nervous about being visited and let it be known that they did not want anyone to visit them. "They better not visit me," one worker said, "Cause I'll call the cops." Whenever organizing committee members heard that someone had expressed a preference not to be visited, the union held off and respected that person's wishes. But as more and more workers experienced the visits as positive events, some of the workers who initially said they did not want to be visited changed their minds and told organizing committee members it would be all right if someone came by. The positive nature of the interactions people experienced during house visits broke down workers' fears about intimidation or violence by convincing them that whatever the Teamsters had done in the past, Local A was a different kind of union.

The substantive communication that took place during the house visits was also important in this respect because workers' perceptions that union representatives were being "straight up" helped build trust. Workers feared the union in part because they viewed it as an outside organization with its own motives and power structures. Developing trust helped workers decide that the organization was not going to bully them or try to intimidate them as the Teamsters had done and that the union's leadership was honest rather than corrupt. Because Hardy understood the importance of trust — unlike the UFCW organizers Linda Markowitz[6] studied — she emphasized that if the house callers didn't know the answer to something, we were not to pretend. "Whatever you do, don't bullshit people," Hardy instructed. "If you don't know, say you don't know, but you can find out. Then find out and follow up. You'll be amazed at how grateful people will be if you actually do what you say you will." It was also important to be honest when the answer wasn't what people wanted to hear. For example, a common question was, "What can the union do about the staffing in this place?" The answer was that staffing was the most difficult issue to deal with directly and that it was almost impossible to negotiate staffing guarantees into a contract. Of course, it helped to mention that the SEIU was at the forefront of political efforts at the state and national level to change the legal minimum staffing requirement, but we had to admit that forming a union was not necessarily going to translate into an immediate improvement in staffing. I found, as Hardy predicted, that giving straight answers on issues like this one was much better than making promises that the union could not deliver. Workers did appreciate being told the truth, and their respect for the union usually went up, not down, when they received an honest if disappointing answer.

House callers were careful not to promise specific raises. As I noted in Chapter 2, sometimes I was asked, "How big a raise will we get if we vote for the union?" I was trained always to answer this the same way: "No one can promise that you will get a specific wage increase. How much you can improve things is going to depend on how united you are, how much you stick together, and what you're willing to agree to in the end." We would then show workers a copy of the wage scale at Greenleaf, a Hewitt sister home represented by Local A, located about 20 miles from Rosemont. Starting wages for nursing assistants at Greenleaf were more than $1.50 more than at Rosemont, and unlike Rosemont, which had no official scale, Greenleaf's wage scale ramped up so that after three years of service nursing assistants were making close to $10 per hour. Workers' eyes always lit up when they saw the Greenleaf wage scale. "I've been working here six years, and I'm making $7.60 an hour," one said. "At Greenleaf I'd be making $10.32. Damn." Admittedly still far less than a princely sum, the Greenleaf wage — in this part of western Pennsylvania — would mean for many the difference between working poverty and a living wage.

Organizers and committee members on house visits also emphasized that it was unrealistic to think that Rosemont workers would get the Greenleaf wage scale in their first contract. Greenleaf had gradually won these increases over several contract rounds. The goal would be to gradually equalize Rosemont and Greenleaf through coordinated bargaining. "There's no way they're going to get a dollar an hour more in their first contract," said Hardy. "We have to make sure they understand that. They'll get more if they stick together, but it's going to be a gradual process." But even though the union was careful not to promise that workers could have exactly what Greenleaf had, giving workers a copy of the Greenleaf wage scale and talking about it allowed the union to accomplish several things at once. First, it helped give the lie to management's claims that the company simply could not afford to pay them more. Since Greenleaf and Rosemont were in most respects identical and owned and operated by the same company, simply showing workers how much less they were making at Rosemont was important in itself. Second, it allowed union organizers to talk about the very idea of a formal wage scale. Workers were quick to agree that one of the many petty injustices at Rosemont was that since how much people made was a big secret, management could reward its favorites with wage increases that others were denied. There was always scuttlebutt floating around about particular workers who had just been hired at higher rates than some long-term employees were getting. With a wage scale, everything would be out in the open and aboveboard, and wage increases would go by seniority. Workers could always see that this would be a good idea and a real improvement over their current setup.

Because nearly everyone had personal, positive contact with union staff during the second campaign, when management showed antiunion movies with old news footage of violence during Steelworker or Teamster strikes, most workers were no longer impressed. "All they have to show us is stuff that happened in the past," one worker said. "This here union is completely different from all of that old-time stuff. What I want to know is why they can't come up with any examples [of violence] that are recent or from this union."

Overcoming Do-Nothing Unionism

Workers' fears about the union "taking our dues money and running" were much alleviated by the opportunity house calling gave to explain clearly how dues worked. During the mandatory antiunion meetings, management representatives had claimed that union dues would cost workers more than $500 per year and had left workers with the false impression that dues deduction would begin immediately if they voted to form a union. House visits were an ideal way of combating this misinformation, since the first question people asked would often be, "They told us that union dues were $500 a year. No way can I afford that. Is that right?" Conducting house visits enabled organizers to explain carefully that Local A dues were $11 a month for the first year of the initial collective bargaining agreement; thereafter, any workers earning less than $13,000 annually would continue to pay $11 per month, while those above $13,000 would pay 1.4 percent of their monthly base wage ($18.66 per month, or $224 per year, for a full-time worker earning $8 per hour).

Organizers and committee members doing house visits used these opportunities to drive home the point that the union did not collect any dues until *workers* approved the first contract. In other words, workers would not pay a dime until they approved a contract they were happy with. There was, organizers told workers, no reason they should approve a contract that did not *at least* provide raises sufficient to cover the cost of their dues. How big a raise would be required to do that? A 10-cent raise in the first contract would cover the cost of dues. Any increases above that would be theirs.

When the issue of protecting bad workers arose, house callers used such opportunities to explain that unions have a legal obligation to represent every worker in a bargaining unit — but that certainly does not mean that union workers cannot be fired. We explained that when a worker covered by a collective bargaining agreement is fired or disciplined, he or she has the right to appeal. If the worker insists on filing a grievance, the union is required to represent him or her. But this is no guarantee that the employee's grievance will be upheld. A labor-management meeting is held to see if the issue can be resolved through discussion. If the company holds firm on its course of action, as a last resort the employee is entitled to an arbitration hearing. This means that the company must prove its case against the employee to a neutral third party, an arbitrator acceptable to both the company and the union. If the company cannot prove that the employee did what he or she is accused of, or that the punishment fits the crime, the arbitrator can erase the discipline or prevent the firing. The idea is that under a collective bargaining agreement the employee has rights of due process that cannot be violated. This does *not* mean that a bad employee cannot be fired—it just means that the employer is required to prove its case against the employee. The employer must have and show "just cause" for the dismissal to be upheld.

In the context of the events that had been occurring at Rosemont over the past year, this issue was actually something of a slam-dunk for the campaign. House callers could say, "Look at all of the people who have been fired or disciplined in the last year. Did they all deserve it? Or were some of them management's scapegoats who paid for management's failure to provide enough staff?" Almost everyone agreed that the latter was the case. Once they were satisfied that people who really deserved to be fired could still be fired, this objection usually became a nonissue for undecided workers.

This issue also had a flip-side for workers who had been members of a union in the past but felt that the union had not done enough for them. A worker named Dave, for example, revealed during a home visit that he had previously worked for another nursing home represented by another SEIU local and that he had been fired—in his view unjustly. "The union didn't do a thing," he said. "They said there was nothing they could do." Dave's story revealed why. He had been an inexperienced worker given the difficult task of showering a combative resident. In the shower room, the resident had grabbed his arm with one hand and started hitting him with the other. Dave had yelled for help, but received no aid. At last, not knowing what else to do, Dave sprayed cold water in the resident's face to get him to release his grip. He was then fired for abusing a resident. "Man," he said. "I didn't know what else to do. He was beating *me* up! And the cold water didn't hurt him, it was just to get him to let go." He couldn't understand why the union had not been able to save his job.

The union's member organizer, Carol Green—an experienced nursing home worker—who accompanied me on this house visit, explained to Dave gently that while she understood exactly how he felt and why he'd reacted as he did, he'd done the wrong thing. "Cold water," she said, "can be a real shock to the system for an older person. It can cause cardiac arrest. I know you didn't mean to do anything wrong, but they had to fire you for that. That falls under the legal definition of abuse, and they had no choice." She talked to him about different ways of restraining residents in such situations without putting them at risk—methods he admitted he now knew as a more experienced worker. In the end he agreed that while he might have had a grievance against the company for failing to train him properly and failing to provide enough staff to assist him with a combative resident, he could understand why his union had not been able to prevent his firing. Carol, for her part, agreed that his union steward should have done a better job of explaining the situation to Dave at the time—although as she said later, "At the time, Dave was probably so upset that he just couldn't accept that he'd screwed up no matter how many times they explained it to him." The visit was a success: from that point on, Dave was a solid and highly visible union supporter.

Collective actions contributed something that face-to-face organizing alone could not, crucial to overcoming experiences and images of do-nothing unionism: a growing feeling of solidarity and power, a sense that the workers were symbolically taking control of the nursing home. The way that the actions built on one another over time transformed the union from an abstract notion of an external organization into a present assemblage of active nursing home workers that was impossible to ignore. This growing sense of collective identity and power made the initial objections of people who worried that the union would not change anything seem palpably absurd.

The building process began with the button days. During the first few button days, only the strongest union supporters would wear prounion buttons; everyone else was afraid to put them on. But the bravery of the leaders was catching: each day, more and more buttons appeared until nearly everyone but the staunchest union foes was wearing them. Next came union T-shirts. By a lucky coincidence, the nursing home's uniform included purple T-shirts, the same color as SEIU shirts. Therefore workers could come to work in SEIU shirts and still be in uniform.

The petitions were a third step, and the marches on the boss that they led up to became turning points in the campaign. On the day that the laundry/dietary petition was about to be delivered, I stood outside with rank-and-file committee members who were about to go in and deliver the petition shortly after shift change. Their excitement was visible as they discussed the logistics of how they were all going to drift toward the boss's office at the same moment. Their effort to confront the boss together was something no group of workers had done in living memory at Rosemont. They went inside, and about 15 minutes later we saw the administrator's car and that of the DON both come tearing out of the parking lot. We got the story later: apparently the bosses had been so petrified of the delegation that they had fled the facility rather than receive the petition! At first some in the delegation were upset and disappointed — until they realized that the bosses had fled because they had been *afraid* of dealing with the workers all together in a group. This realization was electrifying. The members of the delegation took on semihero status within the facility.

After this, rank-and-file workers were able to lead even more daring actions, like taking control of management's antiunion meetings. Instead of listening quietly to management's antiunion presentations, the idea was to use these mandatory meetings as a forum for fighting back. The committee helped prepare a list of "awkward questions for management," such as "Why are you wasting time and money with antiunion meetings when you know we don't have enough time or staff to give the kind of quality care we want to give?" and "Could you do the work we do or live on the wages we make?" They divided the list up so that each question would be posed by a different worker. Then they decided to make their point in an even stronger way. When management was about to begin one meeting, a worker put up her hand and asked, "Do you mind if we get comfortable first?" Upon receiving the affirmative answer, workers began turning their chairs around and facing the back of the room, turning their backs to the boss. This meeting ended up in bedlam, with the administrator losing his cool and yelling at the workers, while they for their part kept demanding answers to their questions.

These actions turned the tide. Shift-change leafleting sessions turned into regular but impromptu union rallies, as people coming off their shift joined the leafleters on the lawn by the roadside instead of driving off. In the weeks preceding the vote, leafleting days usually meant that 15 or 20 people would be hanging out on the lawn in high spirits, cheering and exchanging "V" signals to those workers going in for the next shift. By the time the election was held, the only question was how large the union's margin of victory would be.

CONCLUSION

The success of Local A's 1998 campaign to organize Rosemont nursing home and its defeat the previous year highlight a number of contributions from existing studies of movement unionism. These campaigns confirm the importance of utilizing multiple tactics in a coordinated way.[7] They demonstrate that non-NLRB organizing drives are no panacea in the absence of a comprehensive grassroots organizing strategy. They also clearly show the importance of involving rank-and-file volunteers in member-to-member organizing.[8] And the 1998 campaign also highlights the ability of disruptive tactics to build workers' confidence, sense of collective power, and solidarity.[9]

Beyond this, the analysis presented here also speaks to a common criticism of social movement unionism — that American workers are too conservative and individualistic to be attracted to a movement offering collective mobilization and progressive politics.[10] If it had been possible at the outset to poll Rosemont workers about their views of unions in general — and their need for a union at Rosemont in particular — no doubt the responses would have been very ambivalent overall. And yet, a few short months later, large majorities of Rosemont workers were enthusiastically participating in shop floor collective actions as part of the 1998 organizing drive. This suggests that workers' initial political orientations and views of unions are *not* an insurmountable barrier for social movement unionism. Indeed, the analyses presented here demonstrate that the success of grassroots organizing tactics is rooted in their very ability to overcome workers' existing experiences and images of business unionism. Face-to-face organizing and collective action tactics succeed insofar as they allow organizers and rank-and-file activists to confront workers' servicing expectations and deal with workers' ingrained fears and objections about organized labor. They achieve this not merely by talking about unions — although that is important — but by building a rank-and-file campaign that puts into practice (at least temporarily) a different sort of unionism. The new and positive union experiences that result, the experience of these campaigns shows — more than any specific tactic — are the keys to success.

This argument also shows both the value and the limits of existing theories of social movement participation. We can identify, in the preceding analysis, many of the processes that movement theorists discuss as factors favoring participation. The campaign relied heavily on interpersonal recruitment and communication networks that it set out consciously to create — and success clearly could not have been achieved without these networks. Framing activities were also important: much of the campaign's activity consisted of face-to-face, persuasive communication between organizers or rank-and-file volunteers and ordinary workers. What David Snow and Robert Benford call "prognostic" issue framing[11] was particularly important because the central problem of the campaign was the necessity of convincing workers that forming a union was a viable way to solve some of their work-related problems. Finally, consciousness-raising through participation in collective action built solidarity in precisely the manner identified by Eric Hirsch and Rick Fantasia.[12] But none of these concepts explains the difference between success and failure, participation and nonparticipation, at Rosemont. Success was achieved not simply *because* the campaign constructed networks, engaged in framing, or organized actions but because, *through* these activities, the campaign was able to deal successfully with workers' negative perceptions and experiences of unions and give them hope that the union stood for something worth belonging to.

Organizing and Organization

When one compares the two campaigns discussed in Chapters 2 and 3, an obvious question that arises is why the union took such a conservative, traditional approach in its first campaign. Local A, after all, had been organizing private sector nursing homes for over a decade, and Hardy, though new to Local A, was already an experienced SEIU nursing home organizer. She and the local were quite familiar with the repertoire of grassroots tactics that were eventually employed in the second campaign, so why not use these tactics from the start?

One view, offered by Local A staff director Joe Reilly, is that the union tried to use these tactics in the first campaign but simply was not able to because (a) not enough workers were willing to get involved in the committee the first time around; and (b) without an accurate list of workers' addresses, house calling proved difficult during the first campaign. This explanation may seem plausible, but I am convinced that it is wrong. In my view, the reason more workers did not get involved in the committee during the first campaign was that the union did not work hard enough to build it. During the second campaign, interns conducting house visits encountered numerous workers who would have been excellent committee material but who had simply never been approached during the first campaign. No one had made it clear to them individually that their participation in the committee was crucial to the success of the campaign. "I went to a few meetings," one such worker said, "But there didn't seem to be any reason to keep going."

The accurate-list argument is similarly unsatisfying. As noted in Chapter 3, when the interns returned to the field less than one year after the first election, they found that only about a third of the workers on the Excelsior list were still employed at Rosemont. So while the list was helpful in identifying and visiting some long-term employees, it was no help at all with the newer workers. These newer workers were visited and brought into the campaign by utilizing the efforts of existing committee members. The first campaign had access to enough potential rank-and-file activists to build its committee in much the same way.

The real reason that the first campaign was run so conservatively was that Joan Hardy was the only full-time organizer on staff at the local, and she was trying to manage two campaigns at once. The local did have three organizing interns on staff in the summer of 1997, but we were deeply involved in the campaign that forms the subject of Chapter 5 and could not do the kind of fieldwork at Rosemont that was really required. Splitting her time between Rosemont and a blood bank campaign made it impossible for Hardy to really build a proper committee at Rosemont, let alone conduct house calls in a comprehensive way. Hardy had to choose where she would place most of her effort, so she concentrated on the blood bank campaign. The following summer, in 1998, Hardy again had two campaigns to manage, but this time she had persuaded local president Janet Zimmerman to hire interns specifically to work on new organizing and also to take on Carol Green on a half-time basis to help the interns with Rosemont. The additional organizing help made the difference and made it possible for Hardy to run two grassroots campaigns at once.

By the time Rosemont workers won their certification election in September 1998, Joan Hardy had put together a string of victories at several nursing homes and a local blood bank. Armed with these successes, she approached Zimmerman about expanding the organizing staff. As a first step, Hardy wanted permission to hire Carol Green full time. As a nursing home worker, an experienced veteran of the Megacorp wars (see Part III), and a longtime SEIU activist, Green was an excellent choice. Zimmerman, however, said no, arguing that the local could not afford to take on more full-time staff. Since the local had just spent nearly half a million dollars remodeling its offices, this decision may have reflected a real financial issue, but the choice of expenditures raised questions about Zimmerman's priorities. Hardy was deeply disappointed with the decision. Hardy's vision for the local included a full-scale organizing program, not just one staff organizer. "A local this size should have three or four full-time organizers," she said. Still, not about to give up, she gently pressed the issue at every opportunity over the next year; in the spring of 2000, Zimmerman finally agreed to allow Hardy to bring Green on staff.

Despite her change of heart, Zimmerman clearly maintained a somewhat ambivalent attitude toward new organizing. On the one hand, she wanted to do enough of it so that her local could point to its organizing efforts with a certain amount of pride. Since the early 1980s, when the SEIU international initiated its nursing home campaign, Local A had been organizing nursing homes at a rate of one or two a year. The local had never had more than one permanent organizer on staff, so it was never a major focus for the local as a whole, but it was something that Zimmerman thought was important enough to do. On the other hand, Zimmerman had deep reservations about whether it made sense to put a lot of financial resources into new organizing. Face-to-face organizing is extremely labor-intensive, and for every victory there are a handful of campaigns that never get off the ground. Even when the union wins, additional staff time is required to negotiate new contracts before the union ever sees any dues. Indeed, it is ironic that while management charges that the union's motivation for its organizing campaigns is its desire to collect dues, in reality new organizing costs so much relative to the dues that might eventually be collected that there is not much incentive for union presidents like Zimmerman to view it with enthusiasm.

This is especially true with low-income occupations like nursing home workers. Also, as some writers have pointed out, a constant influx of new members does not necessarily benefit a local union president, especially if these new members are active and militant.[1] Local union presidents have their power bases, and new members can only help destabilize that base. Hence Local's A's overall orientation — which, while it did not ignore new organizing, clearly subordinated it to the representation of existing members — was understandable, even if this orientation was not optimum when considered from the point of view of the movement as a whole.

One implication of the place of new organizing in the overall scheme of things at Local A was that while an emphasis on grassroots organizing and collective action had been the basis for victory in the second campaign, this emphasis was not really being carried through either into the period of contract negotiation or, after the contract was settled, into the administration of the new contract. During the bargaining period, the union did not capitalize on the organization building it had already accomplished in order to mobilize workers further to increase pressure on the company at the table. Instead, the negotiations were a period of demobilization. Likewise, after the contract was settled, the union grafted the unit, which was won through grassroots collective struggle and social movement organizing tactics, onto its existing representational structure. In other words, while the union was able to make use of face-to-face contact and collective action as a set of organizing tactics, it lacked a way to maintain the level of shop floor organization it had built during the campaign beyond the organizing phase. Once Hardy handed the shop over to a staff representative, internal organizing ceased. June McMurray and several other new rank-and-file stewards did a commendable job of taking on the new representational tasks — they learned how to deal with grievances on their own rather than relying on the staff representative — but the mode of representation that the union now initiated still conceived of representation as a set of bureaucratic tasks rather than as inseparable from organizing and mobilization (as SEIU doctrine would have it). Whereas the organizing campaign itself was clearly distinguishable from business union practice, the way the new unit was being administered had strong elements of top-down servicing.

This approach — returning to a servicing model in the wake of grass-roots, participatory organizing campaigns — is a common approach among organizing unions.[2] However, Linda Markowitz has found that even if the quantity and quality of participatory democracy decline after such campaigns come to an end, rank-and-file leaders retain both their attachment to the participatory ideals forged in the campaigns and the leadership skills they learn during those campaigns.[3] This is important because it suggests that organization building during campaigns can have lasting effects. It can reduce the burden of representational activities on staff, thus potentially freeing up more staff for organizing. And, even more important, as we will see in Part III, the organizational capacities built during initial organizing campaigns can be reactivated and further developed during subsequent mobilizations.

But before we get to Part III, we must turn our attention to another issue, one raised by the basic tension between the grassroots nature of organizing struggle and the demobilizing character of representational structures: the organizational legacies of existing business unionism. That subject is examined in more detail in Part II, to which we now turn.

PART TWO

Dealing with Organizational Legacies

The New Urban Politics
of Allegheny County, Pennsylvania

Part I argued that workers' lived experiences of business unionism have become a primary obstacle to new labor mobilization. It also showed how face-to-face organizing and collective action tactics enable social movement unions to successfully confront and deal with negative experiences of the movement. The question posed at the end of Part I — why would an SEIU local familiar with the advantages of social movement organizing ever mount the kind of old-style campaign employed in Local first attempt to organize Rosemont Pavilion — raised a second issue: the organizational legacies of labor's business union history.

In Part I, organizational issues appeared in the margins of the analysis. The focus in that analysis was on the relationship between the organizers and the organized and the processes by which new organizing tactics succeeded in reconfiguring workers' lived experience. It was possible to set aside questions about the local union organization for two reasons. First, the organizational requirements of a small, single–work site campaign are not overwhelmingly great, and second, new organizing campaigns can create their own mobilizing structures such as a rank-and-file organizing committee without having to struggle against preexisting union structures. We now analyze two campaigns in which neither of these things is true, in order to examine the relationship between the organizational legacies of business unionism and attempts to introduce social movement tactics. These campaigns were forced upon Local A by a profound shift in the political landscape of Allegheny County in the 1990s. We begin by sketching this context.

Since Pittsburgh's economic disaster of the 1980s, the question of how to compete in a global economy has consumed that city's business and political leaders and informed much of local public debate. Even as the tax base shrank, numerous projects aimed at making Pittsburgh more attractive to investors, visitors, and tourists siphoned funds away from public services in favor of corporate subsidies. The city of Pittsburgh committed millions in subsidies toward construction of a new downtown convention center; new ballparks for the Pittsburgh Pirates and Steelers; new upscale retail space and apartments downtown; a new regional history center; trolleys for a "tourist transportation" business; and a proposed pedestrian footbridge over the Allegheny River to link Point State Park with the new baseball and football parks.[1]

Efforts to shrink county government and cut taxes were also underway throughout the 1990s. Democratic administrations reduced the number of employees on Allegheny County's payroll from over 10,000 in the late 1980s to 7,000 by the mid-1990s.[2] A Democratic administration cut county tax rates by 16 percent (from 37.5 mills to 31.5 mills) in 1994 and enacted another cut of nearly 10 percent (to 28.5 mills) in late 1995.[3] Republicans upped the ante, however, during the 1995 county election campaign, promising a further across-the-board property tax cut of 20 percent, to be paid for with privatization initiatives and contract concessions from 11 unions representing county employees. The Democrats announced that they intended to match the Republicans' promise of a 20 percent property tax cut but argued that it should be phased in gradually over four years instead of introduced all at once. Like the Republicans, the Democrats also promised to further streamline county departments and eliminate "unnecessary" jobs.[4]

Both parties framed the issue of tax cuts in terms of the demands of interurban competition. During the 1995 commissioners' race, for example, Democratic candidate Colleen Vuono argued that Allegheny County needed a 20 percent property tax reduction because it would make the county more competitive in attracting people and capital to the region, saying, "Part of the reason we're losing residents and losing business is because of the taxes."[5] The views of the Republican candidates were the same. In a letter to the *Pittsburgh Post-Gazette* published two days before the election, Larry Dunn and Bob Cranmer wrote, "We believe that an immediate 20 percent cut in property taxes is the only sure way to send the message to the world that Allegheny County is open for business. We want to compete with other cities and counties for new jobs." The letter added that "by totally changing the economic atmosphere (with a taxpayer-friendly property tax rate) businesses and jobs will come to Allegheny County."[6]

Republican victory in the county elections of November 1995 thus meant only the acceleration of a neoliberal agenda that had already been defining county politics throughout the decade.[7] As in other U.S. cities, the rise of neoliberal urban politics in Pittsburgh in the 1990s meant that unions representing county workers would have to respond to a new kind of challenge. On their first day in office, Dunn and Cranmer instituted the promised tax cut, thereby shrinking county revenues by 20 percent. To pay for these cuts, they announced a two-pronged plan. One prong would involve exacting contract concessions from unionized county workers; the other prong would involve the privatization of the Kane Regional Centers, the county's four public nursing homes. Both efforts were instrumental to the commissioners' plan to eliminate jobs. The contract concessions they sought were aimed at giving the Board of Commissioners the ability to consolidate departments, contract out, and lay off staff without regard to seniority (and without bargaining over such changes). The privatization of the Kanes centers was intended to produce immediate cash for the county in the form of annual lease payments from the new operator.[8]

Between 1996 and 1998, therefore, Local A engaged in two successive struggles — first against the proposed privatization of the Kane

Regional Centers and then against the contract concessions the new commissioners were demanding from all county workers. In the campaign against privatization, members quickly mobilized and joined with external allies in the community, even though Local A's Allegheny County chapter had no preexisting rank-and-file structure in place and even though members were used to traditional, top-down, bureaucratic servicing. But in the local's second campaign (on which I worked as an organizing intern), mobilization proved to be much more difficult, and community allies could not be mobilized at all. The central questions of Part II, therefore, are simple: How and why could Local A so easily deal with workers' servicing expectations and the absence of mobilizing structures during the struggle against privatization? Why, just a few months later in the contract campaign, did servicing expectations and organizational difficulties become a much more difficult dilemma for the local, and how did the local deal with these problems in the new context? And finally, why was the local able to mobilize community allies in the first campaign but not the second?

The public perception (all too accurate in many cases) that unions are narrow special interests rather than broad-based organizations pursuing social justice agendas flows, a number of writers have argued, from the ideology and practice of business unionism.[9] As a result, being associated with labor often hurts a cause more than it helps, a point that has been made by scholars sympathetic to organized labor as well as by labor's opponents. What I want to do in Part II is show how business union ideology shapes the way unions deal with the organizational legacies of business union practice. Chapter 4 shows that in the antiprivatization campaign, all participants viewed privatization as a social justice issue rather than a union issue. As a result, rank-and-file expectations about servicing did not come into play, and the rank and file was so motivated to mobilize that internal union structures supporting mobilization were not needed. In addition, the social justice interpretation of the privatization issue led external constituencies to seek out the union to see how they could aid in the struggle against privatization. The net result was that Local A could adopt social movement tactics *without* dealing directly with members' servicing expectations or its own organizational shortcomings.

In the contract campaign, by contrast, all participants viewed the issue as a *union* matter. Chapter 5 shows that because of this, workers and community allies alike viewed the contract problem as a matter for the union's staff hierarchy to deal with. To create a rank-and-file mobilization around the contract issue, therefore, Local A was now forced to struggle with its own organizational legacies — and workers' resistance to change — more directly. As we will see, the local accomplished a limited mobilization in spite of these difficulties by creating temporary mobilizing structures that *bypassed* existing representational staff.

Part II also advances my broader argument about the value of studying movements in terms of their obstacles and efforts to overcome them rather than in terms of explanatory factors. Just as existing theories of movement participation could not explain why Rosemont workers decided not to form a union in 1997 but reversed their decision in 1998, existing theories of social movement organization do not explain why organizational legacies were so much more problematic in Local A's Allegheny County contract campaign than in its antiprivatization campaign. This is because most research on movement organization treats organization as an independent variable rather than as a problem to be solved in context.

To understand this, we need to take a brief look at a long-standing debate over the role of organization in social movements. On the one side are proponents of the classic "Weber-Michels" hypothesis of organizational transformation, with its inevitable processes of oligarchization, conservatization, and "goal transformation" as leaders gradually shift their emphasis from protest to organizational maintenance, the security of their own positions, and accommodation to elites.[10] This position was reinvigorated by Piven and Cloward's seminal *Poor People's Movements*, which attempted to show that the histories of the unemployed movements of the 1930s, the industrial workers' movements of the 1940s, and the civil rights movement of the 1960s all revealed formal organization leading inevitably to oligarchization and conservatism in goals and tactics. Spontaneous grassroots disruption, Piven and Cloward argued, was what yielded concessions from dominant groups.[11]

Beginning in the late 1960s and early 1970s, however, a number of writers in the resource mobilization (RM) tradition began challenging the Weber-Michels model. These theorists argued that Weber-Michels described only one of several possible outcomes for movement organizations;[12] that at least some movement organizations do not suffer the Weber-Michels fate;[13] and that under some circumstances professional movement staff can facilitate, rather than inhibit or replace, volunteer activism.[14] Moreover, empirical research within the resource mobilization and political process traditions showed convincingly that the grassroots disruptions advocated by Piven and Cloward were not so spontaneous. Research on the civil rights movement, for example, showed that organizations like black churches, community groups, and social movement organizations like the Student Non-Violent Coordinating Committee (SNCC) and the Congress Of Racial Equality (CORE) played key roles in organizing grassroots protest.[15] As the resource mobilization and political process perspectives came to dominate research in social movements, then, researchers within these perspectives developed a consensus that organization was necessary for the creation of sustained grassroots protest.[16]

Still, resource mobilization and political process theorists could not deny that organizations often did behave exactly as the Weber-Michels model would predict. Nowhere is this more clear than in the labor movement — where, as we have already seen, business union organization emphasizes member servicing and routine administration of the contract, discourages rank-and-file participation in the movement, and positions itself as either "apolitical" or politically moderate. Resource mobilization and political process theorists attempted to resolve their differences with the Weber-Michels camp, therefore, by making a distinction between formal and informal organization and arguing that informal organization facilitates protest while formal, hierarchical organization represses it.[17]

However, this argument ignores the important role that formal organizations *have* often played in fomenting and sustaining grassroots protest. The role of black churches in the civil rights movement is an obvious example, but even more salient for our purposes is the role of the contemporary AFL-CIO and national unions like the SEIU in pushing local unions to undertake disruptive and contentious grassroots protest tactics.[18]

As a general explanatory factor, therefore, bureaucratic organization is ultimately ambiguous in its significance. While formal, bureaucratic organizations sometimes discourage mobilization, sometimes they support it. And sometimes bureaucratic organizations can even move from discouraging mobilization to supporting it.[19] Organization as a factor cannot tell us why organization becomes an obstacle to mobilization in some contexts but not others, and it cannot help us understand *how* movement actors deal with organizational problems when they arise. A satisfactory explanation of how and why Local A dealt so differently with its business union legacies in its two Allegheny County mobilization campaigns must therefore view organization as a *problem* to be solved in context — in this case, the context of business unionism, understood as both an ideology *and* a set of organizational practices. Only through such an analysis can we understand why workers and community groups responded differently to the threat of privatization and the threat of contract concessions — and why the union's organizational legacies posed a more difficult set of problems in the contract campaign than in the antiprivatization effort.

FOUR

"Save Our Kanes"

Bypassing Organizational Structures

In September 1996, the Republicans floated their detailed plan to lease the four regional John J. Kane Centers to a private entity, Alleco, specially created for that purpose. Alleco would lease the Kanes for $23 million annually and be responsible for all operating costs — although the long-term debt burden remaining from the centers' construction in the early 1980s would still be borne by the county. Alleco and the Republican commissioners publicly warned the unions that if they did not agree to concessionary contracts with the county before privatization took place, Alleco would not honor the expired contracts.[1] Alleco's business plan promised not to slash existing Kane workers' wages and benefits but reserved the right to downsize in the future. Also, according to the plan, new hires would be brought in at lower wages and with fewer benefits.

But while the interurban competition for jobs and investment can be directly invoked in support of tax cuts and business subsidies, proposals to dismantle public provision of needed services require specific rationales. To justify their proposal to privatize the Kane Regional Centers, Republicans deployed neoliberal ideas about the superiority of private markets over public administration. Alleco, they claimed, could do the job more efficiently than county administrators, without harming Kane residents in any way.[2] The Kanes were overstaffed, they argued, relative to private sector nursing homes — particularly in departments other than nursing (i.e., maintenance, housekeeping, dietary, and laundry). Kane management was burdened with arcane and inflexible work rules that stood in the way of efficiency. Worst of all, they claimed, the Kanes were beginning to lose money — a problem that would only worsen in coming years because of recent changes in state reimbursement rules. In sum, privatization would allow the county to more efficiently meet its legal obligations to provide for the elderly and disabled — by getting rid of unnecessary staff, negotiating better deals with contractors, and using staff more flexibly.[3]

These claims were developed in a report commissioned by Dunn and Cranmer, which explored the county's options for privatizing the Kanes. The report, released in April 1996, recommended that all four Kanes be privatized to achieve maximum savings; second, it suggested that the county could realize a one-time cash windfall as well as substantial annual savings should it "shift ownership and/or operational responsibility" to a private organization created for the purpose of leasing or buying the Kanes.[4] The report also asserted that privatizing the Kanes would neither jeopardize the county's statutory obligation to serve Allegheny County's poorest and most disabled citizens nor negatively affect the quality of care at the facilities. The report's approach and its favored privatization method (creating a "charitable foundation" for the purpose of buying or leasing the facilities) became the blueprint for the county's plan.

Local A was not in a position to mount an attack on ideas about how Pittsburgh should compete for jobs and investment in the new postindustrial economy. Even though the Republicans' tax cut threatened to cripple the county's ability to maintain necessary services and necessitated an austerity attack on unionized public workers, the union could not directly challenge the tax cut because it was very popular politically. The commissioners' specific claims about the virtues of privatization, on the other hand, were ripe for contestation. The union's strategy, therefore, would be to mobilize a grassroots coalition around the idea that "efficiency" really meant cutbacks and that cutbacks would unacceptably harm the Kanes' elderly and infirm residents. Even if the tax cuts could not be directly contested, the union hoped that public sympathy for these innocents would neutralize the Republicans' arguments about costs and efficiency.

The union's plan to build a grassroots community coalition against privatization represented exactly the sort of strategy that the SEIU, and the AFL-CIO under John Sweeney, had been trying to promote, and that many academic observers of labor had been calling for.[5] But in building such a coalition against privatization, Local A faced serious obstacles related to the history of business unionism. Organized in more labor-friendly times in the early 1970s, the union's county chapter had evolved a bureaucratic- servicing model of unionism in which paid union staff, rather than rank-and-file leaders, played the most important role. Workers generally reported grievances directly to their union staff representative, bypassing rank-and-file work site stewards. As a result, many of Local A's work sites and departments had not bothered to elect stewards. In some work sites, too, only a few of the workers had actually joined the union. Staff representatives also tended not to educate workers about the contract, preferring instead to play the role of "expert" over whether issues were grievable or not. For workers, therefore, the grievance process consisted of calling the union representative, relating the problem, and waiting to hear back about how or whether the grievance was resolved.

In itself this was an extremely demobilizing state of affairs, but workers' lack of knowledge of the contract also meant that many of their complaints were not grievable. The logic of the representational structure meant that staff representative Fred Jones received a constant deluge of phone calls about all kinds of complaints, only some of which were grievable. Often Jones would simply not respond to such calls. This may have been his strategy for managing the volume of requests he received from the more than 1,000 workers he represented, but placing a call to your union representative and then not hearing back from him understandably creates feelings of disappointment, disillusionment, and alienation. Even worse, it was common knowledge that Jones did not work very hard in his post. He spent large portions of his day socializing with cronies at the central labor council rather than on real union business. And if he didn't work particularly hard Monday through Thursday, he often bragged that he never worked on Fridays.

Because so much power was centralized in the hands of the staff representative, the union itself did not have accurate, up-to-date records of which bargaining-unit employees had joined the union and which had not; nor did the union have a ready list of stewards and contact people in each department. The staff representatives responsible for various departments had their own knowledge of who the key people were in many departments, but there was little institutional knowledge.

Local A's clerical units at the Kanes were no exception to these arrangements: like other county departments, the Kanes did not have a functioning work site steward structure, with well-trained stewards capable of organizing and carrying out a strategy of grassroots protest. Complicating matters was the fact that most Kane workers were represented by another union, the Laborers' Local X. Local X was even more firmly wedded to its tradition of business union organization and was extremely wary of involvement in a public antiprivatization campaign. Unlike Local A, Local X had no previous experience with public protest campaigns. Local A had already been involved in a series of difficult grassroots, social movement style struggles against Megacorp Enterprises (Part III), and it was largely this experience of struggle that led the local to conclude that a similar approach was now necessary to fight Kane privatization. The leadership of Local X had no tradition of public struggle, having relied mainly on close relations with Democratic politicians over the years. Despite the open hostility of the Republican privatizers toward the county unions, Local X feared that a public protest strategy would irreparably damage relationships with the commissioners and make it difficult to ultimately negotiate contracts. Thus, while the leadership of Local X eventually agreed to allow Local A to try to mobilize Kane workers, Local X did not want to be publicly identified with the campaign or to participate directly in the mobilization effort. Therefore, Local A would have to mobilize Kane workers without the benefit of any kind of effective work site infrastructure.

Local A could not directly overcome these business union legacies, particularly those involving Local X. But the union was able to successfully *bypass* these problems of internal union organization and create a grassroots mobilization because of the special appeal the issue of privatization held for three constituencies: Kane workers, an older generation of Kane activists, and Pittsburgh's progressive religious community. As we will see, each of these constituencies had its own reasons for seeing Kane privatization in humanitarian — rather than economic — terms, and each group brought a different sort of credibility to the campaign to stop privatization.

KANE WORKERS: DEFENDING OUR RESIDENTS

Kane workers themselves were acutely aware of the privatization plan. They were particularly concerned about the possibility of staff cuts because staffing had already been affected by a countywide early retirement plan enacted in the spring of 1996. Many Kane workers had taken the buyout, but these workers had not been replaced. As a result, Kane units were now working shorthanded more often. The Kanes had historically kept a day and evening shift ratio of one nurses' aide for every 10 residents — but since the buyouts, workers whom I interviewed claimed that it had become more difficult to find replacements for workers who called in sick. By the fall of 1996, they said, it was common for day shift nurses' aides to be given 12 residents to care for, and on the evening shift the ratio sometimes approached 1 to 20. Workers I spoke with generally reported that while they were still able to meet the basic physical needs of their residents, as a result of the buyouts they were no longer able to take time to talk with their residents, comfort them, read to them, or comb their hair. As a day shift worker at the McKeesport

Kane said, "It seems like we had more time in the past to talk to the patients, when we always had 10 residents each. Now since we're short-staffed so often, we're more rushed." An evening shift worker at the same facility agreed: "If we had more time, we could read to them. These are the things that we used to do before we got so short-staffed. They say there are volunteers who can do that sort of thing. But there aren't enough, and on the 3:00 to 11:00 shift there aren't any volunteers. They come on daylight shift only." Another evening shift worker at the Glen Hazel Kane said: "There used to be enough time and enough staff that you could give someone an extra shower, or if someone was upset you could ease their problems, or walk someone who needed assistance. You don't have that kind of time now."

Kane workers therefore paid very close attention to the Republican commissioners' public claims that the Kanes were overstaffed, that their workers were overpaid, and that they enjoyed benefits and perks unheard of in the private sector. They understood very clearly that privatization would be likely to cause further cutbacks in staffing, wages, and benefits. They were outraged by the commissioners' attack on the Kanes because, they felt, the Kanes' staffing patterns (one nurses' aide for every 10 residents on the day shift) and relatively good wages and benefits (about $10 an hour for starting nurses' aides) were key ingredients of the facilities' low employee turnover and generally good care. As one Kane worker said:

> I get to take care of the same people every day, so I know them
> and their needs very well. And most of our workers have been at
> the Kanes for a long time. There's very little turnover. If you cut
> people down to six dollars an hour, a lot of people will leave. For
> six dollars an hour, it would be a lot easier to flip hamburgers, and
> not be dealing with the emotional stress of taking care of very sick
> people.

Kane workers were particularly worried about the effects of future cutbacks on residents. Dozens of workers I spoke with were visibly upset about the effects of the buyouts, the likely effects of future cutbacks, and the effect of talk of privatization on residents' morale. One worker's bitter comments captured a theme I heard often: "The residents wonder why we can't spend as much time with them as we used to. They ask us, 'What did I do to make you not love me anymore?' They think it's something they did wrong. It's heartbreaking. And all you can do is tell them it's not their fault and go on to the next patient. They deserve better."

The key point is not only that workers were angry about privatization but also that they viewed privatization as an issue that connected them directly to their residents in opposition to the county board of commissioners. In some ways, the reaction of Kane workers to the privatization proposal confirms arguments that public service workers form natural alliances with their clients based on their common interest in the expansion of social provision.[6] But while sociologists like James O'Connor and Paul Johnston may be correct about the basis for this alliance, nursing home workers' natural affinity for their clients and their sense of common interest with them do not completely explain why these workers acted *independently* against privatization, why they saw it as an issue requiring a direct response, regardless of what the union did about it. As one Kane worker said, "We were protesting [privatization] right out on the street here, before the union even got involved in it. The day the plan was announced we all went outside at lunchtime and marched."

Kane workers acted independently of the union because they did not view privatization as a "union" (i.e., bargaining or grievance) issue, or even as an issue of job survival, but as a moral issue demanding a response: How should county government view the mission of the Kane Centers and, perhaps more important, Kane residents themselves? Ironically, it was precisely because Kane workers did *not* view privatization as a union issue that the union was able to mobilize them so easily. Given the history of business union organization in the Allegheny County chapter, had Kane workers viewed the issue as within the union's normal representational purview, they would more likely have expected it to deal with the problem on their behalf. But because they viewed the issue differently, Local A was able to mobilize them in opposition to privatization even without an easily activated internal union structure.

Thus, when the union began announcing rallies, workers turned up in fairly large numbers, with very little organizational effort on the part of the union. In late September 1996, about 75 Kane workers from Locals A and X turned out on short notice to an antiprivatization rally. Several weeks later, hundreds of workers responded to Local A's call to attend a Wednesday night meeting of the county board of commissioners. In January 1997, Local A successfully organized three days of rallies and marches; noisy crowds of workers descended on the Allegheny County courthouse each day. Between these large events, several dozen workers turned out for each biweekly county commissioners' meeting— to harass the county administration and to use the portion of the meetings designated for "public comment" as a platform to denounce Kane privatization.

The mobilization of Kane workers contributed a crucial piece to the overall response to the Republicans' assault on the Kanes. The sheer scale of workers' rallies and protests, combined with careful attention to media outreach, resulted in extensive coverage by all local television networks and both Pittsburgh's daily newspapers. The *Post-Gazette*, which editorially favored Kane privatization, described the scene at one rally as a "buzz-saw of opposition," during which the crowd "chanted slogans like 'Hey hey, ho ho, Dunn and Cranmer got to go'."[7] The *Post-Gazette* story continued, "By the end of the evening, after several union officials and others spoke against privatization, Democratic commissioner Mike Dawida had donned a union cap. Cranmer was livid and Dunn, who appeared to be flustered during most of the meeting, had left through a side door."[8]

All three local television networks also covered the meeting, giving extensive play to the rambunctious scene inside the meeting and interviewing workers outside the meeting as well. The media coverage emphasized workers' concern for their residents in addition to their own opposition as workers and played up the angle of nursing home residents who faced an uncertain future. In this frame the workers appeared as advocates for the residents. One worker was shown on WPXI, the local NBC affiliate, saying, "I'm very opposed to [privatization] because we're very dedicated workers and I don't feel we should be put out in the streets. And our patients, our poor patients, some of them are asking questions about where we're gonna go, and where they're gonna go." Another gave an emotional statement to the cameras, with tears in her eyes as she referred to the Kane Centers' historical mission: "The [Kane] hospitals used to have a motto that said, 'We'll take the poor and we'll take the indigent.' Now they want to run [the homes] as a business. . . . Well, businesses don't take in the poor."

During the public comment portion of a mid-October commissioners' meeting, workers proposed that instead of privatizing the facilities, the county should initiate a program of quarterly meetings with employee groups at each center "to explore ways of cutting costs and raising revenues." The idea was ignored, allowing 50 workers to claim in an October 17 letter to the editor of the *Post-Gazette* that the Republican commissioners were not interested in working with Kane employees to solve the Kanes' problems.[9] Again the TV networks gave extensive play to the workers' protests. The president of Local A appeared on the KDKA (CBS affiliate) local news addressing the commissioners, pleading, "I come and I ask you, please stop the attack on us, on the unions that represent the working men and women of Allegheny County [loud cheers from over a hundred workers]." Several other scenes of protesting workers were shown, and then Commissioner Dunn was given only a few seconds to rebut the protesters. He said, "[The Kanes] will get more federal funds and state funds than now. So [privatization is] a way of financing them better so care will stay the same."[10] The coverage gave a Kane worker the last word: "[Kane residents] have become family — when they hurt, you hurt."

Despite the success of these events, the counterattack by the two Republican commissioners illustrates the limitations of mobilization by

Kane workers alone and the importance of the union's effort to build a broader community coalition: they began portraying the workers and unions as motivated purely by self-interest in the face of difficult but necessary change. In response to one early protest, Commissioner Dunn said, "They're concerned about their jobs, and that's understandable." Cranmer added, "We want a positive relationship with the unions, but times are changing." As the campaign developed, the commissioners took a harder line, portraying the unions as obstructionist. "If the unions stand back and don't negotiate, then as far as I'm concerned, we turn this thing over to Alleco," Dunn threatened in January 1997. "The employees have had their chance. If their leaders don't do the right thing, then we're going to turn it over to Alleco and let Alleco negotiate with them."[11]

Further, the Republican commissioners and the county's law firm began pointedly attacking "wasteful" labor agreements as the source of inefficiency at the Kanes, slamming Kane workers' free cafeteria lunches and differential rates ($0.25 an hour) for assignments off their normal units. "You'll find no counterpart to that in the private sector," complained John Lyncheski, the county's chief negotiator to local television news cameras. "It's just inefficient and wasteful, frankly." Alleco chairman James Roddey blasted the Kanes for what he called overstaffing in nonmedical departments like dietary and housekeeping. "The quality of care is not the issue," he said. "We've got three people for every position in [the] dietary [department]."[12]

It is important to recognize that these attacks did not come out of nowhere but built on an antiunion discourse that opponents of public sector unions had been using since the mid-1970s. As Paul Johnston has observed, city officials in San Francisco were the first to learn that they could successfully blame "greedy" unions and overpaid public workers for fiscal crises and tax increases.[13] San Francisco's strategy was subsequently duplicated in cities across the country. Johnston views this backlash as a purely public sector phenomenon — but it is interesting to note the similarity between the portrayal of public sector unions as greedy special interests bankrupting municipal governments and the portrayal of industrial unions as greedy special interests whose continual demands for higher wages made it impossible for American industries to compete with foreign competitors in the 1980s. In other words, the Republican commissioners in Allegheny county were not just mobilizing an existing discourse about the greed and inefficiencies caused by *public* sector unions. Rather, in charging the county unions with obstructionism, selfishness, and wastefulness, they were tapping into deeply resonant images about unions in general. These images are particularly resonant in the Rust Belt, as we saw in Part I, in part because even many working-class victims of deindustrialization share this view of unions as being at least partially responsible for it.

Thus we can see that although, on one hand, the nature of the issue in this case allowed Local A to mobilize Kane workers directly (even though the union was organizationally weak), on the other hand this mobilization was not capable — by itself — of dealing with the negative images of unions mobilized by the Republican commissioners. The union did attempt to respond to the Republicans' charges, disputing James Roddey's claims about overstaffing. It argued that the free lunches had been proposed by the county in the 1970s in lieu of a pay increase and had been accepted by the unions to help the county save money. The modest off-unit differential, union officials pointed out, was designed to reinforce the Kanes' philosophy of developing long-term relationships between residents and their primary caregivers and to discourage managers from assigning workers to take care of residents whose needs they did not know well. But these rebuttals received little attention in the media.

ADVOCATES FOR THE ELDERLY: INDEPENDENT CREDIBILITY

Research on union organizing has found that labor-community coalitions are usually ad hoc creations forged in crisis rather than ongoing

alliances.[14] More recent research on labor-community organizing suggests that this is still largely true.[15] In the struggle against privatization at
the Kane centers, Local A did create just such an ad hoc coalition.
However, in doing so it drew on a set of crucial organizational links that
it had been investing in since 1991. From the beginning of the campaign
the union had enlisted a group called the Alliance for Progressive Action
(APA) to help organize an effective labor-community coalition. The APA,
founded in 1991, was an umbrella group for more than a dozen progressive and civil rights organizations in Allegheny County. Local A was a
founding member of APA and had contributed funding since its inception. Other APA members included the Rainbow Coalition, Act/Up, the
United Electrical Workers (UE), and a number of civil rights organizations. Longtime Local A organizer Wendy Newman had been involved
with APA since 1991 and, at the time of the battle over the Kanes, was in
the process of leaving the local to take a full-time job at APA.

One way APA staff broadened the base of antiprivatization opposition
was to begin meeting with a number of activists who had spearheaded a
reform effort at the old Kane Hospital nearly two decades earlier. These
activists were former workers at Kane Hospital who had gone public in
the late 1970s with a damning report called "Kane: A Place to Die." Their
central contention then was that low wages, understaffing, and high
employee turnover at Kane Hospital led to low worker morale, patient
neglect, and patient abuse. Their exposé had received national attention,
had led to changes in federal government regulation of county nursing
homes across the country, and had ultimately resulted in the demolition
of Kane Hospital and the construction of the four regional Kane Centers
in the early 1980s. These activists were justifiably proud of their reform
efforts and of the new Kanes' continuing record of quality care; like Kane
workers, they understood that the Kanes' vastly improved reputation was
the result of their good staffing ratios, decent wages and benefits, and low
staff turnover. The old Kane activists were thus very concerned about the
commissioners' plans to privatize the Kanes, fearing that a private operator would undo precisely the improvements in staffing, wages and

benefits, and turnover that they had fought so hard for two decades ago. One of the original Kane activists who now led the group's efforts against privatization later related, "I ran into [another former Kane activist] at the supermarket, and we said, you know, we should really do something. So we called the union." APA and Local A staff began meeting with these activists in September 1996. Together, they formed a new group, called the Committee to Save Kane, and began planning to organize residents' family members and to circulate petitions.

The members of the Committee to Save Kane played on their former positions as courageous whistle-blowers at the old Kane Hospital and current identities as advocates for the elderly, garnering an aura of impartiality that current Kane workers could not command. When the Committee to Save Kane held a press conference announcing its opposition to privatization and outlining its concern that any attempt to cut costs would necessarily rely on reduced staffing, wages, and benefits, press reports were respectful, treating its members as independent advocates for the elderly.[16] Coverage noted that committee members included a regional director of the National Council for Senior Citizens and the president of the local chapter of the Steelworkers Organization of Active Retirees.[17]

The Republicans found it much more difficult to respond to the Committee to Save Kane than to the mobilization of Kane workers themselves because it could not portray the committee's members as having a vested interest in the outcome of the battle over privatization. Whereas Kane workers were vulnerable to an attack that drew on negative images of unions, the committee was credible precisely because of its public independence from the union. This independence was actually somewhat of an illusion given how closely union officials worked with the committee to plan its events and activities (not to mention the fact that the APA's Newman was a former organizer for Local A). But the Republicans never managed to pierce this veil. They might have been able to score some important points had they uncovered the behind-the-scenes links connecting the Committee to Save Kane, the union, and the

APA, but as it was, they were reduced to arguing weakly that privatization foes had been "'sold a bill of goods' by union leaders with a stake in [Kane jobs]."[18] Claiming that advocates for the elderly and retired had somehow been duped by the Kane unions was not nearly as effective as being able to blast the unions directly. As a result, the commissioners were forced to respond more substantively to the committee's arguments than to those that Kane workers had made. Sounding defensive, the Republicans denied that there would be any job cuts directly involving patient care, but their denial admitted that in fact job reductions were likely through attrition and possibly even layoffs.[19]

The Committee to Save Kane also contributed to the campaign in other ways. When committee members independently discovered that the Kanes were busing nurses' aides from one facility to another to beef up staffing during a state inspection—thus casting doubt on claims of overstaffing—they went public with the information. The Laborers' Local X, which represented these nurse's aides, had known about the practice but had chosen not to go public or even communicate this knowledge to Local A. Committee members spent hours discussing these discoveries and their analysis of privatization with several television reporters, and this paid off in the form of an in-depth television news report on staffing changes at the Kanes since the Republicans had taken office.

But perhaps the most important Committee to Save Kane activity was its effort to contact and organize the family members of Kane residents. Through its organizing efforts, the committee was able to turn out a contingent of residents' family members to protest at the commissioners' biweekly public meetings and at union rallies. The family members were extremely effective and enthusiastic advocates for the Kanes, and their opposition to privatization was genuine and heartfelt. At commissioners' meetings I attended, dozens of family members—mostly middle-aged and elderly women—formed a rowdy caucus. At every opportunity, they yelled at the commissioners, saying, for example, "Shame on you! How can you do this to my mother?" At one meeting, Commissioner Cranmer inadvertently stepped on their toes when he criticized Kane workers. The family members were outraged. "[Kane workers] are the nicest people anywhere!" one white-haired lady shouted angrily. "They take care of my sister every day and she loves them dearly! Don't you say anything bad about them!" Cranmer was clearly flustered by all this, and neither Republican commissioner ever figured out how to respond effectively to the family members' vocal opposition: they simply could not dismiss family members' concerns as "selfish."

RELIGIOUS LEADERS: MORAL AUTHORITY

The value of alliances between unions and churches has been commented on by a number of labor observers.[20] The Catholic Church and many Protestant denominations assert the importance of workers' rights to bargain collectively to achieve economic justice.[21] The involvement of clergy in union campaigns can help legitimate the struggle by enhancing its moral authority.[22] This independent moral authority was a crucial element in Local campaign against the privatization of the Kanes.

In addition to its work with the Committee to Save Kane, the APA also helped coordinate opposition from progressive church leaders. The APA had already been in the process of organizing the Pittsburgh Area Religious Task Force on the Economy, recruiting church leaders who had historically supported labor causes and issues and who were generally concerned about problems of economic inequality and injustice. When the commissioners announced their plans to privatize the Kanes, the APA and Local A suggested Kane privatization as the Religious Task Force's first major project. "They needed something to get started on, they needed something concrete to work around," says the APA's Newman. The union put together a fact sheet on privatization emphasizing how Alleco's plan would be likely to affect the quality of care, and Newman and Janet Zimmerman, the president of Local A, presented the issue to the task force. They proposed that the task force convene public hearings on the issue, take testimony, and then issue an opinion.

The Catholic, Presbyterian, Baptist, and Jewish clergy who made up the Religious Task Force responded enthusiastically to this proposal. The idea of holding public hearings was particularly attractive because, rather than being asked automatically to side with the unions, the clergy were being asked to form their own independent view and issue a thoughtful opinion rather than knee-jerk support. Clearly, though, the sympathies of this progressive group of clergy were with workers and residents from the outset. As the Reverend Phil Wilson, a task force member, later said, "You know, a lot of us visit parishioners at the Kanes on a regular basis. I have always been impressed with the staff there, and whenever I am visiting, they always seem to be working very hard. So to me, and to a number of other clergy, the things the Commissioners were saying about the Kanes being overstaffed just didn't make sense." Also, Wilson added, "Some of us have been around long enough to remember the old Kane Hospital — and we didn't want to see a return to those kinds of conditions."

The hearings held by the Religious Task Force on March 5, and their subsequent opinion statement, added a crucial final piece to the puzzle of resistance. The hearings themselves offered another opportunity to mobilize "disinterested" expert opinion. Written testimony from Linda Rhodes, former Pennsylvania Secretary of Aging, was introduced, emphasizing the Kanes' record of providing high-quality care to a vulnerable population. She wrote of having received many calls, as Secretary of Aging, "from Pittsburghers who asked if there was anything I could do to get their family members into one of the Kane Regional Centers because they knew that the care was so good but the waiting lists were so long." MIT-trained economist Stephen Herzenberg warned that nursing home markets and reimbursement schemes did not reward care quality in the private sector, contributing to understaffing and the spread of a low-wage, high-turnover model of labor relations. Finally, widely respected Democratic County Controller Frank Lucchino testified that short-term budget considerations rather than concern for quality were driving the privatization plan. Lucchino noted that the GOP commissioners were eager to receive a $23 million lease payment from Alleco to help ease the county's self-imposed budget crisis. Moreover, Lucchino testified, to come up with the lease money, Alleco would necessarily have to cut jobs, wages, and services at the Kanes.

Again, the Republicans had difficulty responding effectively to these claims. *Post-Gazette* coverage of the Religious Task Force hearings gave extensive play to Lucchino's financial analysis of the privatization proposal, which James Roddey, Alleco's chairman, was not able convincingly to refute.[23] Roddey and Commissioner Cranmer repeated their denials that privatization would lead to cuts in the medical staff at the Kanes, but they now seemed to be outnumbered by a myriad of experts claiming the opposite.

On March 24, 1997, the Religious Task Force on the Economy issued its opinion on Kane privatization and its appeal to the board of commissioners to reconsider the plan. Its statement, quoted in the *Post-Gazette*, expressed concern about "increased social costs, the loss of public accountability, the stripping of public assets, the potential for corruption, the jobs of Kane workers and the undercutting of union organization."[24] The statement went on to say that "[w]e are deeply concerned about reductions in the quality and availability of patient care. As religious people, we believe society has a duty toward the poor, the elderly, the infirm and the isolated."[25] Sister Mary Carol Bennett, of the Sisters of Mercy Peace and Justice Office, also commented that "[privatization] is a dollar move to cut the bottom line figure. And the only way you're going to do that is to cut services and to cut jobs."[26] The press conference concluded with a call for parishioners and the general public to contact the commissioners to oppose privatization.

According to the APA's Wendy Newman, the Religious Task Force's contribution to the campaign was, organizationally speaking, the weakest piece of the puzzle. "Frankly," she said, the Religious Task Force was "somewhat smoke and mirrors. But it ended up being a very important piece, because [the clergy] had a certain moral authority that had a very real impact." Indeed, the extensive publicity surrounding the appeal by the Religious Task Force on the Economy seemed the final straw for Commissioner Larry Dunn. Dunn had been quiet throughout the month of March, but he decided several hours after the task force made its appeal — six days before his original deadline for a final decision on Kane privatization — to quash privatization at least until the end of the year.

CONCLUSION

In the preceding analysis, I tried to show that existing bureaucratic organization could not usefully be viewed as a factor that straightforwardly hindered or helped Local A's mobilization campaign to prevent the privatization of the Kanes. In this case, as we saw, business union organization did not prevent or stifle mobilization because, within the terms of business union ideology itself, the campaign did not seem to involve purely "union" issues. Workers, religious leaders, and advocates for the elderly all viewed privatization as a direct threat to the well-being of nursing home residents rather than as a union matter. As a result, the union was able to mobilize its rank-and-file members without any organizational infrastructure at all, and it was able to create new external structures through the APA to activate community allies. These external mobilizing structures were of course important to the outcome of the campaign, but the larger point is that they were available to the union only because the privatization issue seemed to transcend the interests of the union and its workers.

The finding that organizational legacies really were *not* a problem in the context of an issue that appealed to workers and community groups alike as a human rights issue has important implications for social movement unionism. It suggests that in many cases — especially if they are creative and clever about how to frame the conflict — unions will be able to construct many grassroots mobilizations without engaging in thoroughgoing organizational reform efforts.[27] On the other hand, however, to the extent that mobilization is possible without serious organizational change, unions are likely to lapse immediately back to a bureaucratic-servicing mode once the campaign ends. Indeed, the campaigns to save the Kanes had no long-term impact on the level of organization within the affected bargaining units — a fact that *did* become problematic in the union's next campaign.

Aimed at winning new contracts for all its county workers (including Kane employees), the contract campaign presented a quite different aspect. In its contract struggle, Local A would not be able construct *any* issue of broad-based appeal, similarly capable of mobilizing credible allies and neutralizing neoliberal assumptions and discourse. Like the antiprivatization campaign, the union's contract campaign revolved around grassroots social movement–style organizing and protest — but unlike the privatization effort, in the context of a contract campaign the union's internal business union structures presented serious obstacles to sustained mobilization. Moreover, the existing organizational links to the progressive community via the APA were now no help in activating these allies. As a result, worker mobilization around the contract issue was much weaker politically, and much of its success hinged on the union's ability to ride the coattails of the earlier victory on privatization.

FIVE

"We Want a Contract"

Confronting Business Union Organization

Even though public opposition had put Kane privatization on hold by the spring of 1997, 3,500 workers represented by 11 county unions were still working under the terms of expired contracts, with no thaw in negotiations likely any time in the near future. The county's labor counsel was still demanding a variety of give-backs and concessions from the unions and insisting that all negotiations begin with a set of completely new documents erasing existing contract language on seniority rights, scheduling, and numerous other issues. Publicly, county negotiators portrayed county employees as overpaid and underworked and blamed the county's fiscal dilemma on a bloated county payroll. Not mentioned was the fact that most unionized county workers earned only around $20,000 annually or that upper-level managers had received large bonuses and raises since Republicans Dunn and Cranmer had taken office. Finally, the county repeatedly told the unions that no substantive discussions were possible until the unions agreed to a new, two-page "management's rights" clause. The county's proposal would have given it the right to privatize or contract out any county function without bargaining with the unions and to unilaterally change workers' schedules and job assignments — or lay them off — without notice. The management's rights clause was important to the county because Pennsylvania labor law requires public employers to negotiate with unions over any proposed privatization or contracting out, even if these subjects are not mentioned in collective bargaining agreements. Therefore, to gain a free hand in this area, the county hoped to force each union to accept the management's rights clause and in this way to make an end run around its defeat on Kane privatization.

Despite the success of Local A's public organizing efforts in defeating Kane privatization, leaders of the other county unions favored returning to a strategy of quiet lobbying and behind-the-scenes pressure in order to settle the county contracts. Janet Zimmerman, president of Local A, believed that such a strategy would not lead to a successful conclusion to county bargaining; she believed that the commissioners would need a stronger push.

The issue of contracts for county workers, however, did not inspire the same sort of community activism that Kane privatization had done. The activists and religious leaders who had helped generate a groundswell of opposition to privatization were not only less interested in county workers' contract situations but also in less of a position to issue morally charged public statements on the issue. Kane privatization had raised the specter of cruelty to innocent old people; the county's demands for contract concessions on seniority rights, scheduling, and contracting out, on the other hand, did not appeal in the same way to a ready-made social justice constituency. County workers' stalled contract negotiations simply did not seem to portend human suffering of the same magnitude as nursing home privatization and cutbacks. Even though county workers stood to lose important seniority and educational benefits, not to mention their legal right to bargain over privatization and contracting out, the union was not able to construct an appealing public discourse about the commissioners' attack or generate the same kind of emotional punch that the specter of Kane privatization had offered. As a result, the union could not rely primarily on external linkages with progressive organizations in its contract battle and was forced to rely on leverage from within.

But without a ready-made counterideology to deploy, mobilizing county workers to fight for fair contracts required more intensive organizing than mobilizing angry Kane workers had done. Kane workers had been keenly aware of the privatization issue and its potential effects on themselves and Kane residents, and they were eager to show their anger publicly. Kane and other county workers, in contrast, generally did not understand the bargaining situation at the outset of the union's internal organizing effort and had no independent analysis of the contract issue that made mobilization around the contract idea seem necessary. On the contract issue, Kane workers and other county workers both expected their paid representatives to negotiate new contracts on their behalf. In this struggle, therefore, unlike the privatization struggle, mobilization would not happen spontaneously — and the union's existing internal organizational structure would become a real obstacle to sustained mobilization.

There were two reasons for this turnabout. First, rank-and-file workers' lack of a mobilizing perspective of their own meant that to mobilize workers around the contract issue, the union would have to deal with their lived experience of business union representation, their expectation that it was the union's job to negotiate new contracts. (In fairness, it must be said that this expectation was one that the union hierarchy had long inculcated by conducting top-level negotiations without rank-and-file participation or input.) And second, the inability to mobilize external allies meant that to mount any sort of campaign, the union would also be forced to deal with several important organizational legacies: the bureaucratic inertia of entrenched representational union staff and the lack of organization and leadership at the work site level.

The president of Local A, Janet Zimmerman, clearly did not want to permanently solve these problems. Such an attempt would have necessitated, first of all, an unpleasant struggle with entrenched organization (i.e., with Jones and his allies at the central labor council). But more important, building a rank-and-file organization in the union's largest and most important chapter was simply not something Zimmerman really wanted to do. In 25 years, Zimmerman had never been opposed in a presidential election, and her control of the local rested in part on her ability to hand-pick executive board members drawn from a pliant and complacent Allegheny County chapter. The organizational weakness and disorganization of the Allegheny County unit, in other words, generally suited Zimmerman quite well, since it was part of her strategy for controlling the local. Building a permanent rank-and-file organization in Allegheny County to facilitate routine rank-and-file participation in the governance of the union could only undermine that control.

Zimmerman therefore faced a dilemma. On one hand, among the leaders of Allegheny County employees' unions, she alone seemed to understand that a grassroots campaign was necessary if the county unions hoped to escape concession bargaining unscathed. Moreover, the idea that Commissioners Dunn and Cranmer were going to take away from her members what she had spent 25 years obtaining infuriated her, and she was determined to resist. On the other hand, however, Zimmerman had no desire to potentially upset her own applecart by building an independent rank-and-file organization in the very chapter whose pliancy she had depended on for a quarter-century as a central part of her governing strategy. Therefore she sought to steer a middle course. She would try to create a contract mobilization through a series of stopgap measures that would not, she hoped, change the organizational functioning of the Allegheny County chapter in a lasting way. In place of a permanent work site structure, a temporary network of departmental contact people would be assembled for the duration of the campaign. And union reps who were unwilling or unable to organize a grassroots campaign would simply be bypassed by a temporary campaign staff composed of interns (of which I was to be one) and a small number of loyal volunteers from the rank and file.

ORGANIZATIONAL LEGACIES
Rank-and-File Repertoires

A number of observers have pointed out that the "servicing" model — in which paid staff perform all representation work *for* members — leads to worker passivity and to the equation of a strong union with one that offers "good service."[1] This is a problem that plagues all attempts to transform local unions, and it reared its head in Local Allegheny County contract campaign. Unlike the privatization threat, which Kane workers saw immediately as a threat to mobilize around, the contract issue did not inspire the same reaction among either Kane workers or other county workers. To be sure, workers were quite upset about the fact that they had been working under expired contracts for nearly two years. But their anger was directed as much at the union as at the county for "taking so long" to settle the contract. These workers' long-standing experience of business union–style representation led them to view contract negotiation as something that the union did for them every three years. For more than two decades, back-room negotiations between top-level union staff and county officials had produced new contracts. Now workers were asking what the union was doing and why they did not have new contracts. Kane workers, in fact, were particularly angry, since in their view they had already worked to defeat the major stumbling block to new contracts, the issue of Kane privatization. After they'd done so much work, why could the union not now deliver new contracts?

I experienced this anger directly on numerous occasions during the campaign, during lunchtime work site organizing meetings as well as in smaller meetings with work site leaders, stewards, and contact people. Early in the planning stage of the campaign, for example, I met with work site leaders at one of the Kanes to discuss the contract campaign and to plan for a lunchtime membership meeting at their site. Before I could even take a seat, I was confronted with an angry barrage of questions and accusations. The group demanded to know why there hadn't been any new negotiating sessions between union negotiators and the county, and they accused the union hierarchy of not taking the negotiations seriously over the past 20 months. I explained, as I had been told to explain, that the first priority had been preventing privatization and that now that the union had successfully put down that initiative it was ready to put pressure on the commissioners to settle the contracts. This was a false step that sent the group into paroxysms of anger. "The union DIDN'T stop privatization — WE did!" one worker hissed. "And the union has been promising to get us new contracts for two years now! When are they going to live up to that? When are they going to get off their asses and do their goddamn JOBS over there?" Finally recognizing that I was out of my depth, at this point I decided to fall back on the "Hey, I'm only an intern!" defense. Other meetings were not as difficult as this one, but workers' first question — understandably — was always the same: "When are we going to have new contracts, and what is the union doing to get them?"

To cope with this reality — and because it had no reliable means of communication with the rank and file — union officials organized a series of lunchtime work site meetings, held at several dozen county departments and locations (representing about 900 of the local's 1,500 Allegheny County workers) during late June and early July 1997, to answer these questions and to seek workers' participation in its contract mobilization campaign. One of the central purposes of the work site meetings was to convey to the rank and file why the kind of bargaining and representation that they were accustomed to were not going to lead to new contracts given the contemporary circumstances and politics of the county. The meetings began with a bargaining report, delivered by a staff representative, explaining the concessions that the county was demanding. After detailing the county's demands on scheduling, contracting out, wages and benefits, and management rights, the presentation emphasized that there were as yet no new contracts because the union could not and would not sign what was currently on the table.

Workers who attended these meeting were universally shocked when they heard the details of the county's bargaining position. No one argued that the union should cave in and accept the county's demands. And once they understood that by continuing to bargain without (1) agreeing to the concessions or (2) allowing negotiations to come to an impasse, the union was preventing the county from legally implementing any of the cutbacks and concessions the commissioners wanted to impose, workers began to appreciate the union's bargaining strategy. This understanding led workers to a different set of questions: How can the union change the county's bargaining position? How can the union get the county to drop its concessionary demands?

At this point the meeting was turned over to the interns and member organizers, who were prepared to answer these questions. The interns' "rap" began with a brainstorming session aimed at getting the workers to think about possible sources of power and leverage, such as (1) the union's ability to influence the public's perception of the commissioners, of the union, and of its issues, and the importance of getting the union's side of the story out to the public; (2) the union's ability to influence the commissioners' perception of its unity and determination. "If the commissioners think we're divided and weak," the rap went, "they won't have any incentive to change their bargaining position." Finally (at the insistence of the local president), the rap emphasized (3) that the union could increase its political clout through donations to its political fund, known as COPE. Although the third point above was essentially a tacked-on plea for money and was sold on the basis of gimmicks like union jackets and members-only discount packages, the central thrust of the rap was to try to convince workers that the union could no longer win new contracts without the involvement of the rank and file. To create media coverage of the union's issues, the union needed rallies and events that the media would cover as news. To convince the commissioners that the union was united against the concessions, the union needed mass attendance at rallies and events.

To coordinate these actions, interns and member organizers handed out sign-up sheets asking rank-and-file workers to commit to participating in specific activities, with space for the workers to check off the ones they were willing to do. At the bottom, the form asked for workers' names, addresses, and home phone numbers so that the union could follow up with workers who volunteered to do specific things. Discussion of the proposed activities emphasized how each helped the union exercise its power and exert pressure on the county commissioners. Workers understood the logic of the appeal and readily signed up to participate in rallies, button days, and other activities. And not only did they sign up, they participated at rates that exceeded the expectations of the staff. Rallies at commissioners' meetings routinely attracted 60 or 70 workers, hundreds of workers signed petitions demanding contracts, and more than 500 workers attended a large rally on July 31, 1997, which was dubbed "Solidarity Day."

Despite these successes, however, it must be emphasized that workers' willingness to participate in the union's contract campaign did *not* imply that they were now eager for a more participatory, grassroots model of day-to-day unionism. Years of experience with a traditional model of servicing unionism had taught workers to view the union, not as the sum of their collective participation, not as something that they created through their mutual support, but rather as something outside themselves, an external service to call on whenever there was a problem. These ingrained dispositions persisted even in the context of the contract campaign.

This could be plainly seen at meetings involving Art Lazarra's work sites. Lazarra tried very hard to convince workers that on a day-to-day basis they could and should respond directly and collectively to work site problems instead of just filing grievances and waiting for a procedural resolution. Lazarra always stressed that direct work site actions were particularly important now that grievances were piling up instead of being resolved in an orderly fashion. He used several examples to show how effective this sort of response can be.

In one of his favorite stories, Lazarra told of a hot, muggy day in late June when the air-conditioning in one of the county offices had broken down. The workers asked their supervisor if they could remove their ties because of the heat, but the supervisor said no. One of the stewards called Art, but instead of filing a grievance (which wouldn't have resulted in immediate relief in any case), Art suggested that all the workers should march down to the office of the row officer (the elected official in charge of their department), give him their ties, explain the problem to him, and tell him that they were prepared to alert the media to the working conditions if they were forced to continue wearing their ties in 90-degree heat. The strategy was successful — faced with collective protest and the threat of negative publicity, the row officer overruled the workers' supervisor and allowed the workers to remove their ties. In fact, for the rest of the week, until the air-conditioning was fixed, the workers were allowed to report to work in shorts and T-shirts.

This story never had the intended effect in any of the meetings Art attended. Workers invariably responded not with enthusiasm but with baffled incomprehension, as if he was missing the point. Every time Art would make his pitch and give an example, workers would counter with a grievance and ask when the union was going to do something about it. They always seemed both puzzled and annoyed by Art's responses. As I watched this on numerous occasions, I could almost hear the workers thinking, "What's going on here? Why isn't he listening to us? We keep telling him about these problems and instead of promising to take care of it, he keeps trying to push them off on us." Often workers actually said in frustration things like "Why am I paying dues if the union isn't going to help me with these problems?" These exchanges always ended with Art and the workers exasperated and annoyed at one another. Lazarra interpreted their responses as an inability to understand their situation, what they were up against, and what they needed to do about it; workers in turn interpreted Lazarra's suggestion that they rely on their collective power to solve work site problems as an abdication of responsibility by the union.

Why did workers approve of and participate in the union's collective action strategy on the contract campaign but respond so negatively to Art Lazarra's suggestion that they apply the same principles to work site grievances? The answer is that these were two very different ideas. Unlike spontaneous work site resistance, the protests that the campaign organized were relatively easy to participate in precisely because they took place *outside* the workplace — on the steps of the county courthouse, for example, or at commissioners' meetings. Acting up *in* the workplace, on the other hand, implies a potentially tense confrontation with the boss, which is an entirely different matter. Moreover, public rallies and activities offered safety in numbers, almost an anonymity of participation. In contrast, asking a few isolated workers to stand up to the boss requires them to go out on a limb in hopes that other workers will back them up. My point is certainly not that a more participatory model of work site unionism is not possible but rather that rank-and-file workers accustomed to a servicing approach will not embrace such threatening new ideas without a great deal more sustained support, leadership, and encouragement than was forthcoming in this campaign. This supports the finding that moving from a servicing approach to a model in which rank-and-file members take more responsibility for day-to-day representational tasks can actually be *more* staff intensive than the servicing model itself, at least in the short term.[2]

Bureaucratic Inertia

In addition to the problem of member resistance, union staff also resist movement away from a servicing approach.[3] Once again, Local A's Allegheny County contract campaign was no exception: the union's bureaucratic-servicing history shaped the development of the contract campaign from the beginning. Of the three staff reps responsible for the 1,500 Allegheny County workers represented by Local A, the most senior, Fred Jones, was firmly entrenched in the bureaucratic proceduralism that had served him so well over the years, and he had little talent or inclination for organizing. Jones may have recognized that a pressure campaign was necessary to move the contract negotiations forward, but he clearly wanted as little to do with it as possible, and he hoped to return to his standard representational activities as soon as the campaign ended.

Jones's refusal to fully support the campaign was an important reason for the union's use of student interns to do most of the legwork of the campaign. This in itself caused some problems, since workers who were already angry at the union were not pleased that the union would send some wet-behind-the-ears intern, who knew nothing about the way the union functioned (or didn't function), to talk to them. A union staff member representing public employees in two neighboring counties warned me about this:

> Steve, you're going to have a tough row to hoe out there. I mean, some of those people are just tired of hearing the same thing at contract time, and then nothing ever changes. And, hey, no offense to you, but what the hell are we doing sending you out there any-way? You have no idea of what's been going on in the last two years or what their problems are. I mean we hire interns and we send them out there to do Jones's job for him, and we expect our members not to be pissed off at us.

I soon found out what he was talking about, since I was on my way to the Kane planning meeting described earlier, at which I found myself a convenient target for workers' frustration, in over my head, and in a situation where everything I could think of to say only made matters worse. The use of college and graduate student interns in a primary rather than a supporting role in this campaign was thus not only somewhat inappropriate (as Steve Early has suggested)[4] but also a symptom of the unwillingness of the local union president to deal directly with staff resistance.

Jones's lukewarm response to the campaign was not universal among the staff. As indicated above, unlike Jones, Art Lazarra believed that the new context of Allegheny County labor relations demanded a radical response from the union. In Lazarra's view, the organizing campaign should not seek merely to temporarily mobilize workers in pursuit of contract agreements, only to return to the status quo; rather, the campaign should be a first step toward organizational reform and restructuring. Lazarra wanted to introduce a functioning work site steward structure so that future mobilizations could be accomplished without having to start from scratch every time. But as consistently as Lazarra tried to introduce the issue of organizational reform into discussions about the campaign, Jones just as consistently tried to focus the campaign purely on short-term mobilization, member recruitment, and member donations to COPE, the local's political fund.

At one early planning meeting, for example, Lazzara criticized the agenda for the lunchtime work site meetings, arguing that they focused only on short-term mobilization and ignored the underlying organizational problems of the county unit. Lazzara suggested mounting a program of stewards' trainings that would be aimed at increasing the capacities of work site stewards to organize their work sites more effectively. This proposal was tabled after vehement objections from a group of union staff led by Jones, who claimed that we would "not have time" to implement such a program and that the work site meetings themselves already represented "a pretty heavy schedule." Later in the summer, after privately lobbying the president of Local A, Lazarra and another staff person were given permission to hold a stewards' training session for county workers from Allegheny, Butler, Beaver, and Washington Counties — but by that time, it was too late to make stewards' training a major focus of the Allegheny County contract campaign. The training session, held on a Saturday in early September, was indeed poorly attended by Allegheny County stewards because only a few departments were contacted.

The competing agendas of Lazarra and Jones ran right through the organizing activities carried out by the interns and volunteer member organizers. To deal with bitterness on the part of workers who felt the union hadn't been doing enough to get them a new contract, Local A staff director Joe Reilly encouraged us to tell workers that the union recognized its past failure to be sufficiently organized and that the present internal organizing effort represented the union's commitment to change. "We need to change our image of what a union is," Reilly told us as we practiced giving the rap. "You can say that. Instead of seeing it as a sort of insurance company, where we buy a kind of policy with our dues, we need to involve all the workers in rebuilding the union." Along with the other interns, I incorporated this kind of talk into the rap. Buoyed by our own visions of a more participatory model of unionism, we naively promised workers that the union was firmly committed to a fundamental change in how their unit functioned.

This kind of talk made promises that Jones was clearly not very interested in fulfilling. Responsible for delivering a bargaining report to work sites that he represented, Jones would continually turn up late at meetings and then leave early. Workers were at once presented with enthusiastic young interns telling them that the union was committed to rebuilding the union with their help, while their staff rep looked on in boredom and left early — not exactly a convincing combination. It was never clear whether Jones really thought of the meetings as a waste of time or whether, as a fellow intern argued, he was simply uncomfortable with this kind of interaction with the membership. Jones obviously viewed himself as the expert, the guy who could fix things. The contract situation was something he clearly couldn't fix. Perhaps Jones may have felt belittled by the need to turn to the members for help. Either way, the absence of firm staff commitment to the new model of unionism we were promising was clear to rank-and-file members.

Work Site Leadership Vacuum and Top-Down Organization

If the union's bureaucratic history made both ordinary workers and union staff ambivalent about the relationship between the contract campaign and a new model of worker participation, this was also true of the union's volunteer work site leadership. As one staff person said, "You've got to understand that for years and years, the position of steward was basically meaningless. The steward was just a figurehead with no real function." As a result, many stewards had become accustomed to viewing the position as essentially symbolic. These stewards often resisted the idea or suggestion that they take responsibility for organizing work. Understandably, they saw organizing and mobilizing as "the union's job" and often refused to do it. When we visited one steward as part of the planning for a work site meeting for her department, she was taken aback by our request that she circulate "Contract Now!" petitions and flyers about the meeting and post notices about the meeting at her work site. She reluctantly agreed but added, "I can tell you right now that these workers here won't do anything. They just won't get involved." This turned out to be a self-fulfilling prophecy. Like many other stewards, she was not prepared to take on organizing responsibilities, primarily because the union had not provided the necessary training and support.

The traditional organizational irrelevance of the work site steward, the lack of training, and the lack of real responsibility the position entailed also had the unfortunate effect of making the position attractive to the wrong people for the wrong reasons. In many work sites the only workers willing to volunteer for the position did so not because they wanted to represent their fellow workers but because it was a way of being "in the know," of having something over co-workers, or even possibly of gaining a platform from which to harass union staff or other workers. In these departments, a kind of "crowding out" took place in which workers with good leadership potential were kept from getting involved by the presence of self-serving volunteers who bullied, harassed, and intimidated them into staying uninvolved. Conversely, genuinely good leaders who held the position of steward with the best of intentions found the position extremely frustrating. Lacking any clearly defined role, and lacking support from the union's staff representative for plans to organize work sites and departments, such stewards found themselves simply the unfortunate lightning rod for the frustrations of fellow workers. As one such steward commented, "I have no authority, no real purpose. I'm not able to do anything for the workers in my department. I'm just the guy who puts stuff up on the bulletin board. The people in this department either laugh at me, or they bitch at me for everything that's wrong with the union. And I can't change a damn thing."

The union's unwillingness to define clearly a meaningful role for volunteer work site stewards, to provide training and support, and to establish standards of performance for which stewards would be accountable meant that the union depended entirely on *top-down organization* to mobilize workers during the contract campaign. This ultimately limited the union to actions that paid union staff could directly organize and supervise — such as a series of rallies held at evening commissioners' meetings and a large day-long rally and protest at the courthouse dubbed "Solidarity Day." These events were successful and generated generally positive media coverage of the workers' fight for fair contracts (between 50 and 100 workers protested at each of the committee meetings, and more than 500 turned out for Solidarity Day) — but unlike the earlier Kane rallies, these actions required an enormous amount of logistical and organizing effort to create. The union could not simply call a contract rally and expect county workers to show up; indeed, it did not even have reliable means of communication with many county work sites. The contract rallies therefore had to be carefully planned ahead of time. Interns and member organizers had to set up and carry out dozens of work site meetings in order to educate the membership about the bargaining situation and the need for rank-and-file involvement in the contract campaign and to recruit workers' participation in the planned rallies. Workers who signed up for these events were then systematically phone-banked in the days leading up to them.

The one initiative in which the union tried to rely on work site stewards to directly organize a series of actions was "Rolling Thunder Week." The idea was that workers at various departments around the county would picket and leaflet at lunchtime; each day was a different department or set of departments. Interns delivered picket signs, union T-shirts, and union buttons to the work sites ahead of time and gave a schedule of picket locations, days, and times to the television news departments. Several television stations sent out news crews each day of the week to do live coverage for the noon news.

Rolling Thunder Week was not particularly successful. As some locations, picketing went off without a hitch. At others, picketing never materialized. The worst failure occurred on August 25, where picketing was taking place during workers' lunch breaks at the Kane Centers. At one of the sites, the picketing simply did not materialize and no one could say why. At the other location, two union stewards had at the last minute scuttled the action by refusing to participate. Despite the presence of the media (a mobile news unit from one of the local television networks had been setting up in the parking lot since mid-morning), the two women drove off to lunch together in a car containing all the picket signs and materials for the action. Leaderless and without picket signs, the other workers had stayed inside. Worst of all, the news crew did a bewildered live report from the parking lot, saying they'd been told picketing was supposed to have occurred but that no one had shown up. Again, the problem was not the workers themselves but the fact that the union suddenly expected them to take on too much responsibility without providing the necessary training and support.

In addition to these problems, the campaign's reliance on top-down organization meant that it was extremely *inflexible*. Because planning was done centrally in the union office and then brought to the membership through dozens of lunchtime meetings, there was little room for incorporating new ideas for events or activities as the campaign went along. The issue of stewards' training was discussed above, but there were also other examples showing the inflexibility of this type of campaign. Several weeks into the organizing phase of the campaign, Reilly decided that it would be a good idea to start organizing around the Labor Day parade. A strong contingent of Local A workers at the parade, with signs demanding new contracts and criticizing the commissioners for their failure to bargain in good faith, would be sure to garner good media for the campaign. The problem was that more than half of the work sites had already been visited — and we had not made a pitch for a Labor Day action or signed anyone up. We added this item to the agenda for the rest of the meetings that we did, but the Labor Day turnout was predictably disappointing.

Finally, the reliance on top-down organization — and especially the reliance on interns — constrained the union's ability to mount a *sustained* campaign. By the end of August 1997, two of the three interns had returned to graduate school, and the union had exhausted its small supply of "member organizers" willing to take two weeks off work, paid by the union, to work on the campaign. Though the commissioners could not have known it, the union could not have sustained the campaign at the same level beyond August without a regrouping period. Had the commissioners been able to hold firm into the fall of 1997, the outcome of the campaign might have been different. Fortunately for the union, however, time was not on the commissioners' side in the wake of their defeat over Kane privatization. The commissioners had failed to realize $23 million in immediate savings by privatizing the Kanes, and county government was still operating under the constraints of the 20 percent property tax cut. As a result, the county's fiscal situation was spiraling out of control. Vast budget deficits loomed as bond rating agencies, citing the mismatch between the sharp revenue reductions and the failure to find new savings, lowered Allegheny County's rating twice during the summer of 1997. The two Republican commissioners were even called to New York to receive a "scolding" from Standard and Poors in early August.[5] By that point, $76 million in county cash reserves had evaporated, and the Republicans' only plan to deal with a budget deficit of $26.5 million involved the one-time sale of property tax liens. The commissioners were thus under tremendous pressure from bond rating agencies to restore some semblance of order to county finances by the end of the year.

Initially the Republicans had hoped to realize the necessary savings — and indeed ultimately to resurrect Kane privatization — by defeating the county unions on the contract issue. If they could force the unions to accept their proposed contract language on contracting out, they would have a free hand once again as far as the Kanes were concerned. But such a strategy depended on defeating the unions quickly. Local A's contract campaign, culminating in its large "Solidarity Day" rally, demonstrated that a quick union collapse was not forthcoming. As a result, there seemed to be no possibility of resurrecting Kane privatization any time soon; Republican commissioner Bob Cranmer decided it was time to back down. In late August, he joined forces with Democratic commissioner Mike Dawida to oust the Republican chair of the board of commissioners, Larry Dunn, who was not yet prepared to settle. Cranmer would be the new chairman, and Cranmer and Dawida agreed to work together to reach quick settlements with the county unions.[6] These agreements took many more months to reach, but ultimately, all the county unions but one signed nonconcessionary contracts. Local A's contract, ratified by the members in January 1998, included raises, compensation for back raises, improved bumping and bidding rights, and no concessions on contracting out or "management rights."

CONCLUSION

I have argued here that when existing members perceive an issue as a union issue, to the extent that they are accustomed to business union representation they will not spontaneously mobilize in self-defense and may even resist the union's suggestion that mobilization is the only viable approach. Moreover, the organizational legacies of business unionism make it difficult for the union to deal with the problem in a thoroughgoing, sustained, or coherent way. I have also analyzed Local A's use of interns as a strategy for dealing simultaneously with the lived experience of its members and the intransigence of its representational staff, pointing out that while this kind of short-term solution allowed the union to achieve a sort of mobilization, that mobilization was top-down, inflexible, and unsustainable.

Throughout the analyses presented in Chapters 4 and 5, I have shown that while organization was important to both campaigns, existing theories of movement organization could not help us understand the differences between them. Instead, I have emphasized throughout that understanding these two campaigns required viewing organization as a problem that could be solved in different ways depending on the relationship between business union ideology and the issue at hand. This is why, in its contract campaign, Local A was forced to confront and deal with organizational problems in ways that had not been necessary during the antiprivatization effort — and why the union's organizational ties to Pittsburgh's progressive community were no longer a source of support, despite having been central to the outcome of the privatization struggle.

Social Movement Unionism
and the Problem of Power

Each of the two interconnected union campaigns discussed in Part II managed to find temporary solutions to the dilemmas of lived experience and organizational legacies. The Kane campaign, unable to construct a counterideology capable of taking on globalization or the Republicans' tax cut, successfully attacked instead the specific neoliberal arguments in favor of privatization. As a result, it was able to mobilize both workers and allies against privatization — despite its inability to deal with organizational legacies. The contract campaign, unable to really solve the organizational problems of the union's county chapter, nevertheless devised short-term, ad hoc ways of dealing with them. As a result, it was able to mobilize workers (but not allies) in the struggle for new contracts — despite its inability to construct an appealing issue frame that could appeal to external constituencies. The ability to mobilize external allies meant that the Kane campaign developed more leverage than the contract campaign — so much so that contract success ultimately depended on the aftereffects of the Kane campaign. Still, despite their limitations and contradictions, the SEIU's Allegheny County campaigns do illustrate the ability of social movement unionism to build on itself — not only because the second campaign built on the successes of the first, but more importantly with respect to how the experience of these two campaigns influenced subsequent developments in the union.

The Allegheny County campaigns did not lead directly to sweeping organizational change, but Local A did undertake a number of incremental but significant changes as a result of its experience with the Allegheny County campaigns. First, the union hierarchy realized that the presence and growth of nonunion private contractors, taking on more and more functions formerly provided directly by county government, constituted a long-term threat to its county chapters. The competitive advantage of many of these contractors, particularly in the areas of human services, was simply that they paid very low wages.[1] Janet Zimmerman therefore decided that a long-term strategy to deal with privatization would seek to organize these nonunion contract workers and to narrow the pay gap between them and public sector employees. Thus Local A began to support (financially and with donated staff time) a living-wage campaign coordinated by the Alliance for Progressive Action. The campaign's goal is to pass legislation at the county level and in the city of Pittsburgh that would require county service contractors to pay a living wage of $9.12 per hour with health benefits, or $10.62 per hour if employers don't provide health benefits. The SEIU viewed the living-wage campaign as a desirable end in itself but also as an aid to organizing; the union made use of the campaign's research effort to gleam information about contractors that provided mental health and mental retardation (MH/MR) services for the county and began to try to figure out how to organize these workers. In 1998 and 1999, the union successfully organized several small MH/MR contractors, and in the spring of 2000, it was making plans to assemble a permanent organizing team that would focus on human service contractors in Allegheny County.

Second, the union supported a new initiative aimed at developing a labor agenda for local politics. Working Families 2000 is a coalition involving Local A, the SEIU international union, the Pennsylvania AFL-CIO, the Allegheny County Central Labor Council, and a number of other local unions. It has been constructed with the goal of developing a progressive, worker-friendly political agenda for county politics. Coalition members have donated staff and an office at the international headquarters of the United Steelworkers in downtown Pittsburgh. Beginning with the 1999 county elections, the campaign has been attempting to coordinate the political endorsements of local labor unions, to support labor-friendly county politicians, and to articulate a progressive agenda for county politics around four planks: (1) support for the APA's living wage campaign; (2) enforcement of the right to organize, so that tax subsidies or government contracts are not used to fight unionization; (3) fair taxation; and (4) no privatization or contracting out. Ideas such as these could represent the modest beginning of a coherent response to globalization — not so much for what they stand for in themselves but because the very attempt to construct a platform has forced Allegheny County's coalition of labor leaders to confront the context of globalization and political restructuring and think about ways of responding to it.

While the campaigns discussed in Part II succeeded in meeting their immediate goals and also helped lead — directly and indirectly — to further action and reform by and within the union, it must be recognized that the union had certain advantages in these campaigns that are not enjoyed by unions in the private sector. Allegheny County's two Republican commissioners may have been interested in union busting, but their repertoire of union-busting tactics was quite limited compared to those routinely employed by private employers. This is illustrated by the very ability of the union to organize its campaign by holding mass union meetings at the work site itself, a practice that most private sector employers would never allow. The county never disputed the union's right not only to meet with its members on county property but also to use these meetings to actually organize the members to fight their struggle against their employer. Moreover, many departmental managers supported the union and did what they could to help. At one point early in the summer, for example, I was meeting with the steward for the workers in the county mail room. The mail room manager shook my hand and said, "I hope you guys get these people a raise, because they deserve it," and then vacated his office so that the steward and I could use it for our meeting. We commandeered the mail room manager's office for about 30 minutes, discussing issues of importance to the mail room workers and setting the groundwork for a larger work site meeting to be held a few weeks later. At another work site meeting, we found ourselves without enough space or chairs for everyone. The department manager gave us permission to move desks and tables around so as to create a large open space for the meeting, and then he got on the phone with the building maintenance department to request chairs. Within 10 minutes, a maintenance worker (a member of a different union) arrived with more chairs than we needed, and we had our meeting on schedule.

The county, as a public employer, was also much more vulnerable to public pressure than a private employer would have been. Commissioner Larry Dunn backed down from the proposal to privatize the Kanes because he feared the electoral repercussions of making what seemed to be an extremely unpopular decision. Corporate CEOs are not quite so vulnerable to this kind of pressure. Indeed, in the 1980s when USX, LTV, and other major steel firms were closing their plants in Pittsburgh, a massive upwelling of public protest did not prevent deindustrialization from occurring. The corporations simply said that they were sorry but that they had to do what was best for the business — and that the law was on their side.

The issue thus raised is the issue of power: Can social movement unionism go beyond initial organizing victories and public sector successes to build workers' power at the industry level? Can it generate sufficient leverage to win industry-level struggles against employers willing to use the full range of legal (and illegal) union-busting tactics? In short, can its successes be themselves institutionalized? In Part III, I turn to a larger, more difficult campaign pitting the SEIU against a powerful and ideologically inflexible private sector opponent. In such struggles, as we will see, the sheer power of capital, rooted as it is in a legal framework for collective bargaining that does not adequately protect workers' rights, becomes an important obstacle in the struggle for power.

PART THREE

Social Movement Unionism

Challenging the Power of Capital

Megacorp and the SEIU in Pennsylvania

Part I focused on the micro-level processes of building work site solidarity that lie at the heart of social movement unionism. In an analysis whose primary locus was the point of contact between union organizers and rank-and-file workers, I demonstrated first why anger against an employer does not automatically translate into support for unions and second that face-to-face organizing and collective action tactics help social movement union campaigns succeed insofar as they help workers reinterpret their own lived experiences and images of unions.

Part II built on this analysis of solidarity-building processes by moving out from the work site to study the local union itself. Here I argued that mobilizing existing union members long accustomed to business union representation — especially when they are scattered across multiple work sites — requires a union to deal with the organizational shortcomings of its own representational structures as well as with workers' lived experience. I showed that when the union happens upon (or can construct) a mobilizing issue that rank-and-file workers and community allies perceive as a social justice issue *rather than* a union issue, it is possible temporarily to overcome both sets of dilemmas — because community allies don't see the struggle primarily as a narrow labor dispute and because rank-and-file workers do not expect the union to "take care of" the problem. Without such an issue, rank-and-file mobilization requires a difficult internal struggle between representation and mobilization, and it may not be possible to mobilize sympathetic allies at all. From Parts I and II, then, we might conclude that if unions can successfully deal with workers' lived experience, they can build enough solidarity to win certification elections, workplace by workplace, and that if unions can also deal in various ways with the organizational legacies of business unionism, they can mobilize existing rank-and-file workers in struggles that link up workers across multiple work sites and with sympathetic community allies.

But unfortunately none of this matters much unless unions can protect and defend the victories they win through social movement struggle. Somehow unions must recast the balance of power between workers and employers at the industry level, across larger geographic units. Social movement unions cannot avoid such confrontations with capital because their very success in aggressively organizing and mobilizing workers is likely to provoke a counterattack in which capital makes use of all of the legal and extralegal means at its disposal to halt — or reverse — unions' initial gains. For social movement unionism to be truly viable, it must be able not only to establish but also to defend and extend permanent beachheads in hitherto unorganized sectors. This is very difficult because, as discussed in Chapter 1, American labor law allows companies many advantages. There are no punitive damages for committing unfair labor practices, no matter how flagrant; but even more important, companies are allowed to permanently replace workers who strike — unless they can show that their strike was at least partially in response to unfair labor practices committed by the company.[1] Moreover, while the employer is essentially encouraged to discriminate against union activists and is allowed to continue operating during strikes by replacing strikers permanently, unions are legally deprived of their most effective weapon, the secondary boycott. The result is that the balance of power is tilted firmly in the employer's direction.

For most of the postwar period, companies almost never made use of striker replacement. But after Ronald Reagan fired striking air traffic controllers in the early 1980s, companies began making striker replacement a standard part of a union-busting tactical repertoire. In high-profile case after case during the 1980s — at Caterpillar, International Paper, Staley, Phelps Dodge, and Hormel, to name just a few — companies successfully broke unions by making bargaining proposals that the union could not accept, pushing workers into strikes, then using permanent replacement to break the union.[2] For a long time it seemed that labor had no response to this devastating tactic. Going on strike could well mean losing one's job forever. Not surprisingly, the number of strikes declined precipitously during that decade.[3]

In the 1990s, however, there have been some indications that unions are beginning to devise ways of dealing with striker replacement. In particular, Tom Juravich and Kate Bronfenbrenner's analysis of the USWA's successful struggle with the Ravenswood Aluminum Corporation in the early 1990s shows that if unions can establish legally that they are striking over unfair labor practices (thus protecting workers from legal permanent replacement) — and combine this legal strategy with innovative tactics designed to put financial, political, and public pressure on the company from a variety of sources — victories may be possible.[4] Juravich and Bronfenbrenner go so far as to suggest that what they call the "co-ordinated campaign" represents a viable new model for taking on union busting and winning.[5]

By analyzing two phases of a bitter two-year struggle between nursing home giant Megacorp Enterprises and the SEIU in Pennsylvania, Part III of this book builds on Juravich and Bronfenbrenner's analysis in several ways. First, it supports their assessment that the approach pioneered by the USWA in the early 1990s is being adopted by other unions, especially by the SEIU. Second, it provides valuable confirmation that Ravenswood was not merely an isolated case of success. And third, it emphasizes that, despite the way the legal system works against unions, capital does have weaknesses that can be exploited in unexpected ways. Indeed, what I want to show is that the very source of the contemporary crisis for labor — the extreme and ideologically inflexible antiunionism of so much American capital — can, in fact, sometimes be turned against capital and exploited to defend and extend social movement unionism.

Chapter 6 explores how Megacorp's attempt to break the union in the state of Pennsylvania in 1995 forced the SEIU to pursue a strategy of escalating mobilization on a statewide basis. It discusses the difficulties and effects of the union's escalation strategies, showing how the union exploited an apparent weakness — Megacorp's willingness to break the law in order to intimidate workers — with an effective grassroots campaign culminating in a legally protected three-day strike over unfair labor practices committed by the company. In Chapter 7 I show how, in the 13 months following the unfair labor practices strike, the union turned the plight of 400 illegally replaced workers into a social justice issue, the cornerstone of its campaign to drive Megacorp back to the bargaining table. It accomplished this with a strategy very similar to that employed by the USWA at Ravenswood: instead of relying solely on the legal process to eventually reinstate the replaced workers, the union aggressively sought to push the legal process along and drive the company back to the table through a multifaceted pressure strategy combining in-plant organizing, community and corporate campaigns, and political pressure.

Once again, as I advance these empirical arguments about how the SEIU was able to turn Megacorp's massive illegalities into a victory, I want to underline the importance of treating the institutionalization of corporate power as an obstacle that the labor movement must creatively overcome rather than looking for the factors that explain success. Social movement researchers have, of course, a long tradition of interest in questions of power, strategy, and tactics and the conditions under which movements are successful. But the dominant theoretical approaches view these questions in terms of explanatory factors: they suggest that movements are more likely to succeed when the right factors are present — namely, when new organizational resources become available (resource mobilization theories) or when new political opportunities appear (political process theories). These approaches are quite clearly ill suited to helping us understand how the SEIU was able to defeat Megacorp in Pennsylvania during a period of declining organizational resources and unfavorable politics.

We must, therefore, set aside Doug McAdam's argument that tactical innovations become possible only when new environmental opportunities present themselves.[6] Instead, we should adopt a view similar to that of Marshall Ganz, whose study of the United Farm Workers' union demonstrates how resourcefulness can often make up for lack of resources. "Because it is based on the innovative, often guileful, exercise of agency," Ganz notes, "good strategy is often anything but obvious. It can thus be hard to deduce from 'objective' configurations of resources and opportunities and is based rather on novel assessments of them."[7] More important than "objective" factors like resources or opportunities, in other words, may be what Ganz calls the "strategic capacity" of movements — the elements of leadership and organization that enable movements creatively to devise surprising and innovative tactics leading to unlikely successes. However, we must resist the temptation to view strategic capacity as another factor determining the likelihood of success. It is always necessary to analyze the processes through which movements devise and implement innovative and surprising strategies — how, in other words, movements solve strategic problems. Such explanations must be historically and contextually situated. Before we proceed to the analysis of the Megacorp campaign, it will thus be necessary to sketch briefly the context of this conflict.

The year 1995 marked the third round of coordinated collective bargaining between Megacorp and three Pennsylvania SEIU locals (including Local A). By the late 1980s, the SEIU and an independent union (soon to merge with the SEIU as Local B) had organized 14 of 40 Megacorp nursing homes in Pennsylvania — while at the national level, the SEIU had worked out some basic contract language with Megacorp covering seniority, union shop, grievance and arbitration, and other basic issues. All 14 of the unionized homes thus had the same basic contract language by 1989. Since all of the homes also had contracts that expired at around the same time, in 1989 Local B and two locals from the SEIU (including Local A) approached Megacorp with a proposal to engage in coordinated bargaining, and Megacorp agreed. "I don't think they thought about it very hard," recalled Joe Reilly later. "It was just easier for them than dealing with each of the locals separately."

This first round of coordinated bargaining led to a major breakthrough for the unions on wages. Up to that point, starting wages throughout the industry were at or near the then-legal minimum of $3.35 per hour. The unions went into the negotiations asking for a large wage increase. Almost to their surprise, they won a basic increase of $2.25 per hour over three years. As Mark Crawford, president of SEIU Local B, later recalled:

> It was astounding. It just changed our whole nursing home program, and it changed the nursing home industry in Pennsylvania. We also were bargaining with a couple of other companies, Unicare and several others — there were maybe 30 contracts we were bargaining together, across all of the locals. And we ended up winning the $2.25 almost everywhere. And it forced the nonunion parts of the industry to do some significant things on wages.

The wage breakthrough stemmed partly from internal developments within Megacorp. Megacorp itself was going through a period of retrenchment after growing too quickly in the early 1980s. The company had tripled in size to about 1,200 nursing homes nationally but could not easily digest or manage its acquisitions. As a result, quality problems were rampant, and the company was developing a bad name among industry analysts as well as the general public. By the late 1980s, Megacorp was in the process of divesting itself of about 500 homes and trying to solve its organizational problems. This context, according to Crawford, created a window of opportunity for productive bargaining. "The company had decided to take more of a business kind of approach. It was like, look, we made some mistakes, there's some problems here, we want to try to get along. We want to try to figure out how to develop a different kind of relationship."

At the same time, the SEIU was doing its part to capitalize on this opportunity by maximizing the political pressure on the company to do something about its dreadfully low wages. As Crawford explained:

> We had done a lot of community organizing as we organized these facilities. We had created, for example, in a number of these facilities an organization called ABC, the Alliance for Better Care. We were actually meeting with family members of residents and workers to talk about problems of staffing, health and safety issues, and other problems. And we had gotten legislators in different areas very involved in it. We did a public hearing that year that was sponsored by the House Labor Committee on nursing home issues and brought busloads of nursing home workers from all over the state. We also did a major demonstration in Harrisburg that had probably 500 nursing home workers at the state Capitol. So there was a lot of pressure on the company.

The combination of political pressure, grassroots organizing, Megacorp's own sense of vulnerability as it struggled to reorganize, and a strike threat from the union combined to induce the company to agree to the wage increase. The union set a strike deadline to show that it was serious, but before it expired the company agreed to the union's terms. "To be honest, we weren't really ready to strike in 1989," says Local A's Reilly. "The company didn't know that, of course. But I don't think we could have struck more than a handful of facilities successfully at that time."

By 1992, Megacorp had began to reconsider whether coordinated bargaining was such a good idea. "The company began to play its game about, they weren't going to bargain jointly," says Crawford. "[Their chief bargainer] would come to negotiations and say, 'We're here today to bargain for this home' — but it was still kind of half-hearted." And the company was still not ready to brave a strike. "Ultimately, at the end, facing a strike deadline, they backed off and they negotiated a tentative agreement that covered all facilities," Crawford recalls. This time the union won more wage increases, major improvements in health insurance — including subsidized family coverage — and individual retirement savings accounts that the company would contribute to on workers' behalf.

Despite the settlement in 1992 and the very real progress it represented for nursing home workers in Pennsylvania, it was clear to SEIU officials that the window of opportunity with Megacorp was closing. One Local B staff organizer recalled:

> The night we settled the Megacorp contracts in 1992, somewhere between 1 and 5:30 am, we were all sitting around waiting for the company to get back to us. Dale Harvey [then president of B] said something like, "The company's decision now is, do they go to war with us today or next time. They've got to know that they've got to go to war with us sometime." And a lot of us talked about that informally and formally afterwards. I wasn't sure they'd go to war with us . . . but . . . there's a large part of me that feared it, and felt it was a strong likelihood. At Local B the range of opinion ranged from strong likelihood to absolute certainty.

Harvey's insight proved prophetic. But despite fears about the future, the SEIU did not moderate its agenda for the next bargaining round. In the spring of 1995, the international union established a "Dignity Office" in Harrisburg and staffed it with a full-time campaign coordinator. In late May, six months before the Megacorp contracts were set to expire, the three locals organized a two-day "Dignity Conference" of rank-and-file leaders from nursing homes all over the state. Several hundred nursing home workers voted to ratify a platform of bargaining goals for the upcoming Megacorp negotiations as well as for negotiations with other chains. The platform included resolutions to fight for minimum starting wages of $9.00 per hour, family health insurance, organizing rights (card check and neutrality), a pension, staffing language, health and safety language, patient care language, and a master contract. The workers also agreed in principle to support one another until everyone had won the same terms.

For the union, this agenda represented the logical next step forward in a movement whose goals from the beginning had been to bring justice, dignity, and respect to nursing home workers. However, although union leaders understood that Megacorp was likely to resist more strongly in 1995 than it had done during the two previous bargaining rounds, initially they did not quite comprehend how radically the company's stance had changed. A former Reagan appointee to the NLRB had now become a vice president at Megacorp, in charge of the company's labor relations. The new VP for labor relations in turn brought in a former general counsel for the National Right to Work Committee — a high-profile antiunion organization — to take over the legal end of labor relations. "More than we imagined going into it, [the new VP for labor relations] and his crew [were] really in control," commented Mark Crawford. "They were very clearly getting ready for this negotiation." Moreover, the union did not recognize until much later that its own militancy, its own determination to realize its vision of a transformed nursing home industry, had probably been a factor in the radicalization of Megacorp's labor relations department:

> The other thing which I don't think we really analyzed or really understood is that we also had by this point put the company in a position where they really don't have a choice but to take us on. Because we're making them uncompetitive. The state is squeezing Medicaid, and we're pushing higher wages, more benefits, you know and it just, I think what it did is it created enough fear in the operations people of the company — and desperation — that when we start talking about things like master contract and card check that they just sort of allowed the company to put [the new labor VP] completely in charge. And then negotiations become extremely impossible going into that fight. [Mark Crawford]

With a Reaganite vice president for labor relations in control of negotiations, Megacorp's strategy was completely different in 1995.

Unlike in the previous rounds, in which productive bargaining began months before the contracts actually expired, in 1995 the company refused to schedule any bargaining sessions until the contracts actually expired in November. Starting in the spring of that year, Crawford — by that time president of Local B and the three locals' chief bargainer with Megacorp — was sending the company lists of dates when the union was available to bargain, but the company refused to acknowledge them. When bargaining sessions were finally held in December 1995, the company made it clear from the start that bargaining was going to be a charade. Instead of sending one chief bargainer as in the past, this time Megacorp sent a team of eight or nine officials — including regional vice presidents from as far away as Georgia and California — each claiming to have authority to bargain only over specific homes. These company bargainers arrived at negotiations with no knowledge of the existing contract or of the issues and conditions in the nursing homes they were supposed to bargain over. The company insisted on bargaining each home separately from the others, even though their proposals were essentially the same at each home. Indeed, the only differences in the proposals they presented for each home concerned wage rates and length of contract. Megacorp thus made clear its intention to roll back the union's earlier achievements of common expiration dates and common wage rates. And for each home the company proposed a litany of unacceptable proposals: wage freezes, open shop, reductions in health benefits.[8] The union presented proposals of its own, but the company did not respond to any of them. Finally, on December 12, company representatives told the union that they would not bargain with the union's 100-person bargaining committee because it was too "cumbersome" and because the room they had reserved for the day seated only 30 people. When Crawford replied that the union had also reserved a room in the same hotel that would comfortably seat everyone, the Megacorp delegation broke off the talks and walked out. Although Crawford wrote a letter reminding Megacorp that (1) the company did not have any right to determine the size of the union's bargaining committee or whom it would or would not deal with and (2) that a similarly constituted committee had successfully bargained agreements in two previous rounds of bargaining without a single lost day of work,[9] the company did not agree to resume scheduled talks until March 1997. Rather than trying to avoid a strike situation, Megacorp was clearly trying to provoke one.

SIX

"We Will Not Be Silenced"

Escalating Mobilization

While in some ways the situation for the three locals was superficially similar to that faced by Local A in its struggle with Allegheny County in 1997, in reality the Megacorp conflict posed a much more difficult set of strategic and tactical problems for the SEIU. In the Allegheny County campaigns, as we saw, the crucial union victory on privatization flowed from the union's ability to create a groundswell of public opposition. Because elected politicians do not like to feel that they are on the wrong side of an unpopular issue, the mere fact of successfully mobilizing public opposition turned out to be enough to convince one of the two Republican county commissioners to change his position. Generating leverage against Megacorp Enterprises, a private corporation that owned 700 nursing homes in several countries, was a problem of a different order of magnitude. Not only was Megacorp capable of weathering public criticism in a way that Allegheny County elected officials could not, but it was financially capable of waging a much more protracted battle. In Allegheny County the union had time on its side because of the precarious fiscal situation of county finances. Megacorp, in contrast, was clearly capable of financially withstanding even a successful strike involving 20 of its Pennsylvania nursing homes. Also, unlike Allegheny County, Megacorp had a long history of unlawful antiunion activity and was clearly willing to bend and break the law in order to intimidate workers and break their union.

There was one other important difference between the Megacorp conflict and Local A's Allegheny County campaigns. In the county, Local A began with an issue — privatization — that immediately appealed to workers and community groups as a social justice issue. The local then built on leverage gained through mobilization around privatization to achieve a victory on the issue of contracts, which did not appeal to the same social justice constituencies. With Megacorp, the situation was exactly the opposite. The conflict began with a "union" issue — contracts had expired and negotiations had broken down. As previously discussed, this sort of issue does not automatically inspire community support and activism. This is partially because communities often assume that both sides are equally to blame for contract squabbles, but it is also because during 50 years of business unionism, organized labor treated contract negotiations as a business matter between private parties.

Like most unions in the contemporary period, the SEIU was not strong enough to win an economic strike against Megacorp in Pennsylvania. Even if the union completely shut down Megacorp statewide, it would have only a tiny impact on the corporation's bottom line. Therefore, somehow the union had to find a way to translate a "union" issue *into* a social justice issue and then to use that issue to create sources of leverage with far more power than anything Local A created in its Allegheny County campaigns. At the same time, the union had to be highly conscious of the fact that Megacorp's bargaining posture and its threat to use striker replacement would force the union to devise strategies of escalation and mobilization that could create real pressure on the company while at the same time protecting workers from legal replacement.

This chapter outlines the union's three central strategies for turning a "union" issue into a "justice" issue. The first of these, an organizing blitz, failed badly. Two other strategies were more effective. Four months of coordinated mobilization and a three-day limited unfair labor practices strike did not, by themselves, bring the company to heel — but these strategies did allow the union to create a social justice issue that workers and community allies could rally around.

ORGANIZING BLITZ

In August 1995, the SEIU sent more than 200 organizers out into the field across the state of Pennsylvania in a two-week organizing blitz focusing on every nonunion nursing home in the state. The personnel for the blitz were assembled from the staff of the three Pennsylvania locals, volunteers from locals from other states, member organizers on lost time, and organizers from the international union. The organizers house-visited every nonunion nursing home worker in the state during the two weeks. Thus the blitz was aimed not only at Megacorp but also at the other nursing home chains with which the three SEIU locals were bargaining in 1995. The idea behind the blitz was to try to establish organizing committees in as many of the homes as possible — but rather than filing for elections, the union would try to stir people up, then bring them into negotiations all together and demand recognition. The SEIU international union was solidly behind this idea because it was interested in exploring alternatives to NLRB-supervised elections. Indeed, the international union made it clear to the locals that it was willing to contribute substantial resources — both money and personnel — to the Pennsylvania Megacorp campaign only if the organizing blitz was part of the strategy.

Unfortunately, the blitz did not succeed in generating a single new committee. "We did manage to build a committee at one Megacorp home near Philadelphia," Joe Reilly reported, "but it was a home that Local B was already involved in organizing. Everywhere else the blitz was completely nonproductive." Even at the Philadelphia home where a committee was assembled, the strategy had problems. According to Mark Crawford,

> With this program of not filing elections, we were also trying to
> figure out how to keep something together for six months [without
> moving toward an election]. A lot of these homes are places where

they've been picked over several times and they're used to a certain approach. And so they don't understand — when you don't put out cards, they want to know what the hell is going on. And what happened in Philly was that Local F [not an SEIU local] found out that we were there and that we were doing it, and while we're trying to hold people back from going to the board, they come in and say, well that's crazy, and they put out cards and they file for election and they take it away from us.

But why was it so difficult to build organizing committees with the blitz in the first place? This is a very interesting question given recent debates in the literature on new union tactics over "hot shop" versus "strategic" organizing. The literature is full of exhortations for unions to "move beyond" hot shop organizing, but it is not clear exactly what this should mean. Stephen Lerner, for example, points out that organizing individual work sites without an analysis of the industry or a strategy for organizing it is a recipe for failure.[1] Citing the experience of Justice for Janitors in Denver, he calls instead for industrywide campaigns: "Workers became union supporters and activists when they learned that the union's goal was to organize the entire industry in Denver; the result of unionization then would not be unemployment but higher wages and more stability for all janitors."[2]

The SEIU's nursing home organizing experience suggests, however, that the distinction between "hot shop" and "strategic" organizing may be something of a false dichotomy. A "hot shop" is generally viewed as a work site where workers are angry at the boss. "Strategic" organizing is supposed to be able to mobilize workers regardless of whether their shop is "hot" or not, by conveying a persuasive vision of the industry that goes beyond their particular work site. But as I showed in Part I, it is not only the presence of anger at the boss that is important but also the extent to which the union is able to connect with workers face to face and deal effectively with their negative perceptions and experiences of unions. Part I showed that this is possible only when the union is able to build a functioning rank-and-file organizing committee. Nearly all private sector nursing home workers are angry about issues like staffing, patient care, wages, and how they are treated on the job. If a hot shop is one where workers are angry, nearly all private sector nursing homes are hot, nearly all of the time. The point is that—at least in the nursing home industry—the difference between a shop that is "hot" and one that is "cold" may not the be the level of anger of the workers at management but rather the presence or absence of a core group of rank-and-file leaders who are already predisposed to try to form a union and are willing to commit themselves to the effort.

Nothing illustrates this more clearly than the difference between organizing at Rosemont and at its sister nursing home, Clearview, in 1998. Clearview, the only other nonunion Hewitt home in southwestern Pennsylvania at that time, is the nursing home I was sent to work on— along with another intern—in preparation for the Rosemont campaign the union was planning for the summer of 1998. Over the course of several weeks, we visited and spoke with nearly one-quarter of Clearview's employees at their homes. We found that the issues at Clearview were essentially identical to those at Rosemont. Workers were angry about exactly the same things—right down to the company's announcement of changes in the health benefits that would hurt only nonunion employees. We also encountered the same range of reactions to the union itself—some workers slammed their doors in our faces when we identified ourselves as union organizers, most were uncertain about whether they would support a union, and a few workers enthusiastically invited us into their living rooms. The difference between Rosemont and Clearview was that at Clearview, among those who strongly wished for a union, there was not a critical mass of workers who were willing to get involved, to take action, to form the beginnings of a rank-and-file committee. Using snowball techniques and charting the work areas and shifts of the nursing home as we went, we did our best to identify prounion workers who were key leaders, influential workers respected by their coworkers. Our efforts turned up plenty of workers who would support a union campaign; provide information such as schedules, lists, and addresses of coworkers; and even "talk union" at work. But we were able to identify only two workers willing to come to an organizing committee meeting and take on concrete organizing tasks. One of these — management's bravest and most outspoken critic — had recently taken the civil service exam and was planning to leave for a job with the Postal Service. Recognizing that a committee of one was not enough, the union backed off, planning to try again six months later.

The point of the foregoing is to show that even if organizing is strategic, even if it is based on an analysis of the industry, even if it makes good use of rank-and-file member-to-member organizing strategies called for by Steve Early and others — and indeed, even if it is part of an ambitious attempt to organize the industry as a whole, as was the SEIU's 1995 organizing blitz, it is still necessary to find rank-and-file leaders, and to build a rank-and-file committee, in every work site. Even "strategic" organizing cannot make headway in a "cold" shop — and the presence of a critical mass of workers who want to get involved as leaders in a union campaign is essentially outside the control of the union. Nursing homes — especially nonunion nursing homes — turn over rapidly, so the absence of such a critical mass at one moment does not mean that the nursing home will remain cold forever. As Joe Reilly rightly said about Clearview, "Six months from now, we might find something completely different up there." The point is that timing is important, even within the context of a larger effort to organize the industry. The SEIU's statewide organizing blitz in the summer of 1995 failed primarily because it assumed that campaigns could be jump-started without regard to timing.

The organizing blitz not only failed to produce new leverage against Megacorp but also resulted in some negative consequences for the campaign. Local officials felt that, if anything, the blitz may have hardened the company's position even further. "We're going out and organizing, we're blitzing all their homes," said Crawford. "So that's all they see, they don't see anything else. So they sort of see that everything is at stake." But more than this, the blitz gave the company an issue of its own to use against the union, according to Dan Adams, vice president of Local B:

> Management jumped on that. They said this was not about anything except SEIU's desire to collect the dues, from all of these workers, that we can't organize through democratic elections, because the workers don't want a union. That we're trying to force people into joining the union against their will. They said this publicly but also to the workers. They really tried to drive a wedge. And part of the reason we withdrew this issue [organizing rights] even before the strike was that we knew we had to take that issue away from them. Number 1, it wasn't winnable. And number 2, in order to be able to go out and organize a successful strike we had to be able to say that this was bullshit.

Still, some international officials pointed out that even if the organizing blitz didn't produce the needed leverage, some positives could be taken from it. The international's Dignity Campaign coordinator, for example, argued that "there was tremendous apprehension and nervousness about whether our members would fight for organizing rights in the same way they'll fight for economic issues. . . . The blitz brought a lot of new members into the campaign who hadn't been active before. It showed that members would fight for organizing rights."

PROVOKING UNFAIR LABOR PRACTICES
Coordinated Mobilization

As the Megacorp contracts expired at the end of November 1995, the SEIU launched the largest nursing home mobilization it had yet attempted in Pennsylvania. In previous contract rounds, bargaining itself had been coordinated, and the three locals had held joint staff meetings to decide what they wanted the nursing homes to do, but each local had been independently responsible for carrying out its own shop floor activities and actions; there had not been any real attempt to coordinate these actions across the different nursing homes. In the fall of

1995 and through the winter of 1996, the union worked out a calendar of coordinated actions and worked to implement each action at the same time in all 20 nursing homes, believing that coordinated activity would convey a stronger message of unity, strength, and commitment.

The campaign began with a statewide "informational picketing weekend" on Saturday, December 1, the day after the contracts expired. Careful attention was paid to logistical aspects such as sign-in sheets — so the union would know exactly who attended the picketing — and photography. At each home, rank-and-file leaders were assigned to specific tasks like leafleting, security, leading chants, setup and cleanup, and media contact. The message of the picketing was also carefully delimited, focusing on the quality of resident care and staffing at Megacorp homes. Media contacts were instructed to stress that "we are fighting to improve the living and working conditions in nursing homes."[3] The picketing culminated with marches on the boss at each nursing home, in which delegations of workers presented administrators with signed petitions demanding that Megacorp begin negotiating in good faith immediately. Each chapter was then required to give a report at the next staff meeting, detailing the number of signatures on its petition, the number of people who picketed, and the number of people in the delegation for the march on the boss.

The December 1 action was the beginning of 17 weeks of coordinated shop floor mobilization. Each week all of the homes were involved in at least one activity — leafleting, informational picketing, marches on the boss, petitions, letter-writing campaigns, and sticker days — each as carefully planned, implemented, and recorded as the first. Each action had its own theme, focusing on some aspect of patient care, staffing, health and safety, Megacorp's failure to bargain in good faith, or unfair labor practices. The union coordinated its planning and reporting through weekly statewide conference calls with rank-and-file leaders from each nursing home; each week's plan was communicated to the members through a phone tree and face-to-face contact.

Records kept by the union show that the 20 facilities varied in terms of how strongly they participated in the mobilization. The strongest home, Facility #9, reported the results of every action; most homes missed some reports, and the weakest homes sometimes did not report for several weeks at a time. Stronger homes reported substantial participation in every activity — at times participation approached 100 percent at Facility #9 — while at the weakest homes the events sometimes failed to come off. At Facility #11, the union never succeeded in sending a delegation in to confront management in a march on the boss.

Union staff pointed to several factors to explain the differences. First, the weakest homes were the ones where workers liked their administrator — and vice versa. One Local B staff member explained:

> We have a home, [Facility #18], that has been organized a long time.
> They have an administrator there who's really a wonderful person.
> I mean *I* really like him. So it's hard to keep people angry. (SL:
> They're not angry at that person). That's right, and as much as
> they work for Megacorp, they don't see Megacorp, they see the
> administrator and they see what's happening in that facility.

Geography was also a factor. Two of the weakest homes were located in Harrisburg, the state capital, whose labor market is largely driven by the employment activities of state government. "In Harrisburg," Mark Crawford reflected, "it's sort of questionable how much is driven by us and how much is driven by the market. What we've been able to accomplish is not as clear for people. Places like Meyersdale, PA, where you have to drive maybe an hour to find a job that isn't minimum wage, to have a nursing home sitting there where the lowest starting wage rate is $8 an hour, it's pretty clear that the union has done something."

Still, despite variation, the overall level of participation and reporting was impressive. The SEIU was able to mount such a large and complex mobilization for two reasons. First, as Crawford noted in the comment quoted above, Megacorp workers had experienced real changes in their working conditions as a direct result of union victories in the two previous rounds of coordinated bargaining. Because the improvements the union had won had brought turnover down at most of the Megacorp homes, each home had a substantial contingent of workers who had been through one or both previous bargaining rounds. As a result, Megacorp workers' lived experience of unions was, for the most part, fundamentally different from that of the nonunion workers in the Rosemont campaigns and the Allegheny County union members, whose experiences were of traditional business union–style representation and back-room deal making. They viewed the union itself, not with apprehension or skepticism, but with loyalty. As Mark Crawford put it:

> By and large, you've got people that believe in the union. By now we're a known quantity for them. So Megacorp workers see the union as being very active and aggressive — and very honest in pushing issues and trying to set standards. Probably if anything they see us as being a little too aggressive sometimes, pushing them to do more than they want to do.

Perhaps even more important, Megacorp workers had learned, through their own experience, the value of collective struggle. Another Local B staff member commented on this:

> The most important thing is that we've always done coordination, and we've always mobilized from the bottom up — so it was an idea that workers were already used to. They knew that they got better together, and we made sure to always emphasize that the things they won in '89 and '92 came because we did this together. And that stuck with people. People understood that they got [wage and benefit increases] because they were working together with other Megacorp homes.

But if Megacorp workers' lived experience was now a facilitating factor rather than an obstacle to mobilization, so too was their level of existing organization — another legacy of the manner in which the shops were organized as well as of the previous campaigns. Each work site had its own elected chapter officers — a president, a vice president, and a secretary-treasurer. In addition, different work areas and shifts had their own elected rank-and-file stewards, as well as "work area leaders" who did not do representational work but who could be called upon to gather or distribute information. Even the weakest homes had this structure already in place, although the quality and density of the leadership varied. At the strongest homes, the level of internal organization was so high at the outset that very little work was required to jump-start the mobilization. A Local B staff person, describing the capabilities of the leaders in Facility #16, her strongest shop, explained:

> They can pull off anything you want them to pull off. Just give them a few days' notice, and it happens. I don't do their third-step grievance meetings there, I don't do anything. I have never done an arbitration there — they settle everything so they don't have to let it get that far. They keep track of their membership. We have put together every possible committee in that facility. They have a new member organization committee, they have a safety committee, they have a political action committee, and all of the committees are active.

At the other end of the spectrum — but still light-years ahead of the Allegheny County work sites — was Facility #4. The same staff person evaluated their level of organization at the outset of the 1995 mobilization this way:

> They could still do stuff, but they needed more help. I do their third-step grievances, I run their labor-management meetings; their health and safety committee is nonfunctional; I have to keep track of when new members come in and write them letters saying that this person and this person need to be signed up with membership cards. I have to do a lot of work with them. Still, you just have to give them very direct instructions, and then they can do it.

Most of the Megacorp shops fell somewhere between shops like Facility #16 and Facility #9 at one end of the scale and Facility #4 at the other. Thus, unlike the organizing and mobilizing campaigns discussed in previous chapters, the Megacorp mobilization benefited from a preexisting set of work site structures that organizers could plug into. The union did put a substantial amount of effort into shoring up committees in the places that were the weakest and making sure all shifts and work areas had volunteer leaders, but it did not have to start from scratch in any of the work sites.

The preceding discussion of the level of organization in the Megacorp shops at the beginning of the 1995 mobilization illustrates that bottom-up social-movement organizing contributes to organization building at the work site level that facilitates later waves of activism. However, even the Megacorp campaign had to confront obstacles to mobilization related to the organizational history of the union. Indeed, the very fact that the Pennsylvania Megacorp shops were split across three SEIU locals with overlapping geographical jurisdictions reflected some of the organizational baggage of the union and contributed to problems of coordination that plagued the campaign from its inception.

The distribution of Megacorp shops across the three locals reflected the political and organizational history of the union. In the early 1980s, before Local B joined the SEIU, both of the other two locals began organizing private sector nursing homes in response to pressure from the international to participate in the SEIU's nursing home campaign. Both of these locals' traditional base was in the public sector: based in Pittsburgh, Local A represented county workers in southwestern Pennsylvania, while Local C represented state and local public employees in and around Harrisburg. Local B — at that time part of a national heath care workers' union — began organizing Megacorp shops in Pennsylvania at around the same time. When Local B joined the SEIU at the end of the 1980s as a statewide local of health care workers, its jurisdiction over nursing homes overlapped with that of Local A and Local C. On the one hand, Local B argued that as a statewide local — and the local with the most Megacorp shops (10) — it was best suited to dealing with all of the nursing homes. On the other hand, neither of the two older SEIU locals wanted to give up their local nursing home jurisdictions and existing members. As one of 17 vice presidents of the international union, Local A's Janet Zimmerman wielded considerable clout within the SEIU, and she was determined not to be defeated on this issue. A redistricting hearing was held in the early 1990s, but instead of resolving the dispute one way or the other, it gave Local B statewide nursing home jurisdiction without abrogating the local nursing home jurisdictions of the other two locals. No one was happy with this outcome; Zimmerman continued to resent B's efforts to organize nursing homes in and around Pittsburgh, while Mark Crawford of Local B continued to feel that as a statewide local dedicated to health care workers, his local could more easily deal with Megacorp and the other nursing home chains if it had complete jurisdiction.

Crawford's frustration is understandable given the difficulties of coordinating across the three locals during the 1995–97 Megacorp campaign. One problem was that the locals had very different standards of staff accountability. Local B took a methodical approach to the organization of the campaign and demanded not only that its staff members complete their work on time but also that they regularly report the results of their work. As one Local B staff member commented, "I knew if I didn't have my workers doing a march on the boss, on the day that they were supposed to do it — that we'd planned on — that I was going to be asked by Mark [Crawford] why not. And I'd better have a damn good reason why it didn't happen." Moreover, Local B was quite self-conscious about hiring and developing staff who viewed representational work more as an organizing job than as bureaucratic grievance handling. As a result, Local B has historically had higher rates of staff turnover than the other two locals. Crawford offered this observation:

> There are differences between staff people. If you've got a really
> good staff person who's really close [to the rank and file], really
> concentrating on building rank-and-file leadership and empowering
> people and the organization, then you're going to have a much
> stronger shop than if you've got a staff person that's hiding, or
> whatever. (SL: Or who sees the role differently, as handling griev-
> ances rather than building leadership and organization.) Right.
> Absolutely. And that's true within each of our locals. Within our

local, people like that don't last very long. I think at the other locals there are very different cultures.

On the other hand, some of this turnover may have been due more to staff burnout and exhaustion more than anything else. Local B was well known for its tendency to use up staff and burn them out. Like Local X, another local studied by Fletcher and Hurd,[4] where staff burnout was also a problem, Local B operated under the expectation that staff should view their job as all-consuming and commit themselves to the exclusion of everything else. One staff person told me, "If you want to have a family, and spend time with them in the evenings or on weekends, then this job just isn't for you." Demanding this sort of fanatical devotion to the work seems unreasonable to me, and indeed, it seems to run counter to the ideals of the labor movement. I don't see any compelling reason why a movement opposing the exploitation of labor should itself rely on exploitation of labor.

With six Megacorp shops, Local A was the second most important local in the campaign. If Local B represented one unhealthy end of the spectrum, Local A represented the other. Staff representatives at Local A were given much more freedom to define their jobs, and both staff members with Megacorp shops were more oriented toward servicing than toward leadership building and organizing. Moreover, the leadership of Local A did not enforce the same kind of standards of accountability as at B. Here, just showing up was usually good enough. This was a matter of contention not only across locals but also within Local A. Several staff members who worked hard to incorporate leadership building, organizing, and teaching of collective action tactics into their representation functions complained about the lack of accountability within their own local. "The ones who do the least work here get the most help," one staff member complained. "I do my job and I have my shops in order. I don't get any help. But if you don't do your job, instead of there being consequences for that, you just get interns to come in and do it for you."

These organizational differences made coordination difficult. A staff person from Local B related:

> In the first couple meetings we were told to have our charts and our membership lists up to date. It was nothing for [staff reps from the other two locals] to come in with no charts, no lists, and no idea how many people they even represented at any of the places. I busted my ass to get done. . . . I'm doing what I was asked to do. You know, here we would all show up with what we were supposed to have, and you might have one or two that would have [their work done] from the other locals. And then it became like no big deal. And we were always behind because they didn't do it.

To make matters worse, Local C (which had only four Megacorp shops) was under trusteeship during the campaign, and conflicts between Local C staff and the international constantly threatened to eclipse work on the Megacorp campaign itself. Local C's staff union threatened to go on strike against the SEIU and actually set its own strike deadline to coincide with the deadline the union gave Megacorp. Staff members at Local B regarded this contemptuously, as evidence that the staff at Local C were willing to put themselves ahead of the members. "They were willing to screw all of their workers for themselves," said another Local B staffer. "I was so furious. I walked out of the meeting slamming doors with the campaign coordinator running after me. It was very frustrating."

The campaign was never able to solve these problems directly. Local B staff constantly complained about the performance of the other locals' staff to Mark Crawford and to the international's campaign coordinator, who met frequently with the president of Local A and with Local C's international trustee to beg for more accountability. According to Local B staff, after these meetings the work of the other locals' staff would improve slightly for a time, then revert back its previous pattern.

The key thing to understand here is that the international union does not possess the power to give or enforce direct orders to the staff of other locals. The decentralized organization of the labor movement in general, and the SEIU's principle of local autonomy in particular, means that local unions run their own ships — including controlling their own budgets — unless there is substantial malfeasance or violation of SEIU bylaws, in which case the international union is empowered to put the local under the direction of an appointed trustee. Even so, trusteeship is not necessarily a quick fix, as the experience of Local C during the Mega-corp campaign shows. There, the turmoil and internecine conflict persisted, and even though the international union was directly running the local, it could not easily deal with the organized resistance of the staff.

Because neither Local B nor the international union could force Locals A and C to demand more from their staff, the campaign was forced to deal with these problems in other ways during the coordinated mobilization. International staff were assigned to help with homes where there were union staff problems, and staff from Local B worked directly with chapter officers and stewards at some A and C shops.

> They would come to us and ask for help because their staff rep would just send them a piece of paper in the mail saying, this is what you are supposed to do by such-and-such a date. No help with how you actually get it done. And here I am with three [shops], I have seven other places I'm still responsible for, I'm doing every-thing else with them, and yet I have Local A's workers calling me too. So we did the best we could. I spent a lot of time on the phone with Local A stewards, talking them through the steps of what they had to do, helping them figure out how to present things to their workers.

Comments like these might seem self-serving, but when I interviewed rank-and-file leaders at Local A shops, they confirmed these claims. "I hardly ever saw or talked to [the Local A rep]," said one such leader, a central figure in the organization of her nursing home. "She did abso-lutely nothing. We relied a lot on Local B's people, and we got help from different international people who came through at different times. And Joe Reilly [A's staff director, second-in-command at the local] would come out and talk to us. It wasn't his job, but he was there for us more than [the staff rep]."

Dealing with the coordination problems this way did enable the campaign to achieve mobilizations at nearly all of the homes. But how did the coordinated mobilization help the union's cause? No one in the SEIU expected Megacorp to suddenly cave in and rush back to the bargaining table because of activities like informational picketing and sticker days — and to be sure the company did not do so.

But the coordinated mobilization did accomplish something crucial to the eventual outcome of the campaign: it provoked the company into escalating its law-breaking activities. Until the union mounted its coordinated mobilization campaign, the company had committed some relatively minor unfair labor practices like unilaterally changing disciplinary rules and instituting overly broad restrictions on employee speech, and they had illegally disciplined a few employees under these rules. None of these violations was egregious enough for the union to build a public campaign around. After the union began its coordinated mobilization, however, the company escalated in retaliation with a series of illegal actions. Although the union's contracts with Megacorp expired on November 30, 1995, their terms were still legally enforceable as long as at least one side was trying to bargain in good faith. Thus even after November 30, unilateral changes in matters covered by the contract or changes in any matter constituting a mandatory subject of bargaining under the National Labor Relations Act (NLRA) would be illegal.

On December 7, 1995, the week after the union's first large informational picketing action, the company violated the terms of its expired contracts with the union by unilaterally ceasing its payroll union dues deductions at all of its unionized facilities in Pennsylvania. On the same date, Megacorp executives instructed the administrators of these facilities to break the contract provision permitting local union representatives "reasonable access" to the nursing homes. Under this provision it had been customary for union representatives periodically to meet with employees in break rooms. According to the decision of the NLRB administrative law judge in the case, at least 15 administrators complied with this order immediately, and in some instances administrators summoned local police to arrest for trespassing several union staff who tried to exercise their right of access. The company also stopped honoring its contract agreements regarding union bulletin boards at each facility, removing the union bulletin boards in 16 homes. This was far from a minor issue, since the bulletin boards were an important means of communication between the union and the rank and file on a day-to-day basis and constituted an important symbol of the union's presence within the institution. Around the same time, Megacorp also illegally ignored the union's lawful requests for information relevant to bargaining after November 30.[5]

Finally, the company began a campaign of surveillance and intimidation targeting employees who participated in union activities. Supervisors and security guards unlawfully videotaped workers who exercised their rights peacefully to leaflet or informational-picket on public property. Workers who brought union literature into their facilities (a protected right under Section 7 of the NLRA) were prohibited from doing so and threatened with discipline. Supervisors approached selected workers in confidence and tried to persuade them to sign letters resigning themselves from the union, while making subtle threats implying that their jobs would not be secure if they did not. Acting in consultation with their corporate superiors, administrators began punishing key rank-and-file union leaders by reducing their work hours without due cause and in violation of seniority rules, and by issuing bogus reprimands and "write-ups."[6]

It is important to understand that these employer illegalities were not remarkable or exceptional. In fact, they represented what had become, by the early 1980s, the standard response to union organizing. For example, Paul Weiler reported data showing that, while the number of NLRB certification elections did not change very much between 1950 and 1980, unfair labor practice charges filed by unions against employers shot up from 4,472 in 1950 to 31,281 in 1980. In 1950, just over 2,000 workers were found to have been illegally fired for their union activities. By 1980, in a similar number of elections, the number illegally discharged union activists had risen by a factor of five, to more than 10,000. By comparing the number of votes in favor of union representation in 1980 (about 200,000) with the number of workers found to have been illegally discharged (more than 10,000), Weiler calculates that the rising tide of employer illegality translated into a 1-in-20 chance that a union supporter in an election campaign in 1980 would be illegally fired.[7]

Moreover, these illegal tactics did not stop once the election is over. In a follow-up article, Weiler showed that first-contract bargaining-phase unfair labor practice charges against employers rose from just 1,213 in 1955 to nearly 10,000 in 1980.[8] Weiler went on to demonstrate that the "ratio of employer bargaining resistance" (the average number of unfair labor practice charges per bargaining unit) rose from less than half an unfair labor practice charge per bargaining unit in 1955 to nearly three unfair labor practice charges per bargaining unit in 1980.[9] More recent research has confirmed that the flood of employer illegality continues unabated to the present time.[10]

It is also necessary to understand that employers commit these illegalities because the legal remedies against them are so weak. As Megacorp knew when it committed these violations, the union would file unfair labor practice charges that the NLRB would investigate through a lengthy process involving hearings, judgments, and opportunities for appeals. At the time Megacorp committed these unfair labor practices, the NLRB was still rendering decisions about unfair labor practices that had been committed in the early 1990s during the organizing drives at many of these facilities. The NLRB would not decide the case of unfair labor practices during the 1995 bargaining period until two years later — six months after the conflict had been settled. The remedy? After finding in favor of the union on all of the issues discussed above, the board ordered Megacorp to "cease and desist" these unlawful activities, to post a notice in its facilities admitting that it had acted unlawfully and promising not to do so in future, and to make some minor restitution to employees who had been unlawfully disciplined. In other words, even though Megacorp was found to have broken the law again and again, there were no serious legal consequences for Megacorp other than the costs associated with litigation. The failure of American labor law to allow punitive damages against employers who break the law thus encourages this sort of law-breaking by employers, who calculate, rationally, that the costs of such a strategy are outweighed by the benefits of being able to intimidate workers into submission.

The real significance of Megacorp's illegalities during this period is not that they were exceptional — they were not. However, what *was* exceptional was how the union made use of these illegalities as part of its own innovative strategy: it capitalized on — and fanned as much as possible — rank-and-file workers' outrage and incorporated the theme of protesting Megacorp's law-breaking into the mobilization itself. Megacorp workers were extremely angry about the violations — particularly the bulletin board issue, which struck at the most visible symbol of the union's day-to-day presence in the facilities — and the union astutely used this energy to keep the mobilization campaign rolling. By provoking these illegalities, by carefully documenting them, and — most important of all — by protesting them vigorously, the union actually took a major step forward. Before the coordinated mobilization campaign, the union not only had very little to hit the company with publicly but was facing the possibility of having to win a strike that Megacorp was eagerly anticipating and planning to break using permanent replacement workers. The mobilization of protest against Megacorp's illegalities gave the union its first slender straw of hope by laying the legal — and organizational — groundwork for a different kind of strike: a strike not over the contracts themselves or the terms of Megacorp's proposals but in protest of Megacorp's unfair labor practices. In the United States, workers who engage in unfair labor practice strikes, unlike those who engage in strikes over contract issues, are legally protected against permanent replacement.[11] The union's coordinated mobilization strategy provoked a response from Megacorp, which nullified the company's initial legal advantage over the union. Megacorp's escalation allowed the union to mount a protected strike instead of an unprotected one.

Unfair Labor Practices Strike

From April 1 to April 4, 1996, after issuing the legally required 10-day notice of intent to strike, nearly 1,000 SEIU members walked off the job at 18 Megacorp nursing homes across the state of Pennsylvania to protest Megacorp's unfair labor practices. Megacorp immediately sent out letters to all striking workers telling them that although they were still Megacorp employees, Megacorp no longer had positions for them. On April 3, the union issued its unconditional offer to return to work, and workers began preparing to report for the shifts for which they had been scheduled. That evening, management officials called hundreds of workers at home, telling them not to bother to report for work. The next day, security guards posted at the doors of every facility allowed some workers to return to work but turned others away. "We all went up to the door in one big group," said one rank-and-file leader. "I said to the security guard, you're probably not going to let me in, but I want management to know that every one of us was here, in uniform, and ready to report to work. Not one of us is a 'no call, no show.' And I made sure he wrote down all of our names before he turned us away." At the end of the day, Megacorp had turned away nearly 400 workers at the 20 facilities. Over the next few months, the company gradually called some of them back to work—but a year later 135 of the replaced workers were still out.

In the previous section, we saw how workers' lived experience of the struggle against Megacorp worked as a facilitating factor aiding mobilization in the winter of 1995–96. Megacorp workers' experience was that they had mobilized, threatened to strike, and been rewarded in 1989 and 1992. Thus mobilization in 1995 was much easier than it would have been for workers who had not had those experiences. But when it came to organizing the strike itself, Megacorp workers' experience cut the other way. Because of the big settlements won in previous bargaining rounds, Megacorp workers now felt they had more to lose. This time, when it came to organizing a strike threat, workers' experience represented not a facilitating factor but an obstacle to be overcome. According to Mark Crawford:

> In 1989, people were making $3.45 an hour, and there were a lot of workers who were willing to say, well, fuck it, I don't care, I'll go on strike. I'll take them on, because, you know, the worst thing that can happen is that I'll lose my job and I'll get a better one. But now, in '95, these are the best jobs around for the most part. They're certainly the best nursing home jobs in terms of wages and benefits. In a lot of places, the nursing homes all around them are still paying minimum wage, and they're making 8 bucks, 9 bucks an hour. And they have health insurance for themselves and their kids. So people are much more afraid of losing their job now all of a sudden. And they're much more conservative about whether they will strike or they won't strike.

As a result, it was actually much harder in 1995 for the union to get a strike vote in many facilities than it had been in 1989 and 1992. "At my weaker places, I thought very early on that it was questionable whether they would strike," said a Local B organizer. "People were saying, 'You don't fix something that's not broken.' They had no hope for anything more than what they already had. They felt the wages were OK, they had health insurance, there wasn't anything broken." Another staff member responsible for one of the weaker facilities said, "It was sort of scary going into the strike because we had poor turnout for informational picketing, maybe 10 people would do it. They wore stickers but not too many would do marches on the boss. So I was not sure how the vote would go — and I worried that [the strike] would collapse here."

The union dealt with this difficulty in two ways. First, instead of planning for a strike of unlimited duration, the union realized it would be easier to get workers to commit to a three-day limited strike. This in itself caused some problems of coordination because workers at the two strongest facilities were outraged by what they viewed as excessive timidity on the union's part. "That meeting was the worst meeting of my life up to that point," said the staff organizer for Facility #9. "I had people sitting there crying saying, 'I'm not going to be replaced for just a three-day strike. Let's go all out.' They wanted an all-out strike or they were voting it down." Eventually, in the course of a series of emotional meetings, the union was able to convince the Facility #9 rank and file that even though they were able to pull off an unlimited strike, the most important thing was for everyone to act together. Obviously, if only a few facilities stayed out on strike, they would not be strong enough by themselves to win it.

Second, at the weaker facilities, the union worked hard to convince workers that there were substantive issues worth striking over. Even though the strike was officially over Megacorp's unfair labor practices, in reality many workers would not have been willing to risk replacement just to protest Megacorp's illegalities. Instead, the union had to convince workers that the strike was a necessary step in the larger struggle to win specific additional gains:

> Well, we talked to them a lot about pensions, what a pension could mean to them. Are you going to survive on social security when it comes time for you to retire? Talking to them about what would it mean if you had four nursing assistants on your floor instead of two. Would that mean that you would no longer be killing yourself every time you came to work, going home, back hurting, having to go to the chiropractor or whatever you're doing?

In the end, these kinds of appeals convinced enough workers to support the strike that the union was able to win strike votes at 18 of the 20 nursing homes and keep people out for three days, with only a few workers crossing the picket line at most of the homes.

Surprisingly, the fact that the strike had been only for three days became a strength rather than a weakness. Traditionally, striking for such a limited period would be a sign of weakness, and in fact it did reflect the union's inability to pull off an unlimited unfair labor practices strike at a majority of the facilities. But as it turned out, the fact that the illegally replaced workers had made unconditional offers to return to work on

April 4 enabled the union to blast the company for illegally preventing the workers from returning. The fact that the company was willing to run its homes with a hastily assembled collection of scabs and managers rather than accept the strikers' offer to return to work strengthened the union's claims about Megacorp's disregard for the quality of patient care. It put the company in the position of not allowing workers to take care of the residents who needed them, rather than the other way around. In sum, the illegal firings were a major boon for the union. Over the course of the next 13 months, as we will see in Chapter 7, the illegal firings became the centerpiece of the union's strategy to pressure Megacorp back to the bargaining table.

CONCLUSION

This chapter has outlined the innovative strategies developed and implemented by the SEIU's Dignity Campaign in response to Megacorp's union-busting threat. Not all of these strategies were successful in meeting campaign goals, and I have analyzed some of the reasons for the failure of the statewide organizing blitz.

In my view, the tactical creativity of the Pennsylvania SEIU highlights the need for a revised understanding of the problem of structure and agency in social movements research. Tactical or strategic innovation cannot be read off the environment but must be understood as the ability of movement actors to devise novel solutions to tactical and strategic problems. The emergence of new tactics and the timing of their emergence must be located in a historical analysis of the internal politics and organization of the movement itself, focusing on how actors in the movement constructed rationales for various courses of action on the basis of different analyses of the external situation. Only through such an analysis could we explain why the *perception* that the time was right for struggle rose to prominence in John Sweeney's SEIU in the early 1980s and then in the AFL-CIO in the 1990s. Such an analysis is beyond the scope of this book, but I mention it here to show why trying to locate the ultimate causes of the movement's shift in external factors — that is, arguing that the crisis of the labor movement somehow dictated such a course — would give these events an inevitability that they did not have.

But if a historical, agency-centered analysis is necessary to explain new tactics and to understand why new tactics emerge when they do, this is not to say that there is no role for structure in such an analytic approach. On the contrary, a central virtue of viewing mobilization in terms of obstacles and attempts to overcome them (as opposed to viewing it in terms of factors, causes, and effects) is precisely that it allows analysis to focus on agency and creativity *without* succumbing to a voluntarist perspective in which anything seems possible. The world *does* impose its limits. Not all things are possible. Sometimes innovative strategies do not succeed because they cannot surmount the obstacles that are objectively there in the world. And it may not be clear what those obstacles are or how insurmountable they might be until someone attempts to overcome them. In a real sense, mobilizations themselves can reveal the obduracy of the world as well as its malleability. Nothing illustrates this better than the SEIU's failed organizing blitz: here the union *perceived* an opportunity that turned out *not* to be there. In attempting the organizing blitz, the union was testing its theory about a certain kind of organizing, and the answer it got back was that the theory was flawed. Opportunities and limits in the world, in other words, cannot simply be reduced to the level of subjective perceptions or "attributions," as Doug McAdam, Sydney Tarrow, and Charles Tilly would have it in their most recent reformulation of political process theory.[12] There *are* objective opportunities and constraints, but they cannot be known a priori. They only reveal themselves in response to attempts to *change* the world.

SEVEN

"Whatever It Takes, as Long as It Takes"

Exploiting Antiunionism

After the Megacorp strike ended on April 4, 1996, conditions at work did not get any easier for the nearly 600 workers whose unconditional offers to return to work were accepted by the company, because Megacorp's retaliation against workers who participated in the strike was not limited to the 400 who were illegally replaced. Those returning to work returned to an environment in which the company escalated its efforts to punish, harass, and surveil those who had participated in the strike and rank-and-file union leaders in particular. Dozens of strikers saw their work hours reduced when they returned, and when one administrator was asked why strikers' work hours had been reduced, the questioners were told that they had "made the wrong fucking choice" during the strike.[1] Fourteen rank-and-file chapter officers, stewards, and work area leaders were fired on various pretexts — all without any sort of due process — in the next several months. Some of these were employees with perfect disciplinary records over more than a decade of service. One chapter president was fired for having spoken to the press during the strike; other workers were dismissed on trumped-up accusations of neglecting or abusing patients or were charged with breaking new "rules" that man-

agement fabricated after the fact. Another 11 union activists were suspended without pay on bogus charges during the same period.[2]

The union diligently documented these and other continuing legal
violations and filed hundreds of unfair labor practice charges in the
months after the strike. At the same time, the union pursued legal
redress for the 400 strikers who had been permanently replaced. The
first thing the union did in this regard was to make sure all of the
replaced workers succeeded in qualifying for unemployment benefits.
"We all went down to the unemployment office as a group," a rank-and-
file leader recalled. "It was a lot easier on us that way, you know — we
weren't ashamed to be there, we were there because of Megacorp and we
wanted everyone to know it." Megacorp contested the replaced workers'
unemployment benefits, which delayed the process slightly but could
not prevent the workers from ultimately receiving their benefits.

The union also began the process of pursuing a court order that
would require Megacorp to put the replaced employees back to work.
This issue was also contested by Megacorp, which claimed not only that
the strike had been over economic issues but also that the union's 10-day
notice was not valid because the union did not strike at precisely the
time it initially said it would; instead it postponed the strike for 71 hours
before actually striking.[3] This was a legal nonissue, since the NLRB had
ruled in dozens of previous cases that postponements of up to 72 hours
were legal. And since the company's unfair labor practices during the
months preceding the strike had been so blatant, its logic justifying them
so tortured, and the union's documentation so meticulous, the company's claim that the strike was not over unfair labor practices was an
extremely weak one. The union thus had every reason to be confident
right from the outset that eventually it would win a court order requiring the reinstatement of the replaced workers to their original positions
and pay rates, with back pay and interest. In addition the union was
justifiably confident that it would also prevail in winning reinstatement
and back pay for the 14 union activists unfairly fired after the strike, as
well as compensation for those who had been unfairly disciplined.

However, for several reasons the union leaders felt that they could not make the legal process the focus of their strategic efforts to pull Megacorp back to the bargaining table. First and foremost, redress through the legal process might be fairly certain, but would be exceedingly slow. Although Megacorp's challenges to the unfair labor practices strike were specious, they would succeed in slowing down the process of getting the replaced workers reinstated, by forcing the NLRB to hold a whole series of hearings to determine whether the strike was a protected unfair labor practice strike or not. These hearings began in mid-July 1996 but dragged on through September. The company was able to drag them out by calling witness after witness and laboriously reading stacks of documents into the record. The company's own witnesses, supposedly called to support its claim that the strike was not over unfair labor practices, made the union's case, but the company's strategy was aimed at delay more than legal victory, and in this it succeeded. Ultimately, the court order sought by the union would not come down until May 1997 — 13 months after the strike.[4] The unfair labor practice charges filed by the union in the wake of the strike took even longer to resolve; the NLRB did not issue its final decision on these issues until March 2000, just short of four years after the strike.[5]

Megacorp's use of legal delay as a tactic, not only in the 1995–96 contract campaign but throughout the entire history of SEIU nursing home organizing, highlights once again the weakness of U.S. labor law. As one labor attorney in Pittsburgh commented, "Megacorp always exhausts every appeal. They take it as high as they can. And they know they're going to lose in the end, but that's not their point. Their point is to force the union to spend hundreds of thousands of dollars to pursue these cases and to delay justice as long as they can." The delay itself is sufficient in many cases to effectively deny justice. Here Megacorp's strategy was to prolong the resolution of the unfair labor practice charges in order to demoralize workers, wear them down, and destroy their will to fight on.

Therefore, the union could not afford to be passive during this period. Megacorp was already moving forward with its own attempts to decertify the union at two of the most recently organized facilities. These actions were themselves illegal, since they were "founded on the company's own unfair labor practices,"[6] but the threat of decertification would nevertheless become real if workers began to lose faith in the union or confidence in eventual victory. Thus it was critical for the union to build on the momentum of its grassroots mobilization and activism and not allow itself to be demobilized by the legal fight over the unfair labor practices strike or the unfair labor practices themselves.

But by far the most important reason that the union could not rely solely on the legal process was that winning on the legal issues would not, by itself, guarantee any real progress in the larger struggle. If all the union did was reinstate the replaced workers and win the unfair labor practice charges the union had filed before, during, and after the strike, the union would simply find itself back where it had begun with respect to the expired contracts: trying to get back to the table with a bargaining counterpart that was not interested in bargaining productively but rather sought to avoid real bargaining. Thus, just as the significance of the unfair labor practices that the company had committed before the strike lay not in legal remedies but in the sort of new mobilization they permitted, the significance of the 400 replaced workers was not merely that the union could win a legal case that would reinstate them but rather that *because* the union could ultimately win its legal case — because, in fact, the firings were so patently unlawful — the union could use the issue of the 400 replaced workers to extend the struggle to new terrain. The union seized on this issue and made it the centerpiece of a social justice campaign that operated on three fronts: an internal organizing strategy, a community organizing strategy, and a political organizing strategy.

INTERNAL ORGANIZING AND MOBILIZATION

During the year following the strike, the union continued its organizing and mobilizing efforts within each nursing home. Many elements of the repertoire of actions and events deployed at the shop level were the same after the strike as before it — sticker days, button days, petitions, informational picketing, marches on the boss. However, the purpose and context of these activities were now quite different than they had been before the strike. Earlier, the union's goal had been to provoke unfair labor practices and lay the groundwork for its unfair labor practices strike. Now the union had a different set of problems and made use of shop-level mobilization for a different set of purposes.

The first task of continuing internal mobilization and organization was to convey to the rank and file — those who had been replaced as well as those who had returned to work — that the struggle was continuing, that there was important work for them to do. "It's real important to feel you're doing something," said one chapter officer who was replaced for more than six months. "We couldn't let people feel like nobody cared. If everybody had sat back that year, a lot of people would have gotten other jobs, other places, if they could have — and not just part time to hold them off, they would have stayed where they were."

There were also important practical reasons to maintain the level of organization and participation after the strike. Since the company had unilaterally suspended dues deductions, the union was forced to collect dues on its own. If dues could not be collected, the union would appear in an important sense to have ceased to exist. But instead of lamenting the lack of dues deduction, the union viewed collecting dues one on one as an opportunity for continuing the face-to-face interaction that kept it together during the darkest days of the struggle. In the best-organized shops, this strategy was fairly successful, and according to internal union reports, in most shops about half of the members paid their dues throughout the conflict. Only in the weakest shops was dues collection not possible: at the two facilities in which Megacorp attempted to initiate decertification, the union basically collected no dues from the time that dues deduction was suspended in November 1995 until the final settlement in the summer of 1997.[7]

Internal organization was also important after the strike because it enabled the union to continue documenting Megacorp's unfair labor practices. The organizational effort required to keep track of unfair labor practice allegations and collect enough evidence at the time to make the charges stick in a hearing that might not be held for months or years later is remarkable. To facilitate this process, the union set up a toll-free 800 number for workers to call to report unfair labor practices. Operators who manned the line were trained to take detailed notes about each alleged incident over the phone, and those who reported problems were then asked to put their own statements in writing. Staff representatives or chapter officers followed up each of the allegations to collect additional evidence and make certain that workers followed through with written statements.[8]

The union also used its internal organization to carefully document health and safety issues to use against Megacorp. The SEIU in Pennsylvania had developed a working relationship with the U.S. Occupational Safety and Health Administration (OSHA) going back to the early 1990s. The union had developed a program focusing on back injuries and pressuring nursing homes to purchase more mechanical lifts and increase staffing to bring the injury rate down. According to Mark Crawford:

> We were able to get OSHA interested in this, and they actually developed this whole process for going into the nursing home and looking at ergonomics, and back injuries, and where they come from, [such as] the lack of training for people. And they cited Megacorp at five homes, and a number of other companies too. And we worked very closely with them on that whole project.

As a result of this history, the union now decided to activate its internal structure to document any health and safety problems that could be identified and to try to get OSHA involved as a way of putting pressure on Megacorp. In an intensive effort at each nursing home, workers searched for safety problems in every department. The union put together an exhaustive checklist of items for workers to investigate, tailored to each department. Nursing workers investigated whether call bells, night lights, heaters, and fixtures were working in every resident's room; whether emergency lighting and fire alarm and sprinkler systems' maintenance records were current; whether each home had written copies of a disaster preparedness plan. Workers also looked for electrical hazards like frayed electrical cords or exposed wires, or improper use of extension cords in residents' rooms (a violation of state regulations). Dietary workers checked the emergency fire extinguishing system, the temperature of the freezers, and so on.

These grueling inspections turned up reportable problems at several facilities: at Megacorp Facility #4, for example, workers found electrical problems, insufficient training on the handling of hazardous chemicals, and an unrepaired roof. At Megacorp Facility #2, workers reported repeated scabies outbreaks. At Facility #19, workers found hazardous conditions in the kitchen, including freezers that were too warm and a nonfunctional sprinkler system. Armed with such evidence, the union was then able to get OSHA to conduct inspections at these and other facilities. These inspections clearly rattled administrators, who sometimes panicked and refused to allow OSHA representatives to enter the nursing home, forcing them to return with search warrants, in order to buy time to make emergency repairs.[9]

Finally, continued direct mobilization was necessary to convince Megacorp that the rank and file were not going to give up no matter how long Megacorp dragged things out. Much as the 1968 Tet offensive — a military defeat for the Vietcong — helped end the Vietnam War by convincing many Americans that its leaders had been lying about the United States' imminent victory, the way the union refused to let its campaign peter out was important for the message it sent the company about its ability to outlast Megacorp in a protracted campaign. "Megacorp's whole strategy was delay, delay, delay," commented a Pittsburgh labor attorney who handled legal work for the SEIU during the campaign. "They didn't really care if they won or lost [the legal issues] in the end, they were just trying to intimidate the union, to make the union spend hundreds of thousands of dollars on legal fees, and hoping to wear the union down over time." Given this, it was imperative to keep demonstrating to the company that its strategy was not working. The campaign adopted a series of slogans aimed at driving that point home, such as "Whatever It Takes, for As Long as It Takes" and "One Day Longer" [than Megacorp]. These slogans adorned stickers and picket signs and were chanted at every event.

In addition to its shop floor activities, the union also organized periodic protests at Megacorp's district and regional corporate offices and even leafleted and picketed outside the homes of members of Megacorp's corporate board. "We just tried to stay in their face at all levels," said a staff organizer. "We never wanted them to be able to forget about us." A chapter president commented on a March 1997 rally at a district office: "Those people don't see us ordinarily. To [the] corporate [officials] we're not real people, we're just numbers in their big scheme. By storming into their office and making our presence felt, now they have to deal with us. And if they hide, then we know they're scared of us, and we get power from that."

The union's aggressive confrontations with management did seem to make an impact at both the shop floor and corporate levels. Some administrators seemed intimidated by workers' angry "marches on the boss." Administrators and directors of nursing departments often hid or left the premises rather than receive a delegation of angry workers with yet another petition or demand. In one case, described by a rank-and-file leader, workers were even able to browbeat an administrator who had been verbally abusive in several meetings into agreeing to write a written apology and post it on the wall. Also, in the months just after the strike, the union's efforts with "Bargain Now" petitions — especially its success in obtaining signatures from 100 percent of the workers at several facilities, including all of the replacement workers — helped push the company to agree to schedule new negotiating sessions in July 1996.[10] These sessions were not productive, as Megacorp continued to make "offers" including no union shop and no dues deduction, but by presenting such an overwhelming demand to bargain, the union did at least force the company to appear at the table for the first time in months. Most important, however, was the overall message conveyed by the union's persistent visibility: by the time that the 10(j) injunction ordering the replaced workers back to work finally came down in May 1997, Megacorp understood very clearly that further delays — such as an attempt to avoid following the order — would not succeed in denting the rank and file's resolve and commitment to persevere.

This commitment was not produced without difficulty. As the year wore on, it became harder and harder to keep ordinary rank-and-file workers "up." "They did get depressed," one chapter officer admitted. "They would call me up on the phone in tears sometimes, saying that they couldn't go on. And my job was to talk them through it, to give them hope, to keep reminding them that we were going to win in the end, that the union was not going to give up until they won. But I know it was hard to see hope at times."

One of the tangible benefits of the replacements in this respect was that since many of the union's strongest rank-and-file leaders were off the job, they were available to work full time as organizers. The union put several dozen of these workers on its payroll as "member organizers" and gave them central roles in continuing to build the organization in their nursing homes. This offered another way of working around the problem of unaccountable staff at Locals A and C. "Some of our best-organized homes, by the end, were Local A homes, because of the work of the member organizers," said Mark Crawford. "After the strike we basically worked with them and bypassed completely the staff that did-n't want to hold up their end." Member organizers (MOs) were put through an intensive training program, then paid for two days of work per week — but in practice they often worked around the clock, seven days a week. "I was on the phone constantly," said one. "Two in the morning on a Sunday night, I would be talking to people, getting them ready for whatever we were doing next or dealing with whatever prob-lems had come up." The MOs were effective and committed organizers, but their exhortations still had to overcome resistance from the membership as it wearied of the struggle. "People said, 'Hey, at least you're getting paid to do this work,'" another former MO recalled.

> I understood that they were tired, and that it was hard to go on and work on yet another petition or organize yet another informational picket, but it had to be done. I got to the point where I told them that if they wanted my job [as a member organizer], if they wanted to work seven days a week and never get thanked for it, they could have it. No one ever volunteered.

Tensions sometimes ran high between these activists (along with the rank-and-file members who continued to turn out for events) and those whose energy ran out. In March 1997, I attended an informational picket at Facility #1, just outside Pittsburgh, where about 20 workers stood along the roadside with billboards and signs. At the afternoon shift change, some of these workers had to leave the picket line to go into the facility for their shift, and the member organizer for the facility was trying to make sure that people from the day shift stayed to picket. As people drove out of the lot, most stopped and talked to the MO. About half of these drove their cars across the street, where they parked in a nearby lot and joined the picketing. The others, however, begged off, citing various reasons why they could not stay. The MO pressed hard on some of these people, especially several whose excuses apparently did not sound legitimate enough for her. A few of the exchanges were barely civil. When several other workers drove out without stopping, looking the other way when the MO approached, her frustration was evident as she called out to them angrily. It was clear that a good number of workers were exhausted by the struggle and just wanted the whole thing to go away.

Still, despite the exhaustion of significant segments of the rank and file, the union maintained the ability to turn out credible numbers for events at most nursing homes throughout the long year after the strike because of the determination and commitment of the entire cadre of rank-and-file leaders, who took responsibility for mobilizing their shops again and again.

COMMUNITY ORGANIZING AND CORPORATE CAMPAIGN

Just as Local A's campaign against Kane privatization could not rely only on mobilizing workers to produce enough leverage, the struggle against Megacorp after the strike sought to triangulate Megacorp by producing pressure from different sources, including community pressure. In the Megacorp campaign, however, the union's community organizing was much deeper than Kane organizing had been, and pressure from the community took the form not only of moral suasion from community allies but also of financial pressure from the union's corporate campaign activities.

The union made community organizing a central feature of its strategy by creating new organizational structures within each nursing home dedicated to this task. Shortly after the strike, with the assistance of union staff and MOs, each nursing home formed a Fundraising Committee, a Hardship Committee, a Media Committee, and an Outreach Committee. The Fundraising and Hardship Committees worked together on activities like bake sales, pizza and hoagie sales, raffles, dances (complete with door prizes donated by local businesses), craft sales, and yard sales, and they solicited donations from local merchants. Many of these events were very successful, like a "truckload of groceries" raffle at Facility #17 that raised $1,300 in July 1996.[11] The union also regularly made members of the Hardship Committee available to speak to meetings of local groups and congregations about the union's struggle. At such occasions, speakers emphasized the illegality of the mass firings and other unfair labor practices; Megacorp's poor quality and safety record; and the hardships suffered by the workers who had been unlawfully replaced. Union representatives brought to these occasions copies of pamphlets and reports on Megacorp's quality and safety problems, professionally produced by the research department of the international union. Speaking engagements also included a request for donations to the hardship fund and invitations to participate in informational pickets, candlelight vigils, and other events. These contacts helped boost attendance at such actions by attracting contingents from sympathetic local political groups such as Labor and Green Parties, who regularly turned out to support the union.

Media committee members not only functioned as designated spokespeople during events but also took photos and helped produce videos, including several professionally edited short videos with narrated voiceover that Hardship Committee members used as part of their presentation during speaking engagements. Media committees also periodically organized local press conferences to "speak out" on specific quality or safety issues. These events not only were good ways to keep the visibility of the struggle high throughout the campaign but also generated a tangible sense of pride and achievement for the rank-and-file workers who organized them and spoke at them. "I never imagined in my wildest dreams that I could pull something like that off," said one LPN who organized a press conference at her facility. "I mean, I have never been a public speaker. And here I was, standing at the podium with TV cameras and reporters all listening to what I had to say." In addition to these activities, Outreach Committee members worked to turn residents' family members out to these events and worked on the union's efforts to solicit signatures on a petition of community support for the union. Rank-and-file workers went door to door and staked out shopping malls with these petitions. Within three weeks of the strike, several chapters each had over 2,000 signatures from their respective communities, and ultimately workers collected tens of thousands of petitions.[12]

This kind of community organizing helped to support the workers materially during their struggle, helped keep morale high, and helped create the impression that communities all over Pennsylvania were fed up with Megacorp's union-busting tactics. Unlike elected Allegheny County commissioners in the Kane struggle, of course, Megacorp could afford to withstand a certain amount of community opposition. However, even large corporations have to pay some attention to their image, and Megacorp's image was being tarnished by the union's high visibility as it hammered the company on its law-breaking, patient care, and health and safety.

In addition to this kind of pressure through bad publicity, the union also attempted to hit the company in the wallet through its community organizing. One of the union's most successful tactics was its portrayal of Megacorp as a faceless, out-of-state corporation that did not care about the communities it operated in. The union struck a gold mine in this respect when researchers from the international discovered the company's connection to a subsidiary, National Pharmacy Corporation (PCA). Researchers discovered in a comparison of 10 prescription drugs that PCA's prices were 11 percent to 300 percent higher than at other local drug stores. Although residents and their families nominally had the right to insist that drugs administered to their family members be purchased from the pharmacy of their choice, in many cases Megacorp would simply use PCA without asking residents or family members which pharmacy they preferred. By using PCA and charging higher prices for drugs, Megacorp was able to make extra money. The union tackled this issue by organizing a national day of education on November 14, 1996, in which Megacorp facilities all around the country were leafleted to inform family members of the issue.[13] At the Myersdale facility, the union discovered that Megacorp had decided to end a long-standing relationship with a local pharmacy and to bring in PCA instead as its preferred pharmacy. Rank-and-file workers met with the local pharmacy owner and leafleted at the facility and in the community. "It got to be a really hot issue there," said Mark Crawford. He continued:

> You know they're in these small communities in Pennsylvania, it's a huge company, an out-of-state company, and we used that all the time. So you have vocal nursing home workers talking about this huge company that treats people like shit and steals our money and

takes it someplace else. So we used it, and at Myersdale it ended up that Megacorp had to make some arrangement to keep working with the local pharmacy there.

The union also took its message to local hospitals that regularly sent patients to Megacorp homes. "We had a booklet called the Arkansas Report, and we took it in to present to the administrator of [a local hospital]," said a rank-and-file leader who participated in the event. "We had 60 people there and we had a press conference, with Channel 11 and 4 news there. We said, listen, we're not here to cause any trouble, we're just here to present this to the administrator. You know, we're not telling you not to put people [at Megacorp], we just want you to look at this and make up your own mind." This strategy was controversial among the rank and file. "A lot of our workers are proud of the job they do. They were worried that if you cross a certain line by criticizing the patient care too much, it actually reflects badly on them," said Joe Reilly of Local A. A staff organizer from Local B agreed that it was a problem. "We definitely had people who felt that the more successful we were at convincing the hospitals not to send patients to Megacorp, the more likely that they wouldn't have jobs to return to." But although this was an issue, the union was still able to carry these events off by convincing enough workers that the situation was desperate enough to call for desperate tactics. "We knew that if we didn't do it, we were dead anyway," commented Dan Adams, B's vice president. "That's what we told people; we told them that if they *didn't* do it, they might not have jobs to return to. At that point we were trying anything and everything."

Megacorp was clearly stung by these activities. At bargaining during the summer and fall of 1996, the company's representatives pressed Crawford to agree to cease its efforts to publicly portray the company in a bad light.[14] Crawford refused to make any unilateral guarantees. The company also filed suit in a Pennsylvania Common Pleas Court against all three locals, charging that the unions' efforts to discredit the company involved false statements that were causing economic injury to the firm. "For years, the union has employed a variety of tactics, including falsely portraying Megacorp as anti-worker, anti-consumer, unsafe and greedy," said a company spokesperson in a press release. The lawsuit sought compensatory damages, legal costs, and punitive damages. According to a Pittsburgh labor attorney who represented the SEIU, the union never took the lawsuit seriously. "The defamation suit is a version of a SLAPP [Strategic Law Suit Against Public Participants] lawsuit. It's just a way of trying to intimidate the other side. And a lot of times it works, because if you lose, you are facing potentially millions of dollars in damages. But we had been careful all along to make sure that the union said only things that were defensible. We knew that the defamation suit would eventually get dismissed."

POLITICAL ORGANIZING

Political leverage was the third prong of the SEIU's pressure strategy. The union cleverly exploited the issue of Megacorp's law-breaking by appealing to political authorities on all levels to intervene and exert pressure on the company to comply with the law. In doing so the union drew not only on the issue of the replaced workers and the unfair labor practices that had occurred during the contemporary conflict but also on the company's record of health and safety problems, on its refusal to cooperate with OSHA inspectors, and on Megacorp's 10-year history of thousands of labor law violations that had accumulated in a whole series of cases — all won by the union — known as Megacorp I through Megacorp V. The union also emphasized in its presentations to government officials that Megacorp's reckless and illegal permanent replacement of 360 strikers jeopardized the health and safety of the residents and illustrated the company's lack of concern for the quality of patient care.

The union sent delegations of workers to meet and plead with government officials at all levels, both locally in Pennsylvania and in Washington, D.C. In late April 1996, for example, the union bused hundreds of Megacorp workers to Washington to lobby Congress. Lawmakers were presented with several studies that summarized Megacorp's history of illegal union-busting tactics and its record of poor care quality. Numerous local bodies such as city and borough councils, after hearing presentations from rank-and-file workers and reviewing the materials they were given, passed resolutions condemning Megacorp for its illegal behavior and sent letters to Megacorp demanding that the company reinstate the replaced workers and negotiate a good-faith settlement to the contract dispute. Some of these local bodies also issued strongly worded public statements on the issue. Pittsburgh City Council President Jim Ferlo, for example, argued, "No corporation that ignores the impact of firing so many long term employees on nursing home residents and so flagrantly violates labor laws deserves to receive a dime of our tax dollars."[15]

National-level politicians also responded with support for the union. A bipartisan group of 12 Pennsylvania congressional representatives wrote to the CEO of Megacorp, urging him to reconsider the course the company had set. In addition, a number of other members of Congress wrote letters of their own, some expressing their personal annoyance at the company's misbehavior. The overall sense one gets from reviewing these letters is that Megacorp was starting to create genuine anger and opposition among members of Congress — not necessarily a good thing for a company 80 percent of whose revenues originated with the federal government. A letter from Representative Tom Lantos (a Democrat from California) in late June 1996 — sent not just to Megacorp's CEO but also to the entire Megacorp Board of Directors — is fairly typical of these missives. After noting that he had followed the dispute "closely and with considerable concern," Lantos reminded Megacorp that the U.S. government's General Accounting Office had recently cited it as "one of the nation's worst labor law violators receiving federal contracts." Lantos went on to say quite ominously that "[i]t is becoming more and more clear to Members of Congress like myself that labor law violators must be held accountable for illegal conduct and should be debarred from the future award of government contracts and taxpayer money." After this warning, and some further discussion of the replaced workers, the letter concludes by sternly advising Megacorp to change its labor policies.

The union exploited its support from sympathetic politicians not just through the private pressure they could exert on the company but also through their helping to publicly legitimate the workers' struggle. A rally in early May 1996 in support of the replaced workers was attended by 10 U.S. congressional representatives, some from other states. At a Memorial Day protest at the Federal Building in Pittsburgh, Representative Bill Coyne also spoke in support of the workers.

Another avenue for political leverage was to exert pressure on the Veterans' Administration (VA) to stop doing business with Megacorp until the company cleaned up its act. Local VA medical centers had lucrative arrangements with Megacorp nursing homes under which the VA regularly referred patients to Megacorp. In addition, Megacorp held federal contracts with the VA to provide services directly to the government. For the union, this represented another point at which pressure could be exerted: the union organized petitions signed by thousands of Pittsburgh area residents urging the director of the local VA Medical Center to cancel its arrangements with Megacorp. The union also organized a letter-writing campaign aimed at federal VA Secretary Jesse Brown, asking the VA administration to reconsider its federal contracts with Megacorp in light of the company's historical record of repeated and continuing unlawful activities. The union worked both with local organizations of retired veterans, such as the Veterans of Foreign Wars (VFW) and the American Legion, and with the United Steelworkers union's retirees organization to help produce a barrage of letters to VA officials protesting the use of federal money to support a company that would "act as if it was above the law" of a country that veterans had risked their lives to defend.[16] Twenty-three members of the 63-seat State House of Representatives also wrote strongly worded individual letters to Secretary Brown urging him to reconsider the VA's contracts with Megacorp.

In addition to these activities the SEIU got behind specific legislation, at both the state and federal level, threatening to punish Megacorp for its behavior. The Pennsylvania "Megacorp Bill," introduced by a bipartisan group of sympathetic representatives in the state House of Representatives, would have punished companies that illegally replaced striking workers by forcing them to reimburse the state for lost taxes, for the cost of unemployment compensation, and for the cost of providing other social services to families affected by such actions.[17] At the federal level, the union worked with Rep. Lane Evans (D-Illinois), who introduced legislation in the U.S. House of Representatives that would debar labor law violators from future federal contracts. To support and publicize the bill, the SEIU organized a congressional hearing, held in Pittsburgh. I was able to attend it. Seven U.S. senators and representatives, including Republican Senator Arlen Spector of Pennsylvania, attended the hearing. They listened to replaced rank-and-file workers describe the hardships they were suffering. Several labor academics testified about Megacorp's long record of labor law violations. Representatives from the American Legion and the Steelworkers' Organization of Active Retirees (SOAR) also spoke in favor of the bill. All seven politicians present — including Spector, not normally a friend of labor — had harsh words for Megacorp, and all but Spector pledged to support the bill.

Finally, throughout the struggle the union pursued one other source of political pressure by seeking intervention from the Republican governor of Pennsylvania, Tom Ridge. During the strike itself, the union bused nearly all 1,000 of the striking workers to Harrisburg for a huge demonstration at the capital building. A delegation of workers asked Governor Ridge to pressure Megacorp to obey the law and bargain in good faith; the entire assemblage sat down to block traffic briefly in a downtown Harrisburg street. Five months later, in October, the union organized another three-day series of rallies and protests at the state capital. Billed as "Days of Rage," this second wave of protests drew nearly as many workers as the first and culminated in workers' sitting in at the governor's office and getting arrested. This time, Ridge agreed to intervene. He personally convened an off-the-record discussion between the union and the company and appointed a mediator to represent him at all future negotiating sessions.

Union leaders regarded this as a major step forward. The governor's mediator took a fairly active role during subsequent negotiating sessions. For example, according to rank-and-file workers who attended the bargaining sessions, when Megacorp negotiators claimed that they could not schedule another meeting because they had not brought their appointment books, the mediator intervened and prodded them into reluctantly agreeing to return the following day. "The involvement of the governor was crucial," said the international staff person who ran the Dignity Office during the campaign, who felt that the presence of the mediator helped moderate Megacorp's behavior at the table. "If you piss off the people who decide whether you can get public money and how much, you have a problem. If the governor wants to hurt a nursing home operator, he can send inspectors to live in those nursing homes. And, you know, if you're pissing off a Republican governor there's something wrong with your approach."

The union's political organizing on all these various fronts elicited defensive responses from Megacorp. In response to the union's lobbying efforts and the resulting letters and calls to Megacorp from irate lawmakers, Megacorp's CEO initially fired back rather arrogant replies claiming that the company had done nothing illegal, that it was Megacorp who was the victim of an illegal and unfair campaign of intimidation and harassment from the union, and that its use of replacement workers would soon be vindicated in the courts. Megacorp also took out full-page ads in newspapers across the state of Pennsylvania defending its actions and claiming that "Megacorp Caregivers Care."[18] The problem with this strategy was that when the court order finally came down in April 1997 finding that Megacorp had acted unlawfully in replacing the strikers and ordering the company to reinstate them to their original positions, Megacorp could no longer resist pressure from lawmakers to get serious at the bargaining table. Shortly after the 10 (j) injunction was handed down, the company signaled to the union that it was ready to work toward an agreement. By the end of May 1997, the union successfully negotiated agreements in principle, and in early July the new, four-year contracts were ratified by the membership of all three locals.

CONCLUSION

In the views of union officials, Megacorp's capitulation reflected the cumulative effects of multiple, mutually reinforcing, sources of leverage. Taken individually, neither the legal decision on the replaced workers, nor the union's militancy and staying power, nor its use of community organizing to hurt the company financially, nor political pressure, would have sufficed to induce Megacorp to bargain in earnest. Together, however, these tactics succeeded because each piece reinforced the others. The company was faced ultimately with a financial hit, a serious deterioration of its public image, a union that wouldn't go away, and political pressure to move on the issues that escalated the longer the conflict dragged on.

The union's strategy of extending the struggle along these fault lines to create multiple points of pressure, of course, was possible only because of the union's earlier success in feeding Megacorp's antiunion animus by provoking more and more extreme unfair labor practices, culminating in the mass illegal replacements, which became the social justice issue at the heart of the union's poststrike efforts. The interesting thing about this observation is that it turns the tables on conventional understandings of the relative flexibility and adaptability of labor and capital in the United States. The image of organized labor as a slow-moving dinosaur is usually contrasted with that of the flexibility of capital as it rapidly redeploys itself both globally and locally. This image is not without merit, for it is certainly true that "big" labor took a long time to begin responding in a remotely effective fashion to the economic changes of the 1980s and 1990s and to capital's escalated assault on labor that began at the beginning of the 1980s. But the experience of the SEIU in the Megacorp struggle suggests that sometimes labor can be *more* flexible than capital. It suggests that by thinking about labor-management relations in a new way — in particular by reconceptualizing the strike as part of an overall strategy rather than as the only weapon in the arsenal — social movement unionism can deploy its forces and its efforts in a highly creative and flexible manner.

At the same time, the SEIU's Megacorp struggle raises the possibility that that the ideologically extreme antiunionism of so much American capital may represent an important *inflexibility*, a rigidity that creative social movement unionism can not only exploit but influence. It is extremely interesting to observe that in the Megacorp case, the aggressiveness and apparent insatiability of social movement unionism from its inception in the 1980s through two rounds of bargaining helped radicalize the company's labor relations approach — and that this radicalization seemed to go hand in hand with a loss of strategic flexibility in the company's labor relations strategy. By pushing the company to take such an extreme approach — while being extremely careful always to make sure its own legal bases were covered — the union helped ensure that Megacorp would be so blinded by its radicalism, by its absolute hostility toward the union, so convinced that its own extreme views would be upheld by others, that it began to do very stupid things, like antagonize important government officials. In sum, it is possible that the early successes of social movement union organizing are a double-edged sword: they can indeed create a backlash, but to the extent that in doing so social movement unionism also radicalizes capital, the movement may also induce capital to limit its own flexibility — thus setting the stage for further success.

These observations about the dynamic interactions between labor and capital in these campaigns call to mind the observations of social movement theorists about the way movements and their opponents interact with one another and respond to each other's tactical innovations.[19] But outside the general observation that movements interact, that they learn from the tactics of the other side, and that new tactics tend to have a shelf life, this literature — like the larger political process model within which it is situated — does not offer theoretical explanations of success and failure that we can use to explain why and how the SEIU managed to defeat Megacorp in Pennsylvania in the mid 1990s. Once again, it should be clear from the preceding analysis that the success of the Megacorp campaign can be understood only with reference to the way the movement dealt with specific historical and contextual obstacles: the particular outlines of American corporate antiunionism; the details of the legal framework; the concrete organizational difficulties of interlocal cooperation (which are themselves structured by the specificities of union organization as distinct from other kinds of movement organization); and the lived experience of workers who, having achieved concrete gains in living standards, are reluctant to risk losing them.

The Ambiguity of Victories

Unions understandably like to portray their victories as epochal, as absolute. It is rarely so. The SEIU's Dignity Campaign against Megacorp in the mid-1990s was not an exception. On one hand, the mere fact that the union survived with all of its Megacorp shops intact really is a significant achievement; there aren't many contemporary examples of unions surviving an all-out union-busting attempt by a large private employer. In surviving, the union also continued to improve the economic lot of Megacorp nursing home workers in Pennsylvania; the four-year contracts signed in July of 1997 provided for wage increases totaling nearly 10 percent over the four years and improvements in health insurance benefits. In the aftermath of the struggle, there were signs that Megacorp's labor-relations strategy might be moving away from the antilabor extremism of its Reaganite vice president for labor relations. "We're getting some signals that the next round of negotiations is going to be a lot less difficult than the last one was," said the union's Pittsburgh attorney in 1999. "You never know with Megacorp, but there are some signs that when the contracts come up, they may actually come to the table prepared to negotiate successor agreements." This proved to be the case in 2001, when SEIU and Megacorp renewed their contracts without a major battle.

The ferociousness of the union's struggle with Megacorp has had a demonstration effect on other nursing home chains in the state. Chains like Hewitt have never been as ideologically rigid as Megacorp, but in 1995 the union did face considerable difficulty at the table with Hewitt as well. Hewitt eventually did settle in 1996, because, according to Joe Reilly, the three locals' chief bargainer for Hewitt, the company saw where things were going with Megacorp and did not want to go in that direction. In late 1998, when Hewitt's contracts came up again, negotiations went extremely smoothly. "Their attitude in '98 was completely different from what it had been in 1995 and 1996," said Reilly. "They really came to the table in '98 saying that they were serious about bargaining. We bargained all the homes together, we reached agreements on new contracts [including a first contract for Rosemont Pavilion] relatively quickly." In Reilly's view, Hewitt had simply decided that it was not worth it to tangle with the SEIU.

But if the Megacorp campaign of 1995–97 represented a very real victory for the union, it certainly was not a complete one. The union did not get pensions, organizing rights, a master contract, or any of the major planks it initially set out to achieve. Pensions in particular are a very real need for nursing home workers, who labor for what are still very modest wages and accumulate nothing for their own retirement. Pensions have become something of a distant goal. Also, by agreeing in the end to bargain the facilities separately and to accept slightly different wage increases at different facilities, the union took several small steps away from the idea of a master contract. The union's goal of organizing the industry in Pennsylvania and creating ultimately industrywide bargaining structures depends, as a first step, on being able to negotiate with each chain in a unified way, rather than having to conduct separate negotiations for each facility. Finally, if negotiations were easier in 2001, it was not only because Megacorp came to the table prepared to negotiate in good faith but also because the union backed away from the elements of its agenda that scared Megacorp the most. The union also was not certain that it could have duplicated its 1996 strike in 2001. "A lot of people are still exhausted," a Local B staff organizer told me in 1999. "I don't know if we could pull that off again soon." Ultimately, then, what the union accomplished in its two-year struggle with Megacorp was to create a situation in which both sides were prepared to live with the status quo — for a while. Megacorp, for its part, has still not reached the point where it is prepared to accept the union as a permanent partner. "You have to understand," said the union attorney cited earlier, "that the people who run Megacorp think that they should be allowed to run their business without interference from anybody — from unions, from the government, anybody. They haven't changed in that respect in 15 years." Megacorp was certainly chastened by its defeat — and as a result, the next round of coordinated bargaining would go quite smoothly, as neither party wanted to repeat the carnage of 1995–96. But the SEIU realizes that future clashes are inevitable as long as the union is determined to work toward changing the balance of power in the nursing home industry in Pennsylvania.

Social Movement Unionism
and Social Movement Theory

Notwithstanding the many weaknesses and shortcomings of the labor organizing struggles I've analyzed in this book, one thing that stands out is that the people who organized and led them, for the most part, viewed their activities as self-conscious attempts to turn organized labor from an ossified relic into a vital social movement. As I attempted to analyze these episodes, therefore, it seemed only natural to turn for inspiration to the sociology of social movements.

But although I found many useful concepts and ideas in this literature, I found that the most important theoretical approaches in the field did not really help me make sense of the contemporary upsurge in trade union organizing. On the contrary, the turn toward social movement unionism represented a challenge to existing perspectives.

Consider the so-called "new social movements" theories advanced by a number of European writers. These theories take as their point of departure a view of "contemporary" society as a new social form, whose nature is still unclear but which has been given various labels including *postindustrial society*,[1] *post-Fordism*,[2] *the network society*,[3] and *complex society*.[4] In contrast to the old industrial society, whose main axis of conflict was class struggle, the contemporary period is said to be distinguished by a proliferation of new collective actors, new grievances, and new modes of political action.[5] Labor struggles are viewed as having declining significance — because, it is assumed, workers' organizations are more or less secure in their position as "solidly based, institutionally guaranteed bodies of representation."[6] As a result, writers in this tradition have gone so far as to say that class identities and conflicts are no longer useful objects of study.[7]

Clearly, this view of contemporary class relations and the security of workers' collective bargaining institutions is at odds with reality, at least in the United States, where labor unions, and workers, have been under a concerted employer assault for the last two decades. Indeed, Alberto Melucci's overall view that contemporary society reflects "a tendency towards the extension of citizenship and participation"[8] is called into question by the crisis of the labor movement and the growth of non-union, low-wage, at-will employment.

If European new social movements theories proved unhelpful, political process models of social movements developed on this side of the Atlantic seemed equally problematic. There are several different versions of the political process perspective, but they all share the idea of favorable confluences of facilitating factors, whether objective or subjective. In Doug McAdam's classic formulation, for example, macro-structural changes simultaneously create new political opportunities for protest and new organizational resources that can support mobilization; these lead in turn to new beliefs about the possibility of change through collective action, a process McAdam labeled "cognitive liberation."[9] Since then, other versions of the approach have variously emphasized the importance of threats as opposed to opportunities;[10] substituted ideas about framing processes in place of McAdam's original notion of cognitive liberation;[11] and attempted to further incorporate social constructionist concerns by abandoning the ideas of political opportunities and threats as objective categories and focusing instead on the *attribution* of opportunity and threat by movement actors.[12] Despite considerable variation, however, in all cases these writers emphasize the favorable factors, processes, and mechanisms that combine to produce social protest.

What struck me about the labor mobilizations I was studying, of course, was not the presence of favorable conditions, mechanisms, or processes but rather how *difficult* mobilization was, how great the obstacles to it, how complex the problems actors struggled with. Far from being driven by a spreading sense among workers that labor mobilization was both possible and likely to improve their lives, for instance, I found that workers' lack of interest or faith in unions was a key *obstacle* in union organizing efforts. Likewise, I found it impossible to understand union organization as a facilitating factor in the transition from member servicing to grassroots mobilization. Not only had the labor movement's organizational resources been shrinking for a quarter of a century (nowhere more than in southwestern Pennsylvania), but entrenched forms of union organization actually stood in the way of mobilization and posed crucial difficulties, problems, and obstacles. Finally, the political and legal situation for labor could not be less favorable. Indeed, as I discovered when I examined the Megacorp battle, the legal and political power of capital posed nearly insurmountable difficulties for these new union struggles.

From a political process perspective, the campaigns I was studying seemed doomed to failure — but somehow they were succeeding despite the obstacles. Union activists and rank-and-file workers were finding ways of solving these problems and overcoming these dilemmas. To capture these processes, I needed a perspective that did not emphasize what was *favorable* to mobilization but that focused instead on the *difficulties* involved and on the agency of actors in confronting these difficulties. This approach would need to be sensitive to history and its legacies without imposing a predetermined narrative.

In constructing such an approach, I returned to the work of Alberto Melucci for my inspiration. Although Melucci was certainly mistaken in his conviction that labor struggles were no longer important or relevant in contemporary society, his writings nevertheless contain a seminal idea: that collective action should be studied not as an *effect* but as an *accomplishment* — not as something "caused" but as something *constructed* by people whose actions are inherently meaningful. This is an idea that has been repeated widely enough among students of social movements, but so far few have seemed to grasp its main implication: viewing collective action as an achievement rather than an effect means shifting attention from facilitating factors to the "difficulties involved in building unitary action,"[13] the obstacles that must be overcome. It is only by focusing attention on the *difficulties* involved in collective action that the creativity and agency of movement actors can be fully appreciated.

This is the insight upon which I have tried to build my analysis of the contemporary labor movement. In doing so, I have been forced to go beyond the work of most social constructionists (including Melucci) in the sense that my analysis does not focus only on *discursive* obstacles — that is, difficulties involved in the construction of shared meaning. The obstacles to building collective action, after all, are not confined to discursive problems or to questions of solidarity: questions of organization, opportunities, constraints, and power are equally salient.[14]

Specifically, as I tried to make sense of my three sets of organizing campaigns, I realized that I could use each comparison to highlight a series of nested obstacles that came into play at different levels of analysis: first at the level of solidarity, next at the level of organization, and finally at the level of strategy and power relations. In this sense, my theoretical schema of nested obstacles corresponded roughly to Doug McAdam's original formulation of political process theory. My three levels of analysis are the same as his: an analysis of consciousness at the micro level; an analysis of organization at the meso level; and an analysis of power relations and strategy at the macro level. But in place of his variables (political opportunities, organizational resources, and cognitive liberation) I substituted analyses of obstacles and attempts to overcome them. In doing so, I found a way to incorporate *both* agency *and* structure into the analysis on an equal basis, something that has largely eluded analysts of social movements to date.

In short, taking labor seriously as a contemporary social movement forced me to invent my own mode of movement analysis, one that combined the best insights of two traditions of social movement theorizing while rejecting those that did not help. Substantively, this mode of analysis has enabled me to contribute new insights about "social movement" forms of labor mobilization: why grassroots organizing is so effective (Part I); why business union organization is a thorny obstacle to mobilization in some contexts but not others (Part II); and how unions can sometimes turn corporate antiunionism from a weakness into a source of strength (Part III).

My findings in each of the three sets of comparative case studies presented here provide the basis for genuine optimism about the labor movement. Despite the very real and serious nature of the obstacles, these case studies demonstrate that the SEIU is capable of dealing with them effectively. They show that, within the context of the current legal framework, it *is* possible to organize new workers in a new industry, against implacable employer opposition, and then to defend and extend those victories.

However, this optimism has to be tempered by the recognition that this process is a slow one. The current period is simply not like the 1930s, in which new industries could be organized all at once, at a single stroke. Instead, the experience of the SEIU in Pennsylvania suggests a stepwise process in which initial victories are defended against counterattack and then extended over time. As union leaders acknowledge, it would not have been possible to fight Megacorp in 1984 or 1988 in the same way that the union did in 1995 and 1996. The seeds for the successful strike against Megacorp the mid-1990s, in other words, were sown through more than a decade of organization and struggle. And the struggle to organizing the nursing home industry in Pennsylvania is by no means over: after nearly two decades of organizing and struggle, the SEIU now represents workers at 12 percent of Pennsylvania's private sector nursing homes. This is a remarkable achievement—and it has already resulted in real gains for Pennsylvania nursing home workers regardless of union status—but 12 percent of the industry is not yet enough to push through the union's long-term agenda of dignity and respect for nursing home workers and the residents they care for. Similarly, organizing efforts in other industries will entail decades-long processes involving initial organizing successes, efforts to build and reform organization at the level of the local unions, and repeated struggles to resist employer counteroffensives. This is not going to happen overnight, no matter what the character of the AFL-CIO leadership.

A more serious problem for labor is that, despite the successes of unions like the SEIU, HERE, and the CWA, so far only a few unions are engaging in innovative grassroots organizing aimed at extending unionization to new sectors in the low-wage service economy. Millions of low-wage workers who *might* support union organizing campaigns in the right context simply do not have any unions willing to make a serious attempt to organize them. For unions to make a bigger dent in the "postindustrial" economy, some union or unions will have to take on the challenge of organizing millions of low-wage food service and retail workers. Indeed, the urgency of this challenge is highlighted by the fact that in 2002, despite organizing nearly 500,000 new members — a feat many thought impossible a decade ago — the labor movement still suffered a net loss of 280,000 workers, thanks to the ongoing recession and accelerated job loss in manufacturing.[15] Continued and heavy losses of union members in manufacturing are probably inevitable under the current economic rules of the game. Thus, a crucial barrier to the recovery of the movement is that few unions have so far adopted proven social movement union strategies.[16]

There are signs that this is slowly changing. One very important recent development, for example, is the nationwide campaign by the United Food and Commercial Workers (UFCW) to unionize Wal-Mart, now the nation's largest employer with nearly 1 million workers. Union density and wages in the supermarket industry, long a UFCW stronghold, have been declining over the last decade, partly as a result of competitive pressure on unionized stores from nonunion discount chains like Wal-Mart, whose low wages and brutal exploitation of suppliers allow it to undercut supermarkets that pay living wages. In early 2000, the UFCW went public with a nationwide campaign against Wal-Mart, announcing that meat cutters in a Texas Wal-Mart supercenter had voted to join the UFCW.[17] Instead of recognizing the union, Wal-Mart instead changed how it bought meat in all of its stores nationwide, shifting to prepackaged and precut meats and reclassifying the meat cutters' jobs. The UFCW began informational picketing campaigns at Wal-Marts across the country to protest the company's unfair labor practices. Three years later, in June 2003, the NLRB ruled that Wal-Mart had illegally changed the meat cutters' jobs to avoid collective bargaining and ordered the company to commence bargaining with the UFCW.[18] Whether the union will be able to turn this legal victory into a series of union contracts remains to be seen.

Certainly, the difficulties involved will be very great. When compared to the SEIU's two decades of nursing home organizing, the UFCW's Wal-Mart campaign is still very much in its infancy. The retail and fast-food chains' hostility to unions, their reliance on a contingent, ever-changing labor force, their willingness to allocate huge resources to fight unions, are legendary. And it is true that retail chains and fast-food places can more credibly threaten to close stores in response to union campaigns than nursing homes and hospitals. Indeed, in one of the few cases in which unions attempted to organize workers at a McDonald's franchise, the campaign was defeated when the franchise owner closed down the restaurant, only to open a new one — union-free — down the street.[19]

Yet 20 years ago no one in labor's mainstream thought it possible to organize low-wage nursing home workers. Nursing home giant Megacorp was no less rabidly antiunion than Wal-Mart, its workers no less contingent and disposable. Because the SEIU's solutions to organizing problems in this industry had not been invented yet, the prospects for success looked exceedingly dim to many observers. Similarly, although Wal-Mart and the other low-wage retailers look like a very difficult nut to crack at present, part of the apparent invincibility of these firms lies in the fact that, until recently, no union has worked very hard to solve the organizing problems they present.

If the labor movement is to rebound, then, its resurgence must be built on the conviction that union organizing is always possible so long as people who work can't afford decent health care, housing, transportation, and leisure. But whether U.S. labor as a whole will manage to translate such a conviction into a series of innovative solutions to the problems of organizing is not a question that will be answered overnight. The struggle to reorient American labor toward organizing and grass-roots struggle in pursuit of economic and social justice will be played out over the first few decades of the 21st century.

APPENDIX

In this study I have attempted to adopt the standpoint of participants in social movement union campaigns. Doing so forced me to turn traditional modes of explaining social movements upside down. Instead of trying to explain mobilization, its development, and its outcomes in terms of the presence or absence of facilitating factors, adopting the standpoint of participants forced me to see the world as it presented itself to participants: as a series of problems to be solved or obstacles to be overcome. This does not mean that I necessarily agreed with participants about the nature of the obstacles that had to be overcome or the problems that needed solving. Movement participants, activists, and leaders can misunderstand their situations, and sociologists do not have to accept the views of the people they study uncritically. Neither, incidentally, does my approach mean studying only movements one likes. The sociologist ought to be able to view the world in terms of obstacles and attempts to overcome them even when studying movements for which personally he or she has nothing but distaste. What adopting the standpoint of participants always does mean is that the analyst must try to understand movement actors in their contexts: how movement actors are going about trying to formulate and achieve their identities, means, and ends, what the difficulties are in the process, and how actors respond to the difficulties.

Further, it must be stressed that I took the standpoint, not of movement participants in general, but of particularly situated actors within the movement. In this study, I chose to take the standpoint of the local union organizer because it allowed me to look "down" at the nitty-gritty tasks of organizing itself, "laterally" at conflicts and difficulties within the local union organization, and "up" at local union leaders and larger questions of strategy and power. This was not the only standpoint that could have been taken. It would be equally possible to take the standpoint of rank-and-file workers in organizing campaigns or the standpoint of local union presidents. However, the choice of standpoints does limit the gaze of the sociologist in different ways, and to study a movement fully one must be able to distinguish among — and pay attention to — different levels of action: the micro, or interpersonal, level; the meso, or organizational, level; and the macro level, or level of social and political power. One must also be able to examine embedded processes at these three levels over time, in their situationally and historically specific contexts. Only by doing this, I felt, could I hope to understand the *relationships* between each of these levels within particular instances of struggle. Hence my choice of standpoint was not random; it was chosen to give me access to all three levels of action.

As an ethnographic study of collective action, this research simply could not have been done without employing participant observation as a method of study. I learned this lesson, interestingly enough, by at first attempting to base the project primarily on interviews with union officials and workers. When I first arrived on the scene in early 1997, the Megacorp campaign was in its final months. This conflict drew my interest as an exciting example of service sector union struggle, and even though I had not been present for the duration of the campaign, I thought it would be possible to understand it by interviewing participants. In the spring of 1997, therefore, I conducted semistructured interviews with officials and staff from Locals A and B and with three or four rank-and-file workers who were active in the campaign.

The tapes of these interviews contain almost nothing of real value. The interviews gave me a basic familiarity with the chronology of the campaign and very little else. I got no information about the internal conflicts between the locals, no sense of how difficult it had been to bring workers to the point where they were willing to commit to a three-day unfair labor practices strike, no inkling of the failure of the "bargaining to organize" strategy, and no understanding of the significance of the union's coordinated mobilization as groundwork for an unfair labor practices strike; nor did I even grasp the strategic importance of the strike as one over unfair labor practices rather than economic issues.

Instead, the story that emerged from these early interviews was mainly a glowing tale about how the heroic Megacorp workers were determined to stand up to the company for as long as it took to win justice. This was a story I could read in any of a hundred union press releases, flyers, or T-shirt slogans. It was the story the union presented to the media as part of its own campaign strategy rather than the story of *how* the campaign worked or didn't work. To be sure, I think that many of the Megacorp workers are indeed heroic, but what was obscured in the accounts I was getting were the nitty-gritty details of the often extremely conflictual and difficult relationships between union staff and rank-and-file workers, between rank-and-file leaders and their co-workers, and between staff and officials from the three locals.

In retrospect I can see several reasons why my respondents told me the story they did. One problem was that because I initially lacked any deep knowledge or understanding of union organizing or its difficulties, I simply did not know what questions to ask. The people I was interviewing would often ask me what I wanted to know about the campaign, but at this early stage I couldn't tell them that I was interested — for example — in the dilemmas of coordinating the efforts of three local unions. Perhaps if I had been smarter or more thoughtful it would have occurred to me right away that this might have posed problems for the campaign that would have occupied a good deal of the efforts of the campaign staff, but sadly, it did not!

Another problem was that my respondents had their own interest in presenting the achievements of collective action as if they were completely driven by the workers themselves rather than involving difficult and conflictual processes of internal struggle. For union officials and organizers, presenting collective action as unproblematically driven by the militancy of the workers they represent, and underplaying their own role, is a standard way of talking publicly about militant rank-and-file action. The organizer does not want to stand up in public and say, in effect, "*I* did this"—because the success of rank-and-file collective action really depends on the perception that it comes from the workers themselves. The reality is that often the impetus comes from the union and that in many cases, without the union's organizing efforts, workers might not act collectively at all.

A third dynamic that initially limited my ability to learn about the Megacorp campaign through interviews was the issue of my status: Was I an outsider or an insider? A few officials, Janet Zimmerman and Joe Reilly in particular, treated me as an insider from the start and would probably have told me anything I wanted to know from the beginning, had I known how to ask. I owed their openness to the fact that Stephen Herzenberg, a former student of a member of my dissertation committee, was the director of the Keystone Research Center in Harrisburg, Pennsylvania. Keystone is a progressive think tank funded primarily by Pennsylvania unions; an SEIU official sits on its board. Herzenberg was a known and trusted friend of Zimmerman and Reilly, and his recommendation guaranteed me a certain level of trust from the outset. But even though Zimmerman told her staff that it was all right to talk to me, others within the union who did not know Herzenberg treated me, understandably enough, as an outsider. And as an outsider, I was entitled to know only the sort of information that the union would ordinarily make public. This was particularly clear when I interviewed Joan Hardy for the first time. At one point she mentioned that she was just getting

off the ground with an organizing campaign at a nursing home. "Wow,"
I said. "That's great! Where is it?" "Well," she said, "I'm afraid I can't
tell you where it is." To her, I was a Berkeley graduate student in
Pittsburgh, interested in the labor movement. Zimmerman had said it
was okay to talk to me, but still she couldn't be sure whether I was really
a friend of the movement.

As it turned out, the nursing home was Rosemont, and two weeks
later I was an intern working with Hardy. We never spoke again about
her refusal to tell me where her campaign was, but once I came on board
as an intern, my status was completely different and there was no longer
any reason to keep secrets. In the end, Hardy became an extremely valuable informant for the study, and she even read drafts of several chapters.
Had I remained on the outside as an interviewer, this kind of access to all
levels of the organization would have been impossible.

I didn't understand these issues too clearly at the time, but I did
understand that my interviews weren't leading anywhere. Frustrated
with my inability to understand the Megacorp campaign in any deep
way, I soon realized that I desperately needed to develop a frame of reference. I needed to understand organizing better, and the only way that
could happen was through direct observation. In May 1997, therefore, I
called Janet Zimmerman, explained my problem, and asked her permission to conduct participant observation within the union. In response,
she proposed that I come to work for the union as an intern. That way I
could get the hands-on experience I needed and learn about the union
from the inside.

This first stint as an intern at Local A lasted from the beginning of
June 1997 through the end of September. During this period, I attended
Rosemont's weekly organizing meetings, but most of my time was spent
working on the Allegheny County contract campaign discussed in
Chapter 5. The first several weeks were spent working with the other
two interns to update the union's membership records and build a data-
base of work site contacts. The rest of the summer was spent organizing
the events and actions of the campaign itself. My fellow interns and I

first met with stewards and contact people from about two dozen work sites to plan the lunchtime work site meetings, which we conducted after being trained by Joe Reilly. Finally, we organized and attended all of the rallies at commissioners' meetings, "Rolling Thunder Week," and the large "Solidarity Day" rally.

My experience during these four months highlights both the advantages and the limitations of participant observation. On one hand, my daily presence in the office during these first weeks enabled me to learn more about the union, particularly about the internal tensions between Fred Jones and several more forward-looking staff, than I could ever have learned from the outside. My realization at this point that Local A was internally torn between backward and progressive elements was initially very disappointing, since from the outside I had thought Local A to be a shining example of the new unionism. Only gradually did I realize that this kind of internal conflict and tension was a central element of the transition from the old unionism to the new and that I was incredibly lucky to be able to study it directly. Moreover, working as an organizer gave me direct access to workers, from whom I heard uncensored versions of how they viewed their relationship with the union as well as their work situations. Because participant observation allowed me to observe firsthand the union's internal dynamics as well as its relationship with workers it represented, during this first period of fieldwork I began to grasp the importance of organizational legacies as a constraint on the new unionism, specifically on the social movement aspects of the Allegheny County contract campaign.

In particular, I gradually began to realize that my very presence as an intern was part of the union's attempt to overcome the resistance of Fred Jones to grassroots mobilization without confronting him directly. This became clear as the interns began to observe firsthand Jones's independence and apparent ability to defy the directives of the union's president. At my first meeting with rank-and-file leaders at one of the Kane centers (described in Chapter 5 as a difficult meeting during which I took the

brunt of workers' anger), one of the things that the workers angrily complained about was Jones's lack of responsiveness. They claimed that he
didn't return phone calls and that when they filed grievances often they
would never hear back from him about the result. When I returned to
the office, I discovered that the other two interns had heard a similar
litany of complaints about Jones. Together, we went to see Joe Reilly, the
staff director, to report the problem. Immediately it became clear that we
had nothing to tell Reilly that he didn't already know. "Look," he said,
rather downcast. "These are problems that are not going to get solved in
this campaign, and may never be solved. I think you have to emphasize
that whatever complaints people have about Jones, the only way they're
going to get a new contract, a fair contract, is by being united, by acting
together, and that you're there to help them do that."

The interns thus got the message that the problems with Jones were
long-standing and that we should not think that were going to be able to
come in and reform the union! But a few weeks later, after Jones had
failed to show up to yet another lunchtime work site meeting, the
interns decided to talk to local president Janet Zimmerman. We told her
that Jones was not cooperating and that his behavior was making it
difficult for us to develop the campaign. She did not seem surprised, and
in fact she indicated that we should not expect him to change, but she
promised to talk to him about it. At the end of the conversation I asked,
"Why do you think Jones is so unwilling to get involved in the organizing effort?" Zimmerman replied, "I don't know, Steve, you'll have to ask
him that." The overall impression Zimmerman gave was that she could
neither control Jones nor be responsible for his behavior. She clearly did
not want to discuss the matter further. In the end, I never did discover
definitively what allowed Jones to act as he did and why Zimmerman was
unable or unwilling to control him. I did learn that Jones was a protégé
of the president of the Allegheny County Labor Council, who was himself a longtime political ally of Zimmerman. It's possible that Jones was
protected by these political connections and that taking Jones on would

have caused Zimmerman political headaches at the labor council that she did not want, but this explanation remains somewhat speculative.

If my participant observation in the summer of 1997 revealed how organizational legacies functioned as an obstacle to mobilization, this four-month stint of fieldwork also highlighted several limitations of participant observation. If the study as a whole could not have been conducted without it, neither could it have been completed using *only* participant observation. First there is the issue of timing. As I struggled to understand what I had seen and done in the Allegheny County contract campaign, it became clear that this organizing effort could not be considered by itself — that it was in fact intimately linked to the earlier mobilization against privatization of the Kanes. I found I could not understand one without the other, particularly because it became clear that the success of the contract campaign owed in large part to the earlier success of the struggle against privatization. I had been present at one or two Kane campaign events — in particular several commissioners' meetings where I got to see the rowdy contingent of residents' family members in action. But since this was the extent of my observations, I found it necessary to reconstruct the Kane campaign using other methods: I interviewed the officials and staff of Local A who had driven it, two members of the Alliance for Progressive Action, and several of the clergy who formed the Religious Task Force on the Economy. In addition, I was fortunate that one of the staff members at Local A had made a videotape containing all of the local television news reports of the protests. Finally, I supplemented the interviews and this videotape material by examining the news coverage of Pittsburgh's two major daily newspapers. The result is, unfortunately, less textured than it would have been had I been able to participate in, and observe directly, the organization of this campaign, but the value of extending observations across time outweighs, in my view, the downside of having a blurrier lens with which to examine things that took place in the past.

A second limitation of participant observation highlighted by my field experience in the summer of 1997 has to do with the limitations of

observation itself when there is less to observe than the researcher orig-
inally hopes. I was frustrated with the fact that the union's Rosemont
campaign was limited essentially to a series of meetings. I attended those
meetings, but there was really no grassroots organizing activity going
on. Because the campaign itself was so limiting, I did try to interview
Rosemont workers during that summer but succeeded in interviewing
just five (although I was able to interview five more later on). At the end
of the summer I did not think that Rosemont would find a place in my
study at all.

When I returned for my second four-month stint of participant
observation at Local A at the beginning of June 1998, I was hoping to
work on a follow-up internal organizing drive in the union's Allegheny
County chapter. In the spring of 1998, during a three-day leadership
development training and conference that Local A held for work site
leaders and stewards from its county chapters, Janet Zimmerman and I
had talked about my returning for the summer, and she had mentioned
the idea of doing a comprehensive leadership development campaign in
Allegheny County. I thought that this was very exciting, since it would
have given me the opportunity to compare the 1997 county contract
campaign with a later effort to fix some of the organizational difficulties
in the chapter. However, by the time I returned to the union this idea
had been put on the back burner. Instead, I was assigned to work on the
follow-up organizing campaign at Rosemont. Once again, initially I was
disappointed, since at this point I was thinking of my study as a comparison of two contract campaigns (Allegheny County and Megacorp),
and I wasn't sure how or whether the Rosemont campaign(s) would fit.
Nevertheless, I spent the summer of 1998 working intensively, and
almost exclusively, on the second Rosemont campaign. As described in
Chapter 3, together with another intern, I conducted house visits,
assembled an organizing committee, and met with the committee at
least once a week throughout the campaign. I also participated in informational picketing and leafleting at the facility and helped plan and
coordinate the various collective activities of the campaign.

The Rosemont fieldwork turned out to be central to the study because it made possible a comparison between the two Rosemont campaigns. Because the opportunities for observation and participation had been so limited the first time around, of course, it was necessary to mine the information I gathered during my house visits in 1998 for clues about the failure of the previous year's campaign. This strategy may have its limitations, but like reconstructing the Kane campaign after the fact, even an imperfect comparison is superior to no comparison. Indeed, it was through this over-time comparison between the two campaigns that I discovered the significance of workers' lived experience of business unionism as an obstacle to face-to-face organizing. As my fellow intern and I went knocking on workers' doors and talking to workers in 1998, what immediately impressed both of us was something that had escaped me entirely in 1997: that workers were as worried about the union as they were about management.

Moreover, it was as a participant observer, not as an interviewer or survey researcher, that I could apprehend how the antiunionism of some workers (and the ambivalence of many more) was *rational* — because it was connected to lived experiences of business unionism. What one can learn as a participant is different from what one can learn as an interviewer — and possibly more accurate as well, precisely *because* the researcher is immersed in the social situation under study. In the context of the organizing campaign, I learned the most not from the reasons workers gave for acting or not acting, but rather from the kinds of questions they asked, how they posed their questions, and how they talked about their own histories. In this manner, I believe I was able to uncover not "attitudes" but the relation between people's most deeply held dispositions and their interpretations of their own lived experience.

The way the research on the two Rosemont campaigns developed also highlights the impossibility of coming into the field with a "research design" and adhering to it. This is a commonplace observation in ethnographic research, but it is perhaps worth repeating. When one studies events in the real world, in real time, it is difficult to know what is going to happen but also what is going to be interesting. The researcher cannot say ahead of time that he or she wants to study this or that and then design a project that captures exactly what is planned. This is so not only because as an actor in the real world the ethnographer has to adjust to the opportunities and possibilities that present themselves, but also because until he or she has spent time in the field it may not be clear what is interesting and what is not. A case in point in this respect is that the significance of the first, failed campaign at Rosemont did not become apparent until the following year, when I found myself working on a follow-up to it. Until then I had been going to write Rosemont off as uninteresting.

The Rosemont fieldwork I did in 1998 was important not only for its own sake but also because by working intensively on this campaign and reflecting on the differences between it and the failed campaign of the previous summer, I developed the crucial perspective on nursing home organizing, the frame of reference that I needed to understand the Megacorp campaign through the materials that were available after the fact. In the winter of 1998–99 I set about interviewing (and in some cases reinterviewing) the leadership and staff of Locals A and B, rank-and-file leaders from both locals who had been member organizers in the Megacorp campaign, and two staff people from the international union. I conducted 23 interviews: 10 staff members (5 from each of the two locals), 11 rank-and-file workers, and the 2 international officials.

This time the interviews were completely different. The shortest of these interviews was two hours, and several lasted up to five hours and had to be conducted in two sessions. One major difference was that by now I had been around for several years, I had been working for Local A, and I had written several policy reports for the Keystone Research Center that had directly benefited both Locals A and B. So I had a level of credibility that I did not have when I first arrived on the scene. (This credibility also helped me gain access to storage boxes of internal files from Locals A and B.) But equally importantly, perhaps, in these interviews, unlike my first attempts, I was able to probe deeply into the difficult and problematic areas of the campaign — not only because I understood in general some of the difficulties of organizing nursing home workers but also because I had a deep understanding of the specific context: in particular, Local A and its internal tensions and problems.

Unlike the first round of interviews, in which general questions about the campaign had elicited generic, often platitudinous responses, this time I was able to ask about specific problems. Earlier, when asking questions like "What were some of the problems or difficulties of the campaign?" I got answers that focused entirely on the company, as if the organizational effort of the campaign itself had been completely unproblematic. Now, however, because I knew what the fault lines of conflict were already, I could ask about specific issues and problems — such as how Megacorp workers experiences' in the first two rounds of coordinated bargaining affected their level of militancy in the third, or about the difficulties of coordinating activities involving shops from all three locals. Such questions often yielded extraordinarily detailed responses, in some cases hour-long discussions of a single issue or dilemma. The key lay in knowing what kinds of problems to ask about, and this knowledge could have been gained only through participant observation.

Substantively, in my second round of interviews I was able to probe the significance of the unfair labor practices strike and thus begin to understand, not only how the inherited legal framework for collective bargaining functioned as an obstacle to union success in the Megacorp campaign, but also how the union overcame it. Initially I had seen the company's use of permanent replacements as a purely *negative* event for the union, missing its positive significance for the campaign: the way it allowed the union to broaden the struggle and to transform its cause into an appealing issue of justice that not only had some legal bite but also outraged the workers and — crucially — their local communities and important political actors at the local, state, and federal levels.

I have protected the confidentiality of all of the individuals mentioned in this study by using pseudonyms for everyone except public figures.

Rosemont Pavilion is of course a fictitious name. Interestingly, the president of Local B didn't care if I used real names or not, but the staff of Local A requested that I not identify their local or staff directly. They did understand that, even though the names were changed, anyone close to the SEIU would probably be able to identify the local and some of the characters, and they were comfortable with this arrangement.

NOTES

PREFACE

1. Quoted in Roy Lubove, *Twentieth-Century Pittsburgh: The Post-Steel Era* (Pittsburgh, Pa.: University of Pittsburgh Press, 1996), p. 1.

2. U.S. Bureau of the Census, *County Business Patterns* (Washington, D.C.: U.S. Department of Commerce, 1974–93).

3. See, for example, John Hoerr, *And the Wolf Finally Came: The Decline of the American Steel Industry* (Pittsburgh, Pa.: University of Pittsburgh Press, 1988); William Serrin, *Homestead: The Glory and Tragedy of an American Steel Town* (New York: Times Books, 1992); Dale Hathaway, *Can Workers Have a Voice? The Politics of Deindustrialization in Pittsburgh* (Pittsburgh: Pennsylvania State University Press, 1993); Lubove, *Twentieth-Century Pittsburgh*.

4. Serrin, *Homestead*, pp. 293–95.

5. Jeremy Rifkin, *The End of Work: The Decline of the Global Labor Force and the Dawn of the Post-Market Era* (New York: Putnam, 1995); Stanley Aronowitz and William DeFazio, *The Jobless Future: Sci-Tech and the Dogma of Work* (Minneapolis: University of Minnesota Press, 1994).

6. Southwestern Pennsylvania Economic Redevelopment Committee, *Pittsburgh Labor Market Study* (Pittsburgh: Southwestern Pennsylvania Economic Redevelopment Committee, 1995).

7. U.S. Bureau of Labor Statistics, "Pittsburgh Area Jobs up 1.8 Percent

since First Quarter 1998," 2000, retrieved from ftp://ftp.bls.gov/pub/special .requests/philadelphia/cesqpit.txt.

8. U.S. Bureau of Labor Statistics, "Current Employment Statistics," 2000, retrieved from ftp://ftp.bls.gov/pub/special.requests/philadelphia/fax_9529.txt.

9. U.S. Bureau of Labor Statistics, "Metropolitan Area at a Glance," 2003, retrieved from www.bls.gov/eag/eag.pa_pittsburgh.htm.

10. Stephen Cohen and John Zysman, *Manufacturing Matters: The Myth of the Post-Industrial Economy* (New York: Basic Books, 1987).

11. Barry Bluestone and Bennett Harrison, *The Deindustrialization of America: Plant Closings, Community Abandonment, and the Dismantling of Basic Industry* (New York: Basic Books, 1982); Robert Reich, *The Work of Nations: Preparing Ourselves for 21st Century Capitalism* (New York: Knopf, 1991); Harley Shaiken, "Advanced Manufacturing and Mexico: A New International Division of Labor?" *Latin American Research Review* 29, no. 2 (1994): 39–72; Steven Dandaneau, *A Town Abandoned: Flint, Michigan Confronts Deindustrialization* (Albany: SUNY Press, 1996).

12. Edna Bonacich, "Reflections on Union Activism," *Contemporary Sociology* 27, no. 2 (1998): 129–32; see also Edna Bonacich, "Intense Challenges, Tentative Possibilities: Organizing Immigrant Garment Workers in Los Angeles," in *Organizing Immigrants: The Challenge for Unions in Contemporary California*, ed. Ruth Milkman (Ithaca, N.Y.: ILR Press, 2000), pp. 130–49, but for an alternate view, see Ruth Milkman and Kent Wong, "Organizing Immigrant Workers: Case Studies from Southern California," in *Rekindling the Movement: Labor's Quest for Relevance in the 21st Century*, ed. Lowell Turner, Harry Katz, and Richard Hurd (Ithaca, N.Y.: Cornell University Press, 2001), pp. 99–128.

13. Susan C. Eaton, *Pennsylvania's Nursing Homes: Promoting Quality Care and Quality Jobs* (Harrisburg, Pa.: Keystone Research Center, 1997).

14. Gooloo Wunderlich, Frank Sloan, and Carolyne Davice, eds., *Nursing Staff in Hospitals and Nursing Homes: Is It Adequate?* (Washington, D.C.: National Academy Press, 1996).

15. Eaton, *Pennsylvania's Nursing Homes*.

16. Service Employees International Union, *Caring Till It Hurts* (Washington, D.C.: Service Employees International Union, 1997).

17. See, for example, Dandaneau, *A Town Abandoned*, and Kathryn Dudley, *End of the Line: Lost Jobs, New Lives in Postindustrial America* (Chicago: University of Chicago Press, 1994).

18. Cited in Howard Kimeldorf, *Battling for American Labor: Wobblies, Craft*

Workers, and the Making of the Union Movement (Berkeley: University of California Press, 1999), p. 167.

19. Milkman, *Organizing Immigrants.*

CHAPTER 1. INTRODUCTION

1. Ruth Milkman, "The New Labor Movement: Possibilities and Limits," *Contemporary Sociology* 27, no. 2 (1998): 125–29; Fernando Gapasin and Michael Yates, "Organizing the Unorganized: Will Promises Become Practices?" *Monthly Review* 49, no. 3 (1997): 46–62.

2. Michael Goldfield, *The Decline of Organized Labor in the United States* (Chicago: University of Chicago Press, 1987); Morris Kleiner, "Intensity of Management Resistance: Understanding the Decline of Unionization in the Private Sector," *Journal of Labor Research* 22 (2001): 519–40.

3. Kate Bronfenbrenner and Tom Juravich, "It Takes More Than House Calls: Organizing to Win with a Comprehensive Union Building Strategy," in *Organizing to Win: New Research on Union Strategies*, edited by Kate Bronfenbrenner et al. (Ithaca, N.Y.: ILR Press, 1998), pp. 18–36.

4. Quoted in Paul Buhle, *Taking Care of Business: Samuel Gompers, George Meany, Lane Kirkland, and the Tragedy of American Labor* (New York: Monthly Review Press, 1999), p. 196.

5. James Gross, *Broken Promise: The Subversion of U.S. Labor Relations Policy, 1947–1994* (Philadelphia: Temple University Press, 1995); Richard Rothstein, "Toward a More Perfect Union: New Labor's Hard Road," *American Prospect* 26 (1996): 47–53; Richard Freeman, "Why Are Unions Faring So Poorly in NLRB Representation Elections?" in *Challenges and Choices Facing American Labor*, ed. Thomas Kochan (Cambridge, Mass.: MIT Press, 1985), pp. 46–64; Sheldon Friedman et al., eds., *Restoring the Promise of American Labor Law* (Ithaca, N.Y.: ILR Press, 1994).

6. William Cooke, *Organizing and Public Policy: Failure to Secure First Contracts* (Kalamazoo, Mich.: W. E. Upjohn Institute for Employment Research, 1985); Kate Bronfenbrenner, "Employer Behavior in Certification Elections and First-Contract Campaigns: Implications for Labor Law Reform," in Friedman et al., *Restoring the Promise*, pp. 75–89.

7. The law lists 12 indicia of supervisory status, only one of which need be exercised (albeit with "independent judgment") for workers to be considered

supervisors without collective bargaining rights. In recent years, management attorneys and antiunion consultants have developed sophisticated strategies to convince the NLRB that more and more professionals and quasi-professionals are supervisors. In nursing homes, for example, RNs and Licensed Practical Nurses (LPNs) are often given token "supervisory" tasks, or revised job descriptions, simply to try to convince the NLRB that they "supervise" nurses' aides and hence are exempt from collective bargaining rights. The federal courts have made this strategy easier by gradually broadening their interpretation of who counts as a supervisor for purposes of bargaining unit formation.

8. Ian Robinson, "Neoliberal Restructuring and U.S. Unions: Toward Social Movement Unionism?" *Critical Sociology* 26, no. 1 (2000): 127.

9. George Strauss, "Is the New Deal System Collapsing? With What Might It Be Replaced?" *Industrial Relations* 34 (1995): 329–49.

10. Eileen Appelbaum and Rosemary Batt, *The New American Workplace: Transforming Work Systems in the United States* (Boston: South End Press, 1994); Stephen Herzenberg, John Alic, and Howard Wial, *New Rules for a New Economy: Employment and Opportunity in Postindustrial America* (Ithaca, N.Y.: ILR Press, 1998); Thomas A. Kochan, Harry C. Katz, and Robert B. McKersie, *The Transformation of American Industrial Relations* (New York: Basic Books, 1986); David Levine, *Reinventing the Workplace* (Washington, D.C.: Brookings Institution, 1995); Charles Sabel, "Bootstrapping Reform: Rebuilding Firms, the Welfare State, and Unions," *Politics and Society* 23, no. 1 (1995): 5–40; Harley Shaiken, Steven Lopez, and Isaac Mankita, "Two Routes to Team Production: Saturn and Chrysler Compared," *Industrial Relations* 36 (1997): 17–45.

11. Robinson, "Neolibereal Restructuring"; Dunlop Commission [Commission on the Future of Worker-Management Relations], *Fact-Finding Report* (Washington, D.C.: U.S. Department of Labor and U.S. Department of Commerce, 1994).

12. David Brody, "Criminalizing the Rights of Labor," *Dissent* 42, no. 3 (1995): 363–67; Friedman et al., *Restoring the Promise*; William Gould, *Agenda for Reform: The Future of Employment Relationships and the Law* (Cambridge, Mass.: MIT Press, 1993); Strauss, "Is the New Deal System Collapsing?"; Paul Weiler, *Governing the Workplace: The Future of Labor and Employment Law* (Cambridge, Mass.: Harvard University Press, 1990), and "Promises to Keep: Securing Workers' Rights to Self-Organization under the NLRA," *Harvard Law Review* 96 (1983): 1769–1827; Michael Yates, *Power on the Job: The Legal Rights of Working People* (Boston: South End Press, 1994).

13. Dorothy Sue Cobble, "Organizing the Post-Industrial Work Force:

Some Examples from the History of Waitress Unionism," *Industrial and Labor Relations Review* 44 (1991): 419–36; James Green and Chris Tilly, "Service Unionism: Directions for Organizing" *Labor Law Journal* 38 (1987): 486–95; Herzenberg, Alic, and Wial, *New Rules for a New Economy;* Howard Wial, "The Emerging Structure of Low-Wage Services," *Rutgers Law Review* 45 (1993): 671–738. Some examples of this idea: SEIU Local 250 in California and AFSCME Local 1199C in Philadelphia both work with multiemployer groups in the nursing home industry to provide training and placement for nurses' aides.

14. Susan C. Eaton, *Pennsylvania's Nursing Homes: Promoting Quality Care and Quality Jobs* (Harrisburg, Pa.: Keystone Research Center, 1997); Stephen Herzenberg, testimony before Pittsburgh Area Religious Task Force on the Economy, March 1997.

15. Other "full-service" proposals include ideas about providing general legal assistance on employment issues to nonmembers or "associate members." I am not impressed with this idea because, as previously noted, U.S. at-will employment law offers so few protections that union lawyers simply would not be able to help most people who have been treated unfairly. Other proposals, such as the idea of sponsoring nonbargaining activities like family counseling (see Strauss, "Is the New Deal System Collapsing?") or portable health insurance and retirement benefits (see Edward Potter, "Love's Labor Lost? Changes in the U.S. Environment and Declining Private Sector Unionism," *Journal of Labor Research* 22 (2001): 321–34; also see Charles Heckscher, "Living with Flexibility," in *Rekindling the Movement: Labor's Quest for Relevance in the 21st Century*, ed. Lowell Turner, Harry Katz, and Richard Hurd (Ithaca, N.Y.: Cornell University Press, 2001), pp. 59–81, are interesting, but while they might encourage people to sign up for these needed services, they do nothing to change the fundamental power imbalance between workers and employers on the shop floor.

16. Quoted in Jeremy Brecher and Tim Costello, "A 'New Labor Movement' in the Shell of the Old?" in *A New Labor Movement for the New Century*, ed. Gregory Mantsios (New York: Monthly Review Press, 1998), p. 26.

17. Robinson, "Neoliberal Restructuring."

18. Ibid., p. 25.

19. Ibid., p. 24.

20. Stephen Greenhouse, "In Biggest Drive since 1937, Union Gains a Victory," *New York Times*, February 26, 1999; see also Linda Delp and Katie Quan, "Homecare Organizing in California: An Analysis of a Successful Strategy," *Labor Studies Journal* 27 (2002): 1–23.

21. Melanie Payne, "Unions Gain in Public Sector as Private Membership Drops," *Sacramento Bee*, March 11, 2002.

22. Tamara Kay, "Bypassing the Captured State: Globalization, Labor Law, and Union Organizing Strategies in Mexico and the United States," paper presented at the annual meeting of the International Sociological Association, Montreal, July 1998.

23. Larry Adams, "Transforming Unions and Building a Movement," in Mantsios, *A New Labor Movement*, pp. 202–15; Paul Johnston, *Success While Others Fail: Social Movement Unionism and the Public Workplace* (Ithaca, N.Y.: ILR Press, 1994); Paul Johnston, "The Resurgence of Labor as a Citizenship Movement in the New Labor Relations Environment," *Critical Sociology* 26 (2000): 139–60; Stuart Eimer, "From 'Business Unionism' to 'Social Movement Unionism': The Case of the AFL-CIO Milwaukee County Labor Council," *Labor Studies Journal* 24, no. 2 (1999): 63–74; Lowell Turner and Richard Hurd, "Building Social Movement Unionism: The Transformation of the American Labor Movement," in Turner, Katz, and Hurd, *Rekindling the Movement*, pp. 9–26; Bruce Nissen, "The Recent Past and Near Future of Private Sector Unionism in the U.S.: An Appraisal," *Journal of Labor Research* 24 (2003): 323–38; Robinson, "Neoliberal Restructuring."

24. Bronfenbrenner and Juravich, "It Takes More."

25. Bronfenbrenner, "Employer Behavior"; Steve Early, "Membership Based Organizing," in Mantsios, *A New Labor Movement*, pp. 82–103; Janice Fine, "Moving Innovations from the Margins to the Center," in Mantsios, *A New Labor Movement*, pp. 119–46; Sam Gindin, "Notes on Labor at the End of the Century: Starting Over?" in *Rising from the Ashes? Labor in the Age of "Global" Capitalism*, ed. Ellen M. Wood, Peter Meiksins, and Michael Yates (New York: Monthly Review Press, 1998), pp. 190–202; Josephine LeBeau and Kevin Lynch, "Successful Organizing at the Local Level: The Experience of AFSCME District Council 1707," in Mantsios, *A New Labor Movement*, pp. 104–18; Stephen Lerner, "Taking the Offensive, Turning the Tide," in Mantsios, *A New Labor Movement*, pp. 69–81; Linda Markowitz, "Union Presentation of Self and Worker Participation in Organizing Campaigns," *Sociological Perspectives* 38 (1995): 437, and *Worker Activism after Successful Union Organizing* (Armonk, N.Y.: M. E. Sharpe, 2000).

26. Roger Waldinger et al., "Helots No More: A Case Study of the Justice for Janitors Campaign in Los Angeles," in Bronfenbrenner et al., *Organizing to Win*, pp. 102–20; Stewart Acuff, "Expanded Roles for the Central Labor Council: The View from Atlanta," in *Which Direction for Organized Labor? Essays on*

Organizing, Outreach, and Internal Transformations, ed. Bruce Nissen (Detroit: Wayne State University Press, 1999), pp. 133–42; Larry Cohen and Steve Early, "Defending Workers' Rights in the Global Economy: The CWA Experience," in Nissen, *Which Direction for Organized Labor,* pp. 143–64.

27. Andy Banks, "The Power and Promise of Community Unionism," *Labor Research Review* 10 (1992): 17–31; James Craft, "The Community as a Source of Power," *Journal of Labor Research* 11 (1990): 145–60; Johnston, *Success While Others Fail;* Ruth Needleman, "Building Relationships for the Long Haul: Unions and Community Organizing Groups Working Together to Organize Low-Wage Workers," in Bronfenbrenner et al., *Organizing to Win,* pp. 71–86; Ronald Peters and Theresa Merrill, "Clergy and Religious Persons' Role in Organizing at O'Hare Airport and St. Joseph Medical Center," in Bronfenbrenner et al., *Organizing to Win,* pp. 164–77; Katherine Sciacchitano, "Finding the Community in the Union and the Union in the Community: The First-Contract Campaign at Steeltech," in Bronfenbrenner et al., *Organizing to Win,* pp. 150–63; Fernando Gapasin and Howard Wial, "The Role of Central Labor Councils in Union Organizing in the 1990s," in Bronfenbrenner et al., *Organizing to Win,* pp. 54–68; Philip McLewin, "The Concerted Voice of Labor and the Suburbanization of Capital: Fragmentation of the Community Labor Council," in Nissen, *Which Direction for Organized Labor?* pp. 113–32; Acuff, "Expanded Roles."

28. Johnston, *Success While Others Fail.*

29. Bronfenbrenner and Juravich, "It Takes More."

30. The argument that social movement unionism is a viable survival strategy for labor may need to be qualified by the issue of sector. In the preface to this study, I made this distinction in justifying my decision to study a service sector union rather than a union attempting to organize manufacturing industries. My argument was that manufacturing industries can be often directly subject to capital mobility in ways that many kinds of service occupations are not. Bonacich has made this argument with respect to garment workers; see Edna Bonacich, "Reflections on Union Activism," *Contemporary Sociology* 27, no. 2 (1998): 129–32. For these workers, she is not certain that increased militancy and grassroots activism is the solution. When they organize, she says, manufacturers move offshore, often to countries where labor organizing involves very real risks to life and limb. For these workers, adopting a class-conscious, social movement form of unionism doesn't address this fundamental problem. Therefore, although proponents of social movement unionism often present this strategy for labor in general, it might well be really effective only for service sector (or otherwise

nonmobile) occupations. It is easy to forget that the plant-closing movement in the 1980s and early 1990s was quite successful in generating grassroots protest, community-labor coalitions, and so on, without managing to save many factories from closure. In Pittsburgh, tens of thousands of displaced steelworkers took to the streets in the late 1980s to try to save several plants, to no avail. The lesson: when capital has the ability to move, and wants to move, militancy loses just as completely as concession bargaining. It is worth noting here also that this conception of social movement unionism — as rooted in postindustrial sectors rather than in heavy industry — turns traditional understandings of the labor movement upside down. Class-conscious unionism has always been associated with industrial workers, who have traditionally been viewed as the "real" working class. This view is so strong that it has led social theorists like Alain Touraine and the late Alberto Melucci to assume that the advent of "postindustrial" society necessarily means the end of labor as a significant social movement. See Alain Touraine, *Post-Industrial Society: Tomorrow's Social History. Classes, Conflicts and Culture in the Programmed Society* (New York: Random House, 1971); Alberto Melucci, *Nomads of the Present: Social Movements and Individual Needs in Contemporary Society* (Philadelphia: Temple University Press, 1989).

31. For an example of the kind of comparative case study approach I'm calling for, see Ruth Milkman and Kent Wong, "Organizing Immigrant Workers: Case Studies from Southern California," in Turner, Katz, and Hurd, *Rekindling the Movement*, pp. 99–128.

32. All names have been changed with the exception of the names of several public officials. The names of the private sector nursing homes involved in these campaigns have also been changed.

33. Lowell Turner, "Rank and File Participation in Organizing at Home and Abroad," in Bronfenbrenner et al., *Organizing to Win*, pp. 123–34.

34. Kim Voss and Rachel Sherman, "Breaking the Iron Law of Oligarchy: Union Revitalization in the American Labor Movement," *American Journal of Sociology* 106 (2002): 303–49.

35. Bill Fletcher, Jr., and Richard Hurd, "Beyond the Organizing Model: The Transformation Process in Local Unions," in Bronfenbrenner et al., *Organizing to Win*, p. 43.

36. Roger Waldinger and Claudia Der-Martirosian, "Immigrant Workers and American Labor: Challenge . . . or Disaster?" in *Organizing Immigrants: The Challenge for Unions in Contemporary California*, ed. Ruth Milkman (Ithaca, N.Y.: ILR Press, 2000), pp. 49–80.

37. Miriam Wells, "Immigration and Unionization in the San Francisco Hotel Industry," in Milkman, *Organizing Immigrants*, p. 119.

38. Ibid, p. 120.

39. Ibid., pp. 119–20.

40. See, for example, Daniel Cornfield et al., "In the Community or in the Union? The Impact of Community Involvement on Nonunion Worker Attitudes about Unionizing," in Bronfenbrenner et al., *Organizing to Win*, pp. 247–58, and Roger Weikle, Hoyt Wheeler, and John McClendon, "A Comparative Case Study of Union Success and Failure," in Bronfenbrenner et al., *Organizing to Win*, 197–212, for brief summaries.

41. Eva Weinbaum, "Organizing Labor in an Era of Contingent Work and Globalization," in Nissen, *Which Direction for Organized Labor?* p. 47.

42. Rick Fantasia, *Cultures of Solidarity: Consciousness, Action, and Contemporary American Workers* (Berkeley: University of California Press, 1988), p. 7.

43. Fine, "Moving Innovations"; Adams, "Transforming Unions"; Michael Eisenscher, "Critical Juncture: Unionism at the Crossroads," in Nissen, *Which Direction for Organized Labor?* pp. 217–46.

44. Voss and Sherman, "Breaking the Iron Law"; Fletcher and Hurd, "Beyond the Organizing Model."

45. Dan Clawson, "Making a Meaningful Labor Movement," *Tikkun* 9, no. 4 (1994): 41–44.

46. Voss and Sherman, "Breaking the Iron Law."

47. But see Johnston, *Success While Others Fail*, for an argument about how effective framing and use of the media helped a public sector strike succeed despite being organizationally weak.

48. Voss and Sherman, "Breaking the Iron Law"; Fletcher and Hurd, "Beyond the Organizing Model."

49. Fletcher and Hurd, "Beyond the Organizing Model."

50. Ibid., p. 43. See also Bill Fletcher and Richard W. Hurd, "Overcoming Obstacles to Transformation: Challenges on the Way to a New Unionism," in Turner, Katz, and Hurd, *Rekindling the Movement*, pp. 182–208.

51. Brody, "Criminalizing the Rights of Labor"; Friedman et al., *Restoring the Promise*; Gould, *Agenda for Reform*; Strauss, "Is the New Deal System Collapsing?"; Weiler, *Governing the Workplace*; Yates, *Power on the Job*.

52. Rothstein, "Toward a More Perfect Union."

53. Barbara Kingsolver, *Holding the Line: Women in the Great Arizona Mining Strike of 1983* (Ithaca, N.Y.: ILR Press, 1989); Julius Getman, *The Betrayal of*

Local 14 (Ithaca, N.Y.: ILR Press, 1997); Peter Rachleff, *Hard Times in the Heartland* (Boston: South End Press, 1993).

54. Edna Bonacich, "Intense Challenges, Tentative Possibilities: Organizing Immigrant Garment Workers in Los Angeles," in Milkman, *Organizing Immigrants*, pp. 130–49.

55. Catherine Fisk, Daniel Mitchell, and Christopher Erickson, "Union Representation of Immigrant Janitors in Southern California: Economic and Legal Challenges," in Milkman, *Organizing Immigrants*, pp. 199–224.

56. Tom Juravich and Kate Bronfenbrenner, *Ravenswood: The Steelworkers' Victory and the Revival of American Labor* (Ithaca, N.Y.: ILR Press, 1999).

57. The SEIU's organization of 70,000 home care workers in southern California and the CWA's organization of thousands of airline ticket takers represent exceptions. In these cases, a non–shop floor strategy was both necessary and possible because workers were organized in large, geographically dispersed bargaining units.

58. See Dan Clawson, *The Next Upsurge: Labor and the New Social Movements* (Ithaca, N.Y.: ILR Press, 2003), for a recent argument that labor revitalization must take the form of a rapid upsurge in response to radically changed conditions, rather than gradual recovery. While such an upsurge is always possible, the case studies presented in this book show that incremental organization of a new industry via social movement unionism is also possible.

INTRODUCTION TO PART I

1. Adrienne Jones, *The National Nursing Home Survey: 1999 Summary* (Washington, D.C.: U.S. Department of Human Services, Centers for Disease Control and Prevention, National Center for Health Statistics, 2002).

2. Tim Diamond, *Making Gray Gold: Narratives of Nursing Home Care* (Chicago: University of Chicago Press, 1992).

3. Gooloo Wunderlich, Frank Sloan, and Carolyne Davice, eds., *Nursing Staff in Hospitals and Nursing Homes: Is It Adequate?* (Washington, D.C.: National Academy Press, 1996); Susan C. Eaton, *Pennsylvania's Nursing Homes: Promoting Quality Care and Quality Jobs* (Harrisburg, Pa.: Keystone Research Center, 1997).

4. Health Care Financing Administration, "Report to Congress: Appropriateness of Minimum Nurse Staffing Standards in Nursing Homes," 2000, retrieved from www.hcfa.gov/medicaid/reports/rp700hmp.html. The federal government has recently concluded, on the basis of this comprehensive, nine-

year investigation, that the majority of the nation's nursing homes meet their states' minimum staffing standards but still do not have enough staff to ensure the basic safety of nursing home residents.

5. Pennsylvania Department of Health, Annual Inspection Report for 1997, Rosemont Nursing Home.

6. The administrator is the highest-ranked management official in the nursing home.

7. Anthony Oberschall, *Social Conflict and Social Movements* (Englewood Cliffs, N.J.: Prentice Hall, 1973); David Snow, Louis A. Zurcher, Jr., and Sheldon Ekland-Olson, "Social Networks and Social Movements: A Microstructural Approach to Differential Recruitment," *American Sociological Review* 45 (1980): 787–801; Doug McAdam, "Recruitment to High-Risk Activism: The Case of Freedom Summer," *American Journal of Sociology* 92 (1986): 64–90; Roberto Fernandez and Doug McAdam, "Social Networks and Social Movements: Multiorganizational Fields and Recruitment to Mississippi Freedom Summer," *Sociological Forum* 3 (1988): 357–82; Roger Gould, "Collective Action and Network Structure," *American Sociological Review* 58 (1991): 182–96, and "Multiple Networks and Mobilization in the Paris Commune, 1871," *American Sociological Review* 56 (1993): 716–29; Doug McAdam and Ronelle Paulson, "Specifying the Relationship between Social Ties and Activism," *American Journal of Sociology* 99 (1993): 640–67; Karl-Dieter Opp and Christiane Gern, "Dissident Groups, Social Networks, and Spontaneous Cooperation: The East German Revolution of 1989," *American Sociological Review* 58 (1993): 659–80; James A. Kitts, "Not in Our Backyard: Solidarity, Social Networks, and the Ecology of Environmental Mobilization," *Sociological Inquiry* 69 (1999): 551–74, and "Mobilizing in Black Boxes: Social Networks and Participation in Social Movement Organizations," *Mobilization* 5 (2000): 241–57.

8. See Bert Klandermans, "Mobilization and Participation: Social-Psychological Extensions of Resource Mobilization Theory," *American Sociological Review* 49 (1984): 583–600, and "The Formation and Mobilization of Consensus," *International Social Movement Research* 1 (1988): 173–96; see also Bert Klandermans, *The Social Psychology of Protest* (Oxford, England: Blackwell, 1997). Also see David A. Snow and Robert D. Benford, "Ideology, Frame Resistance, and Participant Mobilization," *International Social Movement Research* 1 (1988): 197–218.

9. Mancur Olson, *The Logic of Collective Action: Public Goods and the Theory of Groups* (Cambridge, Mass.: Harvard University Press, 1965); Oberschall, *Social Conflict and Social Movements*; Klandermans, "Mobilization and Participation";

Bert Klandermans and Dirk Oegema, "Campaigning for a Nuclear Freeze: Grassroots Strategies and Local Government in the Netherlands," in *Research in Political Sociology*, ed. Richard Braungart (Greenwich, Conn.: JAI Press, 1987), pp. 305–37. The literature views benefits as either collective (affecting everyone) or selective (accruing only to those who participate). Benefits do not have to be tangible or material but can be intangible, intrinsic, and social — such as the belief that one is doing the morally right thing.

10. Rick Fantasia, *Cultures of Solidarity: Consciousness, Action, and Contemporary American Workers* (Berkeley: University of California Press, 1988); see also Eric Hirsch, "Sacrifice for the Cause: The Impact of Group Processes on Recruitment and Commitment in Social Movements," *American Sociological Review* 55 (1990): 243–54.

CHAPTER 2. "SEE YOU NEXT YEAR"

1. Union organizing within the legal framework of the NLRB has several steps. To proceed to a board-supervised certification election, the union must first show that at least 30 percent of employees in a proposed bargaining unit desire union representation. Workers must indicate their desire to join a union by signing "interest cards." When the union is ready to petition for an election, the cards are turned over to the board, which counts them and decides whether they represent at least 30 percent of the proposed bargaining unit. The employer never sees the cards and has no easy way of knowing who signed them.

2. John Lawler, *Unionization and De-Unionization: Strategy, Tactics, and Outcomes* (Columbia: University of South Carolina Press, 1990); Martin Levitt, *Confessions of a Union Buster* (New York: Crown, 1993); Bruce Kaufman and Paula Stephan, "The Role of Management Attorneys in Union Organizing Campaigns," *Journal of Labor Research* 16 (1995): 439–54.

3. This strategy plagued a second organizing campaign the union was also working on in the summer of 1997. Attorneys for the Central Blood Bank of Allegheny County were able to stretch out the bargaining unit hearing for weeks; the election wasn't held until more than three months after the union had petitioned the NLRB.

4. Rick Fantasia, *Cultures of Solidarity: Consciousness, Action, and Contemporary American Workers* (Berkeley: University of California Press, 1988).

5. In the past, Hewitt's response to organizing activity had always been to

bring in antiunion consultants and begin holding mandatory antiunion meetings as soon as it became aware that union organizers were talking to its employees.

6. I'd wanted to interview more than 10 that summer, but unfortunately the arm's-length nature of Local A's campaign made it impossible to make the necessary contacts. Of the 10 that I did interview, three were core union supporters and the other seven were interested in the union but not active. This is not, therefore, a random sample, so the possibility that the people I interviewed were much more angry at management than other Rosemont workers must be considered. My confidence that this was *not* the case — that, in fact, the grievances described here were nearly universal — stems from the fact that the following summer, as part of the house-visiting strategy of the second campaign, nearly every worker at Rosemont was visited at home (I visited 36 myself.) These house visits revealed without a doubt that the grievances and anger discussed in this section were shared by virtually everyone.

7. See Tim Diamond, *Making Gray Gold: Narratives of Nursing Home Care* (Chicago: University of Chicago Press, 1992), for an excellent discussion of the federally required nurse's aide training, which consists mainly of medical terminology and basic anatomy. Experienced nurses' aides need to employ a whole repertoire of tactics, tricks, and techniques for getting through the day, but they do not learn these from their formal training. Also see Nancy Foner, *The Caregiving Dilemma: Work in an American Nursing Home* (Berkeley: University of California Press, 1994), and Barbara Bowers and Marian Becker, "Nurses' Aides in Nursing Homes: The Relation between Organization and Quality," *Gerontologist* 32 (1992): 360–66.

8. This claim was fully supported by the Department of Health's investigation.

9. Anthony Oberschall, *Social Conflict and Social Movements* (Englewood Cliffs, N.J.: Prentice Hall, 1973); see also Oberschall, "The Decline of the 1960s Social Movements," *Research in Social Movements, Conflicts and Change* 1 (1978): 257–89; Charles Tilly, *From Mobilization to Revolution* (Reading, Mass.: Addison-Wesley, 1978); Doug McAdam, *Political Process and the Development of Black Insurgency, 1930–1970* (Chicago: University of Chicago Press, 1982), "Recruitment to High-Risk Activism: The Case of Freedom Summer," *American Journal of Sociology* 92 (1986): 64–90, and *Freedom Summer* (New York: Oxford University Press, 1988); Bert Klandermans, *The Social Psychology of Protest* (Oxford, England: Blackwell, 1997).

10. Richard Freeman, "Why Are Unions Faring So Poorly in NLRB Representation Elections?" in *Challenges and Choices Facing American Labor*, ed.

Thomas Kochan (Cambridge, Mass.: MIT Press, 1985), pp. 46–64; William Cooke, "The Rising Tide of Discrimination against Union Activists," *Industrial Relations* 24 (1985): 421–42; Robert LaLonde and Bernard Meltzer, "Hard Times for Unions: Another Look at the Significance of Employer Illegalities," *University of Chicago Law Review* 58 (1991): 953–1014; Richard Hurd and Joseph Uehlein, "Patterned Responses to Organizing: Case Studies of the Union Busting Convention," in *Restoring the Promise of American Labor Law*, ed. Sheldon Friedman et al. (Ithaca, N.Y.: ILR Press, 1994), pp. 61–74.

11. Commission for Labor Cooperation, *Plant Closings and Labor Rights: A Report to the Council of Ministers on the Effects of Sudden Plant Closings on Freedom of Association and the Right to Organize in Canada, Mexico, and the United States* (Lanham, Md.: Bernan Press, 1997).

12. William Dickens, "The Effect of Company Campaigns on Certification Elections: Law and Reality Once Again," *Industrial and Labor Relations Review* 36 (1983): 560–75; Richard B. Freeman and Morris Kleiner, "Employer Behavior in the Face of Union Organizing Drives," *Industrial and Labor Relations Review* 43 (1990): 351–65; Richard B. Peterson, Thomas W. Lee, and Barbara Finnegan, "Strategies and Tactics in Union Organizing Campaigns," *Industrial Relations* 31 (1992): 371–81; Kate Bronfenbrenner, "Employer Behavior in Certification Elections and First-Contract Campaigns: Implications for Labor Law Reform," in Friedman et al., *Restoring the Promise*, pp. 75–89; see also Kate Bronfenbrenner and Tom Juravich, "It Takes More Than House Calls: Organizing to Win with a Comprehensive Union-Building Strategy," in *Organizing to Win: New Research on Union Strategies*, ed. Kate Bronfenbrenner et al. (Ithaca, N.Y.: ILR Press, 1998), pp. 18–36.

13. The administrator's note to McMurray was probably an unfair labor practice because it's illegal for an employer to ask workers about their union activity. But in the scheme of things this was not a major violation, and Hardy did not make a formal complaint to the arbitrator.

14. Fantasia, *Cultures of Solidarity*; Eric Hirsch, "Sacrifice for the Cause: The Impact of Group Processes on Recruitment and Commitment in Social Movements," *American Sociological Review* 55 (1990): 243–54.

15. U.S. Bureau of the Census, "1990 Census of Population and Housing," Summary Tape File 3.

16. William J. Puette, *Through Jaundiced Eyes: How the Media Views Organized Labor* (Ithaca, N.Y.: ILR Press, 1992).

17. Trevor Armbrister, *Acts of Vengeance* (New York: Warner Books, 1980);

Brit Hume, *Death and the Mines: Rebellion and Murder in the United Mine Workers* (New York: Grossman, 1971).

18. Linda Markowitz, "Union Presentation of Self and Worker Participation in Organizing Campaigns," *Sociological Perspectives* 38, no. 3 (1995): 437; see also Linda Markowitz, *Worker Activism after Successful Union Organizing* (Armonk, N.Y.: M. E. Sharpe, 2000).

19. Olson, *The Logic of Collective Action: Public Goods and the Theory of Groups* (Cambridge, Mass.: Harvard University Press, 1965); Oberschall, *Social Conflict*; Bert Klandermans, "Mobilization and Participation: Social-Psychological Extensions of Resource Mobilization Theory," *American Sociological Review* 49 (1984): 583–600; Bert Klandermans and Dirk Oegema, "Campaigning for a Nuclear Freeze: Grassroots Strategies and Local Government in the Netherlands," in *Research in Political Sociology*, ed. Richard Braungart (Greenwich, Conn.: JAI Press, 1987), pp. 305–37.

20. Stanley Aronowitz, *False Promises: The Shaping of American Working Class Consciousness* (Durham, N.C.: Duke University Press, 1992); Paul Buhle, *Taking Care of Business: Samuel Gompers, George Meany, Lane Kirkland, and the Tragedy of American Labor* (New York: Monthly Review Press, 1999); Kim Moody, *An Injury to All: The Decline of American Unionism* (New York: Verso, 1988); Michael Eisenscher, "Critical Juncture: Unionism at the Crossroads," in *Which Direction for Organized Labor? Essays on Organizing, Outreach, and Internal Transformations*, ed. Bruce Nissen (Detroit: Wayne State University Press, 1999), pp. 217–46.

CHAPTER 3. "IT'S A UNION"

1. Steve Early, "Membership Based Organizing," in *A New Labor Movement for a New Century*, ed. Gregory Mantsios (New York: Monthly Review Press, 1998), pp. 82–103; Bruce Nissen, "Utilizing the Membership to Organize the Unorganized," in *Organizing to Win: New Research on Union Strategies*, ed. Kate Bronfenbrenner, Sheldon Friedman, Richard W. Hurd, Rudolph A. Oswald, and Ronald L. Seeber (Ithaca, N.Y.: ILR Press, 1998), pp. 135–49.

2. This nursing home, another Hewitt property, was also on the union's list of strategic targets. Our task was to house-visit 25 percent of the workforce and make assessments, which we recorded along with our comments on special forms. When we found strong union supporters, we tried to use snowball techniques to find others. If we found enough, the union would try to form an organ-

izing committee and mount a campaign. Otherwise, the experience would still be valuable training for the interns.

3. See James A. Kitts, "Mobilizing in Black Boxes: Social Networks and Participation in Social Movement Organizations," *Mobilization* 5 (2000): 241–57.

4. Commission for Labor Cooperation, *Plant Closings and Labor Rights: A Report to the Council of Ministers on the Effects of Sudden Plant Closings on Freedom of Association and the Right to Organize in Canada, Mexico, and the United States* (Lanham, Md.: Bernan Press, 1997).

5. This erosion has been most evident since 1980. Between 1945 and 1980, there was no year in which the number of work stoppages was less than 1,000, and the average for the period was over 2,000 per year. See Michael Goldfield, *The Decline of Organized Labor in the United States* (Chicago: University of Chicago Press, 1987), p. 41. In 1995, there were only 385 work stoppages, the lowest number since before the Wagner Act was passed in 1935. See Jeremy Brecher and Tim Costello, "A 'New Labor Movement' in the Shell of the Old?" in Mantsios, *A New Labor Movement*, p. 25.

6. Linda Markowitz, *Worker Activism after Successful Union Organizing* (Armonk, N.Y.: M. E. Sharpe, 2000).

7. Bronfenbrenner and Juravich, "It Takes More than House Calls: Organizing to Win with a Comprehensive Union-Building Strategy," in Bronfenbrenner et al., *Organizing to Win: New Research on Union Strategies*, pp. 18–36.

8. Lowell Turner, "Rank and File Participation in Organizing at Home and Abroad," in Bronfenbrenner et al., *Organizing to Win*, pp. 123–34; Nissen, "Utilizing the Membership"; Early, "Membership Based Organizing."

9. Roger Waldinger et al., "Helots No More: A Case Study of the Justice for Janitors Campaign in Los Angeles," in Bronfenbrenner et al., *Organizing to Win*, pp. 102–20; Stewart Acuff, "Expanded Roles for the Central Labor Council: The View from Atlanta," in *Which Direction for Organized Labor? Essays on Organizing, Outreach, and Internal Transformations*, ed. Bruce Nissen (Detroit: Wayne State University Press, 1999), pp. 133–42; Larry Cohen and Steve Early, "Defending Workers' Rights in the Global Economy: The CWA Experience," in Nissen, *Which Direction for Organized Labor?* pp. 143–64.

10. See, for example, Harry Katz, "Whither the American Labor Movement?" in *Rekindling the Movement: Labor's Quest for Relevance in the 21st Century*, ed. Lowell Turner, Harry Katz, and Richard Hurd (Ithaca, N.Y.: Cornell University Press, 2001), pp. 339–49.

11. David A. Snow and Robert D. Benford, "Ideology, Frame Resonance,

and Participant Mobilization," *International Social Movement Research* 1 (1988): 197–218.

12. Eric Hirsch, "Sacrifice for the Cause: The Impact of Group Processes on Recruitment and Commitment in Social Movements," *American Sociological Review* 55 (1990): 243–54; Rick Fantasia, *Cultures of Solidarity: Consciousness, Action, and Contemporary American Workers* (Berkeley: University of California Press, 1988).

EPILOGUE TO PART I

1. See, for example, Roger Waldinger et al., "Helots No More: A Case Study of the Justice for Janitors Campaign in Los Angeles," in *Organizing to Win: New Research on Union Strategies*, ed. Kate Bronfenbrenner et al. (Ithaca, N.Y.: ILR Press, 1998), pp. 102–20; see also Jane Williams, "Restructuring Labor's Identity: The Justice for Janitors Campaign in Washington, D.C.," in *The Transformation of U.S. Unions: Voices, Visions, and Strategies from the Grassroots*, ed. Ray Tillman and Michael Cummings (Boulder, Colo.: Lynne Rienner, 1999).

2. Wade Rathke, "Letting More Flowers Bloom under the Setting Sun," In *Which Direction for Organized Labor? Essays on Organizing, Outreach, and Internal Transformations*, ed. Bruce Nissen (Detroit: Wayne State University Press, 1999), pp. 75–94.

3. Linda Markowitz, *Worker Activism after Successful Union Organizing* (Armonk, N.Y.: M. E. Sharpe, 2000).

INTRODUCTION TO PART II

1. City of Pittsburgh, Mayor's Office, "Mayor's Report, 1998."

2. John Bull, "County May Offer Buyout Packages: Republican Takeover Could Frighten Many to Take Money, Leave," *Pittsburgh Post-Gazette*, November 22, 1995.

3. David Michelmore, "Democrats Match G.O.P. Vow of 20% Cut in County Millage," *Pittsburgh Post-Gazette*, September 16, 1995.

4. Ibid.

5. Bull, "County May Offer Buyout Packages."

6. Larry Dunn and Bob Cranmer, "Our Campaign Is Different," *Pittsburgh Post-Gazette*, November 5, 1995.

7. This sort of neoliberal shift was, of course, not unique to Pittsburgh but could be observed in major cities throughout the United States beginning in the early 1980s. See, for example, Paul Johnston, *Success While Others Fail: Social Movement Unionism and the Public Workplace* (Ithaca, N.Y.: ILR Press, 1994).

8. See ibid. and Kate Bronfenbrenner and Tom Juravich, "Preparing for the Worst: Organizing and Staying Organized in the Public Sector," in *Organizing to Win: New Research on Union Strategies*, ed. Kate Bronfenbrenner et al. (Ithaca, N.Y.: ILR Press, 1998), pp. 261–82. These writers point out that privatization is a central element in the new urban politics. Public sector nursing home workers in particular are dealing with this issue all across the country because counties are seeking to reduce the cost of their legal obligation to provide services to the indigent.

9. Fernando Gapasin and Michael Yates, "Organizing the Unorganized: Will Promises Become Practices?" *Monthly Review* 49, no. 3 (1997): 46–62; William Forbath, "Down by Law? History and Prophesy about Organizing in Hard Times and a Hostile Legal Order," in *Audacious Democracy: Labor, Intellectuals, and the Social Reconstruction of America*, ed. Steve Fraser and Joshua Freeman (Boston: Houghton Mifflin, 1997); Kim Moody, *An Injury to All: The Decline of American Unionism* (New York: Verso, 1988).

10. Hans Gerth and C. Wright Mills, *From Max Weber: Essays in Sociology* (New York: Oxford University Press, 1946); Robert Michels, *Political Parties: A Sociological Study of the Oligarchical Tendencies of Modern Democracy* (1915; reprint, New York: Collier Books, 1962).

11. Frances Fox Piven and Richard A. Cloward, *Poor People's Movements: Why They Succeed, How They Fail* (New York: Random House, 1977).

12. Mayer Zald and Roberta Ash, "Social Movement Organizations: Growth, Decay, and Change," *Social Forces* 44 (1966): 327–40; Joseph Gusfield, "Social Movements: The Study," *International Encyclopedia of the Social Sciences* 14 (1968): 445–52; William Gamson, *The Strategy of Social Protest* (Homewood, Ill: Dorsey Press, 1975).

13. Elisabeth Clemens, "Organizational Repertoires and Institutional Change: Women's Groups and the Transformation of U.S. Politics, 1890–1920," *American Journal of Sociology* 98 (1993): 755–98.

14. Bob Edwards and John D. McCarthy, "Social Movement Schools," *Sociological Forum* 7 (1992): 541–50.

15. Aldon Morris, *The Origins of the Civil Rights Movement: Black Communities Organizing for Change* (New York: Free Press, 1984); Doug McAdam, *Polit-

ical Process and the Development of Black Insurgency, 1930–1970 (Chicago: University of Chicago Press, 1982).

16. See Doug McAdam, John D. McCarthy, and Mayer Zald, eds., *Comparative Perspectives on Social Movements: Political Opportunities, Mobilizing Structures, and Cultural Framings* (New York: Cambridge University Press, 1996). Researchers in these traditions have also explored a series of questions about what sort of organization is best. See, for example, Gamson, *The Strategy of Social Protest*, and Jack Goldstone, "The Weakness of Organization: A New Look at Gamson's *The Strategy of Social Protest*," *American Journal of Sociology* 85 (1980): 1017–42, for a debate about whether organizations should be centralized and formal or decentralized and informal. On the question of whether movement emergence and development are tied more to the presence of external resources and allies or the internal organizational capacities of aggrieved groups, see John D. McCarthy and Mayer Zald, *The Trend of Social Movements in America: Professionalization and Resource Mobilization* (Morristown, N.J.: General Learning Press, 1973), and "Resource Mobilization and Social Movements: A Partial Theory," *American Journal of Sociology* 82 (1977): 1212–41; J. Craig Jenkins and Charles Perrow, "Insurgency of the Powerless Farm Worker Movements," *American Sociological Review* 42 (1977): 249–68; Charles Tilly, *From Mobilization to Revolution* (Reading, Mass.: Addison-Wesley, 1978); McAdam, *Political Process;* and Morris, *Origins.* For debates about whether the relations among movement organizations in a multiorganizational field are a source of movement strength or a source of weakening interorganizational conflict, see Russell Curtis and Louis Zurcher, "Stable Resources of Social Movements: The Multiorganizational Field," *Social Forces* 52 (1973): 53–61; Mayer Zald and John D. McCarthy, "Social Movement Industries: Competition and Cooperation among Social Movement Organizations," *Research in Social Movements, Conflict and Change* 3 (1980): 1–20; Steven Barkan, "Inter-Organizational Conflict in the Southern Civil Rights Movement," *Sociological Inquiry* 56 (1986): 190–209; Suzanne Staggenborg, "Coalition Work in the Pro-Choice Movement: Organizational and Environmental Opportunities and Obstacles," *Social Problems* 33 (1986): 374–90; and Dieter Rucht, "Environmental Organizations in West Germany and France: Structure and Interorganizational Relations," *International Social Movement Research* 2 (1989): 61–94.

17. Aldon Morris, "Black Southern Sit-in Movement: An Analysis of Internal Organization," *American Sociological Review* 46 (1981): 744–67; Suzanne Staggenborg, "The Consequences of Professionalization and Formalization in

the Pro-Choice Movement," *American Sociological Review* 53 (1988): 585–606; Nancy Whittier, *Feminist Generations: The Persistence of the Radical Women's Movement* (Philadelphia: Temple University Press, 1995); J. Craig Jenkins and Craig Eckert, "Elite Patronage and the Channeling of Social Protest," *American Sociological Review* 51 (1986): 812–29; Christian Smith, *Resisting Reagan: The U.S. Central America Peace Movement* (Chicago: University of Chicago Press, 1996); Ruud Koopmans, "The Dynamics of Protest Waves: West Germany, 1965–69" *American Sociological Review* 58 (1993): 637–58; Hanspeter Kriesi, Ruud Koopmans, and Jan Willem Duyvendak, *New Social Movements in Western Europe: A Comparative Analysis* (Minneapolis: University of Minnesota Press, 1995).

18. Kim Voss and Rachel Sherman, "Breaking the Iron Law of Oligarchy: Union Revitalization in the American Labor Movement," *American Journal of Sociology* 106 (2002): 303–49.

19. J. Craig Jenkins, "Radical Transformation of Organizational Goals," *Administrative Science Quarterly* 22 (1977): 568–86; Bert Useem and Mayer Zald, "From Pressure Group to Social Movement: Efforts to Promote the Use of Nuclear Power," *Social Problems* 30 (1982): 144–56.

CHAPTER 4. "SAVE OUR KANES"

1. Mark Belko, "Dunn Gives Ultimatum to Kane Unions," *Pittsburgh Post-Gazette,* January 11, 1997.

2. Mark Belko, "Control of Kanes May Be Shifted," *Pittsburgh Post-Gazette,* September 4, 1996.

3. James McDonough, *John J. Kane Regional Centers: Privatization Options* (Pittsburgh, Pa.: Allegheny Institute for Public Policy, 1996); Jake Hauk, *The Case for Privatizing the Kane Regional Centers* (Pittsburgh, Pa.: Allegheny Institute for Public Policy, 1997).

4. McDonough, "John J. Kane Regional Centers," p. 1.

5. See, for example, Andy Banks, "The Power and Promise of Community Unionism," *Labor Research Review* 10 (1992): 17–31; James Craft, "The Community as a Source of Power," *Journal of Labor Research* 11 (1990): 145–60; Paul Johnston, *Success While Others Fail: Social Movement Unionism and the Public Workplace* (Ithaca, N.Y.: ILR Press, 1994); Ruth Needleman, "Building Relationships for the Long Haul: Unions and Community Organizing Groups Working Together to Organize Low-Wage Workers," in *Organizing to Win: New Research on Union Strategies,* ed. Kate Bronfenbrenner et al. (Ithaca, N.Y.:

ILR Press, 1998), pp. 71–86; Ronald Peters and Theresa Merrill, "Clergy and Religious Persons' Roles in Organizing at O'Hare Airport and St. Joseph Medical Center," in Bronfenbrenner et al., *Organizing to Win*, pp. 164–77; Katherine Sciacchitano, "Finding the Community in the Union and the Union in the Community: The First-Contract Campaign at Steeltech," in Bronfenbrenner et al., *Organizing to Win*, pp. 150–63; Fernando Gapasin and Howard Wial, "The Role of Central Labor Councils in Union Organizing in the 1990s," in Bronfenbrenner et al., *Organizing to Win*, pp. 54–68; Philip McLewin, "The Concerted Voice of Labor and the Suburbanization of Capital: Fragmentation of the Community Labor Council," in *Which Direction for Organized Labor? Essays on Organizing, Outreach, and Internal Transformations*, ed. Bruce Nissen (Detroit: Wayne State University Press, 1999), pp. 113–32; Stewart Acuff, "Expanded Roles for the Central Labor Council: The View from Atlanta," in Nissen, *Which Direction for Organized Labor?* pp. 133–42.

6. See James O'Connor, *The Fiscal Crisis of the State* (New York: St. Martin's Press, 1973); also Johnston, *Success While Others Fail.*

7. Mark Belko, "Privatization Hits Strong Opposition: Commissioners Booed, Questioned by Crowd," *Pittsburgh Post-Gazette*, October 3, 1996.

8. Ibid.

9. Sali Magrini and 50 Other Kane Workers, "The County Has Not Listened to Workers on Improving the Kanes," *Pittsburgh Post-Gazette*, November 11, 1996.

10. Dunn was referring to a provision in Pennsylvania law that requires counties to contribute 5 percent of the total reimbursement for county nursing homes. Private sector nursing homes do not have to contribute the 5 percent, so in theory reimbursements are higher for private sector than for county-owned homes. However, in practice Dunn's claim was not accurate, since the association of county nursing homes has been able to negotiate away the 5 percent contribution. This portion has been paid for with money from the federal-state intergovernmental transfer (IGT), and the counties have never actually had to pay it.

11. Belko, "Dunn Gives Ultimatum." This approach backfired when the unions revealed that they had been trying to set up negotiation meetings with the county's law firm for months, only to be told that the county negotiator's schedule was "virtually full."

12. Ibid.

13. Johnston, *Success While Others Fail*, pp. 35–38.

14. Craft, "The Community."

15. Needleman, "Building Relationships"; Sciacchitano, "Finding the Community in the Union."

16. Mark Belko, "Keep Kane Homes Public, Group Asks," *Pittsburgh Post-Gazette*, January 29, 1997.

17. Ibid.

18. Ibid.

19. Ibid.

20. John Russo and Brian Corbin, "A System of Interpretation: Catholic Social Teaching and American Unionism," *Conflict* 11, no. 4 (1991): 237–66, and "Work, Organized Labor, and the Catholic Church: Boundaries and Opportunities for Community/Labor Coalitions," in Nissen, *Which Direction for Organized Labor?* pp. 95–112; see also Peters and Merrill, "Clergy and Religious Persons' Roles."

21. Thomas Fuechtmann, *Steeples and Stacks: Religion and Crisis in Youngstown* (New York: Cambridge University Press, 1989); Russo and Corbin, "A System of Interpretation."

22. Peters and Merrill, "Clergy and Religious Persons' Roles."

23. Mark Belko, "Lucchino: Privatization of Kanes Just a Quick Fix," *Pittsburgh Post-Gazette*, March 5, 1997.

24. Mark Belko, "Dunn Halts Proposed Transfer of Kanes," *Pittsburgh Post-Gazette*, March 25, 1997.

25. Ibid.

26. Joseph Crumb, "Religious Leaders Put out Call for No Privatization," *Pittsburgh Tribune-Review*, March 25, 1997.

27. For a contrary view, see Kim Voss and Rachel Sherman, "Breaking the Iron Law of Oligarchy: Union Revitalization in the American Labor Movement," *American Journal of Sociology* 106 (2002): 303–49.

CHAPTER 5. "WE WANT A CONTRACT"

1. Bill Fletcher, Jr., and Richard W. Hurd, "Beyond the Organizing Model: The Transformation Process in Local Unions," in *Organizing to Win: New Research on Union Strategies*, ed. Kate Bronfenbrenner et al. (Ithaca, N.Y.: ILR Press, 1998), pp. 37–53, and "Political Will, Local Union Transformation, and the Organizing Imperative," in *Which Direction for Organized Labor? Essays on Organizing, Outreach, and Internal Transformations*, ed. Bruce Nissen (Detroit: Wayne State University Press, 1999), pp. 191–216; Kim Voss and Rachel Sher-

man, "Breaking the Iron Law of Oligarchy: Union Revitalization in the American Labor Movement," *American Journal of Sociology* 106 (2002): 303–49.

2. Ibid.

3. Ibid.

4. Steve Early, "Membership-Based Organizing," in *A New Labor Movement for a New Century*, ed. Gregory Mantsios (New York: Monthly Review Press, 1998), pp. 82–103, suggests that one problem with college interns and college graduate organizers is that they "are not likely to question what it is they are trying to organize workers into" because they lack the experience or intellectual tools necessary to criticize the movement. My experience suggests otherwise. I found three cohorts of college-age fellow interns at Local A to be incisively critical of the gaps between rhetoric and reality that often characterized our activities. Their critiques were rooted in their idealism, their sense that the movement ought to live up to its ideals. I think this sort of idealism — the kind that gets outraged over failures to live up to principle — is extremely valuable to the labor movement and that college-age interns are at least as likely to develop a critical analysis of the movement as rank-and-file workers. I do agree with Early's analysis of the limits of a strategy of "rootless, mobile cadre" of organizers and the importance of member-to-member organizing strategies, but I do not think that this should mean expressing an ironclad preference for drawing leaders from the rank and file — particularly given Voss and Sherman's finding about the relation between outside movement experience and visionary leadership.

5. "County's Former Third Wheel Comes Full Circle," *Pittsburgh Post-Gazette*, August 17, 1997.

6. Ibid.

EPILOGUE TO PART II

1. Living-wage research that the union helped to fund estimated that nearly 4,000 human services workers employed by Allegheny County contractors earned less than $9.12 per hour in 1998.

INTRODUCTION TO PART III

1. Paul Weiler, "Promises to Keep: Securing Workers' Rights to Self-Organization under the NLRA," *Harvard Law Review* 96 (1983): 1769–1827.

2. Barbara Kingsolver, *Holding the Line: Women in the Great Arizona Mining*

Strike of 1983 (Ithaca, N.Y.: ILR Press, 1989); Julius Getman, *The Betrayal of Local 14* (Ithaca, N.Y.: ILR Press, 1997); Peter Rachleff, *Hard Times in the Heartland* (Boston: South End Press, 1993); Richard Vigilante, *Strike: The Daily News War and the Future of American Labor* (New York: Simon and Schuster, 1994).

3. Jeremy Brecher and Tim Costello, "A 'New Labor Movement' in the Shell of the Old?" in *A New Labor Movement for the New Century*, ed. Gregory Mantsios (New York: Monthly Review Press, 1998), p. 25.

4. Tom Juravich and Kate Bronfenbrenner, *Ravenswood: The Steelworkers' Victory and the Revival of American Labor* (Ithaca, N.Y.: ILR Press, 1999).

5. Ibid., p. 205.

6. Doug McAdam, *Political Process and the Development of Black Insurgency, 1930–1970* (Chicago: University of Chicago Press, 1982), and "Tactical Innovation and the Pace of Insurgency," *American Sociological Review* 48, no. 6 (1983): 735–54.

7. Marshall Ganz, "Resources and Resourcefulness: Strategic Capacity in the Unionization of California Agriculture, 1959–1966," *American Journal of Sociology* 105, no. 4 (2000): 1009.

8. Service Employees International Union, *Pennsylvania Dignity Campaign: Bargaining News Flash* (newsletter), November 27, 1995.

9. Letter from Mark Crawford, Chief Bargainer for the SEIU, to Megacorp Enterprises, December 18, 1995.

CHAPTER 6. "WE WILL NOT BE SILENCED"

1. Stephen Lerner, "Taking the Offensive, Turning the Tide," in *A New Labor Movement for a New Century*, ed. Gregory Mantsios (New York: Monthly Review Press, 1998), pp. 69–81.

2. Ibid., p. 74.

3. SEIU, internal memo to Pennsylvania Dignity Campaign Staff, November 28, 1995.

4. Bill Fletcher, Jr., and Richard Hurd, "Beyond the Organizing Model: The Transformation Process in Local Unions," in *Organizing to Win: New Research on Union Strategies*, ed. Kate Bronfenbrenner et al. (Ithaca, N.Y.: ILR Press, 1998), pp. 37–53.

5. National Labor Relations Board, Cases 6-CA-27873 et al., *Decision and Statement of the Case*, 1997.

6. Ibid.

7. Paul Weiler, "Promises to Keep: Securing Workers' Rights to Self-Organization under the NLRA," *Harvard Law Review* 96 (1983): 1769–1827.

8. Paul Weiler, "Striking a New Balance: Freedom of Contract and the Prospects for Union Representation," *Harvard Law Review* 98 (1984): 351–420.

9. Ibid., p. 355.

10. Commission for Labor Cooperation, *Plant Closings and Labor Rights: A Report to the Council of Ministers on the Effects of Sudden Plant Closings on Freedom of Association and the Right to Organize in Canada, Mexico, and the United States* (Lanham, Md.: Bernan Press, 1997).

11. For a court to find that an unfair labor practice strike has taken place, the union must show two things: first, that unfair labor practices occurred, and second, that the unfair labor practices were a cause (though not necessarily the only or most important cause) of the strike. Neither the right of employers to replace striking workers nor the right of workers to retain their jobs if they strike, at least in part, over unfair labor practices is spelled out in labor statutes. Rather, these rights developed through case law, beginning with a 1938 Supreme Court decision, *NLRB v. Mackay Radio and Telegraph Co.*, 304 U.S. 333. This decision rather casually established employers' right to permanently replace striking workers. *Mastro Plastics Corp. v. NLRB*, 350 U.S. 270, 288–89 (1956), on the other hand, established that if the strike was in some way attributable to the employer's unfair labor practices, the strikers were guaranteed their jobs back under the NLRA.

12. Doug McAdam, Sydney Tarrow, and Charles Tilly, *Dynamics of Contention* (New York: Cambridge University Press, 2001).

CHAPTER 7. "WHATEVER IT TAKES"

1. National Labor Relations Board, Cases 6-CA-28276 et al., *Decision and Statement of the Case*, 2000.

2. Ibid.

3. National Labor Relations Board, Cases 6-CA-27873 et al., *Decision and Statement of the Case*, 1997.

4. SEIU, "We're Coming Back!" *Megacorp Bulletin*, May 2, 1997.

5. National Labor Relations Board, Cases 6-CA-28276 et al., 2000.

6. Ibid.

7. This experience is relevant to debates over the role of dues check-off procedures in the labor movement more generally. Many on labor's left argue that

dues check-off procedures weaken the labor movement by substituting a bureaucratic procedure for face-to-face organizing and contact and that the labor movement would be better off collecting dues in person. Doing so, the argument goes, would force unions to be more responsive to their members because in order to collect money from someone it is necessary to talk to them and listen to their concerns. I do not find this argument to be particularly compelling, for several reasons. First, collecting dues manually, by itself, does not guarantee that unions will organize to empower their members; it may be equally likely to lead to a heightened form of servicing — which itself would further reduce the resources that the movement could devote to external organizing. In addition, there is a more practical objection: the experience of the Megacorp campaign suggests that even when, because of the replacements, the union was able to deploy a large cadre of essentially full-time, well-trained, and highly motivated member organizers in the context of a pitched battle that heightened workers' attachments to their union, it was able to collect only about half of the normal dues. And in the weakest shops, where workers were even more vulnerable because they were more intimidated by management, virtually no dues were collected.

8. SEIU, "ULP of the Week: Not Following Seniority," *Megacorp Bulletin*, January 18, 1997.

9. SEIU, *Megacorp Bulletin*, various dates, January–February 1997.

10. SEIU, "Workers March with 'Bargain Now' Petitions," *Megacorp Bulletin*, July 23, 1996.

11. SEIU, "Fundraisers Going Strong," *Megacorp Bulletin*, July 9, 1996.

12. SEIU, *Megacorp Bulletin*, June 18, 1996, and September 6, 1996.

13. SEIU, "National Solidarity," *Megacorp Bulletin*, November 25, 1996.

14. SEIU, "Bargaining Update," *Megacorp Bulletin*, November 15, 1996.

15. Pittsburgh City Council, *Statement in Support of Megacorp Nursing Home Workers*, March 16, 1996.

16. SEIU, "Sample Letter" to Hon. Jesse Brown, Secretary of Veterans Affairs, n.d.

17. SEIU, "Support the Megacorp Bill" (leaflet), 1996.

18. SEIU, "Bargaining Update," *Megacorp Bulletin*, November 15, 1996.

19. Doug McAdam, "Tactical Innovation and the Pace of Insurgency," *American Sociological Review* 48 (1983): 735–54; David Meyer and Suzanne Staggenborg, "Movements, Countermovements, and the Structure of Political Opportunity," *American Journal of Sociology* 101 (1996): 1628–60.

CONCLUSION

1. Daniel Bell, *The Coming of Post-Industrial Society: A Venture in Social Forecasting* (New York: Basic Books, 1973); Alain Touraine, *Post-Industrial Society: Tomorrow's Social History. Classes, Conflicts, and Culture in the Programmed Society* (New York: Random House, 1971).

2. Alain Lipietz, *Towards A New Economic Order: Postfordism, Ecology, and Democracy* (New York: Oxford University Press, 1992); Ash Amin, ed., *Post-Fordism: A Reader, Studies in Urban and Social Change* (London: Blackwell, 1994).

3. Manuel Castells, *The Rise of the Network Society* (Cambridge, England: Blackwell, 1996).

4. Alberto Melucci, *Challenging Codes: Collective Action in the Information Age* (New York: Cambridge University Press, 1996).

5. There are a number of different versions of this perspective. One variant draws on Habermas's notion of the "colonization of the life-world" by system imperatives (see, for example, Jurgen Habermas, *Legitimation Crisis* (Boston: Beacon Press, 1975), and *The Theory of Communicative Action*, vol. 1, *Reason and the Rationalization of Society* (Boston: Beacon Press, 1981), to explain the rise of new *expressive* movements reacting against the progressive instrumental-rationalization of all areas of life. Expressive movements resist these trends by challenging the technocratic control of "private" behavior and by politicizing previously private domains such as sexuality and reproductive rights. A second argument focuses on how the "normal" functioning of modern economic and political institutions produce negative side effects that affect everyone in ways that transcend class, such as threats of environmental catastrophe or nuclear annihilation. These threats generate broad-based movements protesting the unacceptable physical, aesthetic, or health costs of modernity, whose use of extrainstitutional channels of protest reflects the inability of institutionalized politics to deal effectively with the negative consequences of economic growth. A third perspective argues that the rise of "postindustrial" forms of organization creates an expanding category of knowledge workers, service workers, students, and others not directly tied to the "old" class structure of production; these groups constitute a postindustrial social cleavage. The proliferation of new social conflicts thus reflects the multiplicity of new groups (with new identities and interests) arising out of this transition from "industrial" to "postindustrial" society.

6. Melucci, *Challenging Codes*, p. 209.

7. See, for example, Alain Touraine, "An Introduction to the Study of Social

Movements," *Social Research* 52 (1985): 749–87; Alberto Melucci, "The New Social Movements: A Theoretical Approach." *Social Science Information* 19 (1980): 199–226, *Nomads of the Present: Social Movements and Individual Needs in Contemporary Society* (Philadelphia: Temple University Press, 1989), and especially "A Strange Kind of Newness: What's New in New Social Movements," in *New Social Movements: From Ideology to Identity*, ed. Enrique Laraña, Hank Johnston, and Joseph Gusfield (Philadelphia: Temple University Press, 1994), pp. 101–32.

8. Melucci, *Challenging Codes*, p. 219.

9. Doug McAdam, *Political Process and the Development of Black Insurgency, 1930–1970* (Chicago: University of Chicago Press, 1982).

10. Charles Tilly, *From Mobilization to Revolution* (Reading, Mass.: Addison-Wesley, 1978).

11. Doug McAdam, John D. McCarthy, and Mayer Zald, eds., *Comparative Perspectives on Social Movements: Political Opportunities, Mobilizing Structures, and Cultural Framings* (New York: Cambridge University Press, 1996).

12. Doug McAdam, Sydney Tarrow, and Charles Tilly, *Dynamics of Contention* (New York: Cambridge University Press, 2001).

13. Melucci, *Challenging Codes*, p. 42.

14. As Melucci himself observes in *Challenging Codes*, "processes of mobilization, organizational forms, models of leadership, and ideologies and forms of communication," as well as "relationships with the outside, with competitors, allies, adversaries, and especially the reaction of the political system and the apparatus of social control, must be taken into account" (p. 78). Melucci did not conceive these as factor variables but rather as "*meaningful levels of analysis* for reconstruction from within of the system of action that constitutes a collective actor" (p. 78, italics added). However, in my view Melucci failed to follow his own prescription in his own analyses. He does not take historically situated organizational and political obstacles to collective action seriously.

15. Amy Butler, "U.S. Labor Union Membership Decreases by 280,000 in 2002," *Pittsburgh Post-Gazette*, February 26, 2003.

16. Kate Bronfenbrenner, "Changing to Organize: Unions Know What Has to Be Done: Now They Have to Do It," *Nation* 273, no. 7 (2001): 16–20.

17. "UFCW, AFL-CIO Join in Wal-Mart Campaign," *Label Letter, Union Label and Service Trades Department, AFL-CIO* 25 (March/April 2000): 1.

18. "Judge Orders Wal-Mart to Recognize Union Formed by Meat Cutters," *Associated Press State and Local Wire*, June 18, 2003.

19. Eric Schlosser, *Fast Food Nation: The Dark Side of the All-American Meal* (Boston: Houghton Mifflin, 2001).

BIBLIOGRAPHY

Acuff, Stewart. "Expanded Roles for the Central Labor Council: The View from Atlanta." In *Which Direction for Organized Labor? Essays on Organizing, Outreach, and Internal Transformations*, edited by Bruce Nissen, pp. 133–42. Detroit: Wayne State University Press, 1999.

Adams, Larry. "Transforming Unions and Building a Movement." In *A New Labor Movement for a New Century*, edited by Gregory Mantsios, pp. 202–15. New York: Monthly Review Press, 1998.

Adler, Paul, and Robert Cole. "Designed for Learning: A Tale of Two Auto Plants." *Sloan Management Review* 34 (1993): 85–94.

Amin, Ash, ed. *Post-Fordism: A Reader. Studies in Urban and Social Change.* London: Blackwell, 1994.

Appelbaum, Eileen, and Rosemary Batt. *The New American Workplace: Transforming Work Systems in the United States.* Boston: South End Press, 1994.

Armbrister, Trevor. *Act of Vengeance.* New York: Warner Books, 1980.

Aronowitz, Stanley. *False Promises: The Shaping of American Working Class Consciousness.* Durham, N.C.: Duke University Press, 1992.

Aronowitz, Stanley, and William DeFazio. *The Jobless Future: Sci-Tech and the Dogma of Work.* Minneapolis: University of Minnesota Press, 1994.

Banks, Andy. "The Power and Promise of Community Unionism." *Labor Research Review* 10 (1992): 17–31.

Barkan, Steven. "Inter-Organizational Conflict in the Southern Civil Rights Movement." *Sociological Inquiry* 56 (1986): 190–209.

Barnard, Elaine. "Creating Democratic Communities in the Workplace." In *A New Labor Movement for a New Century*, edited by Gregory Mantsios, pp. 4–15. New York: Monthly Review Press, 1998.

Belko, Mark. "Control of Kanes May Be Shifted." *Pittsburgh Post-Gazette*, September 4, 1996.

———. "Privatization Hits Strong Opposition: Commissioners Booed, Questioned by Crowd." *Pittsburgh Post-Gazette*, October 3, 1996.

———. "Dunn Gives Ultimatum to Kane Unions." *Pittsburgh Post-Gazette*, January 11, 1997.

———. "Keep Kane Homes Public, Group Asks." *Pittsburgh Post-Gazette*, January 29, 1997.

———. "Lucchino: Privatization of Kanes Just a Quick Fix." *Pittsburgh Post-Gazette*, March 5, 1997.

———. "Dunn Halts Proposed Transfer of Kanes." *Pittsburgh Post-Gazette*, March 25, 1997.

Bell, Daniel. *The Coming of Post-Industrial Society: A Venture in Social Forecasting.* New York: Basic Books, 1973.

Benford, Robert D. "Frame Disputes within the Nuclear Disarmament Movement." *Social Forces* 7 (1993): 677–701.

Bluestone, Barry, and Bennett Harrison. *The Deindustrialization of America: Plant Closings, Community Abandonment, and the Dismantling of Basic Industry.* New York: Basic Books, 1982.

Bonacich, Edna. "Reflections on Union Activism." *Contemporary Sociology* 27, no. 2 (1998): 129–32.

———. "Intense Challenges, Tentative Possibilities: Organizing Immigrant Garment Workers in Los Angeles." In *Organizing Immigrants: The Challenge for Unions in Contemporary California*, edited by Ruth Milkman, pp. 130–49. Ithaca, N.Y.: ILR Press, 2000.

Bowers, Barbara, and Marian Becker. "Nurses' Aides in Nursing Homes: The Relation between Organization and Quality." *Gerontologist* 32 (1992): 360–66.

Boyer, Richard, and Herbert Morais. *Labor's Untold Story.* New York: United Electrical, Radio, and Machine Workers, 1955.

Brecher, Jeremy. *Strike!* San Francisco: Straight Arrow Books, 1972.

Brecher, Jeremy, and Tim Costello. "A 'New Labor Movement' in the Shell of the Old?" In *A New Labor Movement for the New Century*, edited by Gregory Mantsios, pp. 26–43. New York: Monthly Review Press, 1998.

Brody, David. "Criminalizing the Rights of Labor." *Dissent* 42, no. 3 (1995): 363–67.

Bronfenbrenner, Kate. "Employer Behavior in Certification Elections and First-Contract Campaigns: Implications for Labor Law Reform." In *Restoring the Promise of American Labor Law*, edited by Sheldon Friedman, Richard W. Hurd, Rudolph A. Oswald, and Ronald L. Seeber, pp. 75–89. Ithaca, N.Y.: ILR Press, 1994.

———. "Changing to Organize: Unions Know What Has to Be Done: Now They Have to Do It." *Nation* 273, no. 7 (2001): 16–20.

Bronfenbrenner, Kate, and Tom Juravich. "It Takes More Than House Calls: Organizing to Win with a Comprehensive Union-Building Strategy." In *Organizing to Win: New Research on Union Strategies*, edited by Kate Bronfenbrenner, Sheldon Friedman, Richard W. Hurd, Rudolph A. Oswald, and Ronald L. Seeber, pp. 18–36. Ithaca, N.Y.: ILR Press, 1998.

———. "Preparing for the Worst: Organizing and Staying Organized in the Public Sector." In *Organizing to Win: New Research on Union Strategies*, edited by Kate Bronfenbrenner, Sheldon Friedman, Richard W. Hurd, Rudolph A. Oswald, and Ronald L. Seeber, pp. 261–82. Ithaca, N.Y.: ILR Press, 1998.

Buba, Tony, and Ray Henderson. *Struggles in Steel: A Story of African American Steelworkers*. Pittsburgh, Pa.: Braddock Films, 1996.

Buhle, Paul. *Taking Care of Business: Samuel Gompers, George Meany, Lane Kirkland, and the Tragedy of American Labor*. New York: Monthly Review Press, 1999.

Bull, John. "County May Offer Buyout Packages: Republican Takeover Could Frighten Many to Take Money, Leave." *Pittsburgh Post-Gazette*, November 22, 1995.

Butler, Amy. "U.S. Labor Union Membership Decreases by 280,000 in 2002." *Pittsburgh Post-Gazette*, February 26, 2003.

Castells, Manuel. *The Rise of the Network Society*. Cambridge, England: Blackwell, 1996.

City of Pittsburgh, Mayor's Office. "Mayor's Report, 1998."

Clawson, Dan. "Making a Meaningful Labor Movement." *Tikkun* 9, no. 4 (1994): 41–44.

Clawson, Dan. *The Next Upsurge: Labor and the New Social Movements*. Ithaca, N.Y.: ILR Press, 2003.

Clemens, Elisabeth. "Organizational Repertoires and Institutional Change: Women's Groups and the Transformation of U.S. Politics, 1890–1920." *American Journal of Sociology* 98 (1993): 755–98.

Cobble, Dorothy Sue. "Organizing the Post-Industrial Work Force: Some Lessons from the History of Waitress Unionism." *Industrial and Labor Relations Review* 44 (1991): 419–36.

Cohen, Larry, and Steve Early. "Defending Workers' Rights in the Global Economy: The CWA Experience." In *Which Direction for Organized Labor? Essays on Organizing, Outreach, and Internal Transformations,* edited by Bruce Nissen, pp. 143–64. Detroit: Wayne State University Press, 1999.

Cohen, Stephen, and John Zyzman. *Manufacturing Matters: The Myth of the Post-Industrial Economy.* New York: Basic Books, 1987.

Commission for Labor Cooperation. *Plant Closings and Labor Rights: A Report to the Council of Ministers on the Effects of Sudden Plant Closings on Freedom of Association and the Right to Organize in Canada, Mexico, and the United States.* Lanham, Md.: Bernan Press, 1997.

Conell, Carol, and Kim Voss. "Formal Organization and the Fate of Social Movements: Craft Association and Class Alliance in the Knights of Labor." *American Sociological Review* 55 (1990): 255–69.

Cooke, William. *Organizing and Public Policy: Failure to Secure First Contracts.* Kalamazoo, Mich.: W. E. Upjohn Institute for Employment Research, 1985.

———. "The Rising Tide of Discrimination against Union Activists." *Industrial Relations* 24 (1985): 421–42.

Cornfield, Daniel, Holly McCammon, Darren McDaniel, and Dean Eatman. "In the Community or in the Union? The Impact of Community Involvement on Nonunion Worker Attitudes about Unionizing." In *Organizing to Win: New Research on Union Strategies,* edited by Kate Bronfenbrenner, Sheldon Friedman, Richard W. Hurd, Rudolph A. Oswald, and Ronald L. Seeber, pp. 247–58. Ithaca, N.Y.: ILR Press, 1998.

"County's Former Third Wheel Comes Full Circle," *Pittsburgh Post-Gazette,* August 17, 1997.

Craft, James. "The Community as a Source of Power." *Journal of Labor Research* 11 (1990): 145–60.

Crumb, Joseph. "Religious Leaders Put out Call for No Privatization." *Pittsburgh Tribune-Review,* March 25, 1997.

Curtis, Russell, and Louis Zurcher. "Stable Resources of Social Movements: The Multiorganizational Field." *Social Forces* 52 (1973): 53–61.

Dandaneau, Steven. *A Town Abandoned: Flint, Michigan Confronts Deindustrialization.* Albany: SUNY Press, 1996.

Delp, Linda, and Katie Quan. "Homecare Organizing in California: An Analysis of a Successful Strategy." *Labor Studies Journal* 27 (2002): 1–23.

Diamond, Timothy. *Making Gray Gold: Narratives of Nursing Home Care.* Chicago: University of Chicago Press, 1992.

Dickens, William. "The Effect of Company Campaigns on Certification Elections: Law and Reality Once Again." *Industrial and Labor Relations Review* 36 (1983): 560–75.

Dudley, Kathryn. *End of the Line: Lost Jobs, New Lives in Postindustrial America.* Chicago: University of Chicago Press, 1994.

Dunlop Commission [Commission on the Future of Worker-Management Relations]. *Fact Finding Report.* Washington, D.C.: U.S. Department of Labor and U.S. Department of Commerce, 1994.

Dunn, Larry, and Bob Cranmer. "Our Campaign Is Different." *Pittsburgh Post-Gazette*, November 5, 1995.

Early, Steve. "Membership-Based Organizing." In *A New Labor Movement for a New Century*, edited by Gregory Mantsios, pp. 82–103. New York: Monthly Review Press, 1998.

Eaton, Susan C. *Pennsylvania's Nursing Homes: Promoting Quality Care and Quality Jobs.* Harrisburg, Pa.: Keystone Research Center, 1997.

Edwards, Bob, and John D. McCarthy. "Social Movement Schools." *Sociological Forum* 7 (1992): 541–50.

Eimer, Stuart. "From 'Business Unionism' to 'Social Movement Unionism': The Case of the AFL-CIO Milwaukee County Labor Council." *Labor Studies Journal* 24, no. 2 (1999): 63–74.

Eisenscher, Michael. "Critical Juncture: Unionism at the Crossroads." In *Which Direction for Organized Labor? Essays on Organizing, Outreach, and Internal Transformations*, edited by Bruce Nissen, pp. 217–46. Detroit: Wayne State University Press, 1999.

Fantasia, Rick. *Cultures of Solidarity: Consciousness, Action, and Contemporary American Workers.* Berkeley: University of California Press, 1988.

Fernandez, Roberto, and Doug McAdam. "Social Networks and Social Movements: Multiorganizational Fields and Recruitment to Mississippi Freedom Summer." *Sociological Forum* 3 (1988): 357–82.

Figueroa, Héctor. "International Labor Solidarity in an Era of Global Competition." In *A New Labor Movement for a New Century*, edited by Gregory-Mantsios, pp. 304–19. New York: Monthly Review Press, 1998.

Fine, Janice. "Moving Innovations from the Margins to the Center." In *A New Labor Movement for a New Century*, edited by Gregory Mantsios, pp. 119–46. New York: Monthly Review Press, 1998.

Fisk, Catherine, Daniel Mitchell, and Christopher Erickson. "Union Representation of Immigrant Janitors in Southern California: Economic and Legal Challenges." In *Organizing Immigrants*, edited by Ruth Milkman, pp. 199–224. Ithaca, N.Y.: ILR Press, 2000.

Fletcher, Bill, Jr., and Richard W. Hurd. "Beyond the Organizing Model: The Transformation Process in Local Unions." In *Organizing to Win: New Research on Union Strategies*, edited by Kate Bronfenbrenner, Sheldon Friedman, Richard W. Hurd, Rudolph A. Oswald, and Ronald L. Seeber, pp. 37–53. Ithaca, N.Y.: ILR Press, 1998.

———. "Political Will, Local Union Transformation, and the Organizing Imperative." In *Which Direction for Organized Labor? Essays on Organizing, Outreach, and Internal Transformations*, edited by Bruce Nissen, pp. 191–216. Detroit: Wayne State University Press, 1999.

Fletcher, Bill, and Richard W. Hurd. "Overcoming Obstacles to Transformation: Challenges on the Way to a New Unionism." In *Rekindling the Movement: Labor's Quest for Relevance in the 21st Century*, edited by Lowell Turner, Harry Katz, and Richard Hurd, pp. 182–209. Ithaca, N.Y.: Cornell University Press Press, 2001.

Foner, Nancy. *The Caregiving Dilemma: Work in an American Nursing Home*. Berkeley: University of California Press, 1994.

Forbath, William. "Down by Law? History and Prophecy about Organizing in Hard Times and a Hostile Legal Order." In *Audacious Democracy: Labor, Intellectuals, and the Social Reconstruction of America*, edited by Steve Fraser and Joshua Freeman. Boston: Houghton Mifflin, 1997.

Freeman, Richard B. "Why Are Unions Faring So Poorly in NLRB Representation Elections?" In *Challenges and Choices Facing American Labor*, edited by Thomas Kochan, pp. 46–64. Cambridge, Mass.: MIT Press, 1985.

Freeman, Richard B., and Morris Kleiner. "Employer Behavior in the Face of Union Organizing Drives." *Industrial and Labor Relations Review* 43 (1990): 351–65.

Friedman, Sheldon, Richard W. Hurd, Rudolph A. Oswald, and Ronald L. Seeber, eds. *Restoring the Promise of American Labor Law*. Ithaca, N.Y.: ILR Press, 1994.

Fuechtmann, Thomas. *Steeples and Stacks: Religion and Crisis in Youngstown*. New York: Cambridge University Press, 1989.

Gamson, William. *The Strategy of Social Protest*. Homewood, Ill: Dorsey Press, 1975.

Ganz, Marshall. "Resources and Resourcefulness: Strategic Capacity in the

Unionization of California Agriculture, 1959–1966." *American Journal of Sociology* 105 (2000): 1003–62.

Gapasin, Fernando, and Howard Wial. "The Role of Central Labor Councils in Union Organizing in the 1990s." In *Organizing to Win: New Research on Union Strategies*, edited by Kate Bronfenbrenner, Sheldon Friedman, Richard W. Hurd, Rudolph A. Oswald, and Ronald L. Seeber, pp. 54–68. Ithaca, N.Y.: ILR Press, 1998.

Gapasin, Fernando, and Michael Yates. "Organizing the Unorganized: Will Promises Become Practices?" *Monthly Review* 49, no. 3 (1997): 46–62.

Gerth, Hans, and C. Wright Mills. *From Max Weber: Essays in Sociology*. New York: Oxford University Press, 1946.

Getman, Julius. *The Betrayal of Local 14*. Ithaca, N.Y.: ILR Press, 1997.

Gindin, Sam. "Notes on Labor at the End of the Century: Starting Over?" In *Rising from the Ashes? Labor in the Age of "Global" Capitalism*, edited by Ellen M. Wood, Peter Meiksins, and Michael Yates, pp. 190–202. New York: Monthly Review Press, 1998.

Goldfield, Michael. *The Decline of Organized Labor in the United States*. Chicago: University of Chicago Press, 1987.

Goldstone, Jack. "The Weakness of Organization: A New Look at Gamson's *The Strategy of Social Protest*." *American Journal of Sociology* 85 (1980): 1017–42.

Gould, Roger. "Collective Action and Network Structure." *American Sociological Review* 58 (1991): 182–96.

———. "Multiple Networks and Mobilization in the Paris Commune, 1871." *American Sociological Review* 56 (1993): 716–29.

Gould, William. *Agenda for Reform: The Future of Employment Relationships and the Law*. Cambridge, Mass.: MIT Press, 1993.

Green, James, and Chris Tilly. "Service Unionism: Directions for Organizing." *Labor Law Journal* 38 (August 1987): 486–95.

Gross, James. *Broken Promise: The Subversion of U.S. Labor Relations Policy, 1947–1994*. Philadelphia: Temple University Press, 1995.

Gusfield, Joseph. "Social Movements: The Study." *International Encyclopedia of the Social Sciences* 14 (1968): 445–52.

Habermas, Jurgen. *Legitimation Crisis*. Boston: Beacon Press, 1975.

———. *The Theory of Communicative Action*. Vol. 1. *Reason and the Rationalization of Society*. Boston: Beacon Press, 1981.

Hathaway, Dale. *Can Workers Have a Voice? The Politics of Deindustrialization in Pittsburgh*. Pittsburgh: Pennsylvania State University Press, 1993.

Hattam, Victoria. *Labor Visions and State Power: The Origins of Business Unionism in the US.* Princeton, N.J.: Princeton University Press, 1993.

Hauk, Jake. *The Case for Privatizing the Kane Regional Centers.* Pittsburgh, Pa.: Allegheny Institute for Public Policy, 1997.

Health Care Financing Administration. "Report to Congress: Appropriateness of Minimum Nurse Staffing Ratios in Nursing Homes." 2000. Retrieved from www.hcfa.gov/medicaid/reports/rp700hmp.html.

Heckscher, Charles. "Living with Flexibility." In *Rekindling the Movement: Labor's Quest for Relevance in the 21st Century*, edited by Lowell Turner, Harry Katz, and Richard Hurd, pp. 59–81. Ithaca, N.Y.: Cornell University Press, 2001.

Herzenberg, Stephen. Testimony before Pittsburgh Area Religious Task Force on the Economy, March 1997.

Herzenberg, Stephen, John Alic, and Howard Wial. *New Rules for a New Economy: Employment and Opportunity in Postindustrial America.* Ithaca, N.Y.: ILR Press, 1998.

Hirsch, Eric. "Sacrifice for the Cause: The Impact of Group Processes on Recruitment and Commitment in Social Movements." *American Sociological Review* 55 (1990): 243–54.

Hoerr, John. *And the Wolf Finally Came: The Decline of the American Steel Industry.* Pittsburgh, Pa.: University of Pittsburgh Press, 1988.

Hume, Brit. *Death and the Mines: Rebellion and Murder in the United Mine Workers.* New York: Grossman, 1971.

Hurd, Richard, and Joseph Uehlein. "Patterned Responses to Organizing: Case Studies of the Union Busting Convention." In *Restoring the Promise of American Labor Law*, edited by Sheldon Friedman, Richard W. Hurd, Rudolph A. Oswald, and Ronald L. Seeber, pp. 61–74. Ithaca, N.Y.: ILR Press, 1994.

Jenkins, J. Craig. "Radical Transformation of Organizational Goals." *Administrative Science Quarterly* 22 (1977): 568–86.

Jenkins, J. Craig, and Craig Eckert. "Elite Patronage and the Channeling of Social Protest." *American Sociological Review* 51 (1986): 812–29.

Jenkins, J. Craig, and Charles Perrow. "Insurgency of the Powerless Farm Worker Movements." *American Sociological Review* 42 (1977): 249–68.

Johnston, Paul. *Success While Others Fail: Social Movement Unionism and the Public Workplace.* Ithaca, N.Y.: ILR Press, 1994.

———. "The Resurgence of Labor as a Citizenship Movement in the New Labor Relations Environment." *Critical Sociology* 26 (2000): 139–60.

Jones, Adrienne. *The National Nursing Home Survey: 1999 Summary.* Washington, D.C.: U.S. Department of Human Services, Centers for Disease Control and Prevention, National Center for Health Statistics, 2002.

"Judge Orders Wal-Mart to Recognize Union Formed by Meat-Cutters." *Associated Press State and Local Wire,* June 18, 2003.

Juravich, Tom, and Kate Bronfenbrenner. *Ravenswood: The Steelworkers' Victory and the Revival of American Labor.* Ithaca, N.Y.: ILR Press, 1999.

Kane, Robert. "Long-Term Care in the United States: Problems and Promise." In *Economic Security and Intergenerational Justice,* edited by Timothy Smeeding, Theodore Marmor, and Vernon Green, pp. 287–302. Washington, D.C.: Urban Institute Press, 1994.

Katz, Harry. "Whither the American Labor Movement?" In *Rekindling the Movement: Labor's Quest for Relevance in the 21st Century,* edited by Lowell Turner, Harry Katz, and Richard Hurd, pp. 339–49. Ithaca, N.Y.: Cornell University Press, 2001.

Kaufman, Bruce, and Paula Stephan. "The Role of Management Attorneys in Union Organizing Campaigns." *Journal of Labor Research* 16 (1995): 439–54.

Kay, Tamara. "Bypassing the Captured State: Globalization, Labor Law, and Union Organizing Strategies in Mexico and the United States." Paper presented at the annual meeting of the International Sociological Association, Montreal, July 1998.

Kimeldorf, Howard. *Battling for American Labor: Wobblies, Craft Workers, and the Making of the Union Movement.* Berkeley: University of California Press, 1999.

Kingsolver, Barbara. *Holding the Line: Women in the Great Arizona Mining Strike of 1983.* Ithaca, N.Y.: ILR Press, 1989.

Kitts, James A. "Not in Our Backyard: Solidarity, Social Networks, and the Ecology of Environmental Mobilization." *Sociological Inquiry* 69 (1999): 551–74.

———. "Mobilizing in Black Boxes: Social Networks and Participation in Social Movement Organizations." *Mobilization* 5 (2000): 241–57.

Klandermans, Bert. "Mobilization and Participation: Social-Psychological Extensions of Resource Mobilization Theory." *American Sociological Review* 49 (1984): 583–600.

———. "The Formation and Mobilization of Consensus." *International Social Movement Research* 1 (1988): 173–96.

———. *The Social Psychology of Protest.* Oxford, England: Blackwell, 1997.

Klandermans, Bert, and Dirk Oegema. "Campaigning for a Nuclear Freeze: Grassroots Strategies and Local Government in the Netherlands." In

Research in Political Sociology, edited by Richard Braungart, pp. 305–37. Greenwich, Conn.: JAI Press, 1987.

Kleidman, Robert. "Volunteer Activism and Professionalism in Social Movement Organizations." *Social Problems* 41 (1994): 257–76.

Kleiner, Morris. "Intensity of Management Resistance: Understanding the Decline of Unionization in the Private Sector." *Journal of Labor Research* 22 (2001): 519–40.

Kochan, Thomas A., Harry C. Katz, and Robert B. McKersie. *The Transformation of American Industrial Relations*. New York: Basic Books, 1986.

Koopmans, Ruud. "The Dynamics of Protest Waves: West Germany, 1965 to 1969." *American Sociological Review* 58 (1993): 637–58.

Kriesi, Hanspeter, Ruud Koopmans, and Jan Willem Duyvendak. *New Social Movements in Western Europe: A Comparative Analysis*. Minneapolis: University of Minnesota Press, 1995.

LaLonde, Robert, and Bernard Meltzer. "Hard Times for Unions: Another Look at the Significance of Employer Illegalities." *University of Chicago Law Review* 58 (1991): 953–1014.

Lawler, John. *Unionization and De-Unionization: Strategy, Tactics, and Outcomes*. Columbia: University of South Carolina Press, 1990.

LeBeau, Josephine, and Kevin Lynch. "Successful Organizing at the Local Level: The Experience of AFSCME District Council 1707." In *A New Labor Movement for a New Century*, edited by Gregory Mantsios, pp. 104–18. New York: Monthly Review Press, 1998.

Lerner, Stephen. "Taking the Offensive, Turning the Tide." In *A New Labor Movement for a New Century*, edited by Gregory Mantsios, pp. 69–81. New York: Monthly Review Press, 1998.

Levine, David. *Reinventing the Workplace*. Washington, D.C.: Brookings Institution, 1995.

Levitt, Martin. *Confessions of a Union Buster*. New York: Crown, 1993.

Lipietz, Alain. *Towards a New Economic Order: Postfordism, Ecology, and Democracy*. New York: Oxford University Press, 1992.

Lipset, C. Martin, Martin Trow, and James Coleman. *Union Democracy: The Inside Politics of the International Typographical Union*. New York: Free Press, 1956.

Lubove, Roy. *Twentieth-Century Pittsburgh: The Post-Steel Era*. Pittsburgh, Pa.: University of Pittsburgh Press, 1996.

Magrini, Sali, and 50 Other Kane Workers. "The County Has Not Listened to

Workers on Improving the Kanes." *Pittsburgh Post-Gazette*, November 11, 1996.

Mantsios, Gregory. "What Does Labor Stand For?" In *A New Labor Movement for a New Century*, edited by Gregory Mantsios, pp. 44–64. New York: Monthly Review Press, 1998.

Markowitz, Linda. "Union Presentation of Self and Worker Participation in Organizing Campaigns." *Sociological Perspectives* 38 (1995): 437–54.

———. *Worker Activism after Successful Union Organizing.* Armonk, N.Y.: M. E. Sharpe, 2000.

McAdam, Doug. *Political Process and the Development of Black Insurgency, 1930–1970.* Chicago: University of Chicago Press, 1982.

———. "Tactical Innovation and the Pace of Insurgency." *American Sociological Review* 48 (1983): 735–54.

———. "Recruitment to High-Risk Activism: The Case of Freedom Summer." *American Journal of Sociology* 92 (1986): 64–90.

———. *Freedom Summer.* New York: Oxford University Press, 1988.

McAdam, Doug, John D. McCarthy, and Mayer Zald, eds. *Comparative Perspectives on Social Movements: Political Opportunities, Mobilizing Structures, and Cultural Framings.* New York: Cambridge University Press, 1996.

McAdam, Doug, and Ronnelle Paulsen. "Specifying the Relationship between Social Ties and Activism." *American Journal of Sociology* 99 (1993): 640–67.

McAdam, Doug, Sydney Tarrow, and Charles Tilly. *Dynamics of Contention.* New York: Cambridge University Press, 2001.

McCarthy, John D., and Mayer Zald. *The Trend of Social Movements in America: Professionalization and Resource Mobilization.* Morristown, N.J.: General Learning Press, 1973.

———. "Resource Mobilization and Social Movements: A Partial Theory." *American Journal of Sociology* 82 (1977): 1212–41.

McDonough, James. *John J. Kane Regional Centers: Privatization Options.* Pittsburgh, Pa.: Allegheny Institute for Public Policy, 1996.

McLewin, Philip. "The Concerted Voice of Labor and the Suburbanization of Capital: Fragmentation of the Community Labor Council." In *Which Direction for Organized Labor? Essays on Organizing, Outreach, and Internal Transformations*, edited by Bruce Nissen, pp. 113–32. Detroit: Wayne State University Press, 1999.

Melucci, Alberto. "The New Social Movements: A Theoretical Approach." *Social Science Information* 19 (1980): 199–226.

————. *Nomads of the Present: Social Movements and Individual Needs in Contemporary Society.* Philadelphia: Temple University Press, 1989.

————. "A Strange Kind of Newness: What's New in New Social Movements." In *New Social Movements: From Ideology to Identity,* edited by Enrique Laraña, Hank Johnston, and Joseph Gusfield, pp. 101–32. Philadelphia: Temple University Press, 1994.

————. *Challenging Codes: Collective Action in the Information Age.* New York: Cambridge University Press, 1996.

Meyer, David, and Suzanne Staggenborg. "Movements, Countermovements, and the Structure of Political Opportunity." *American Journal of Sociology* 101 (1996): 1628–60.

Michelmore, David. "Democrats Match GOP Vow of 20% Cut in County Millage." *Pittsburgh Post-Gazette,* September 16, 1995.

Michels, Robert. *Political Parties: A Sociological Study of the Oligarchical Tendencies of Modern Democracy.* 1915. Reprint, New York: Collier Books, 1962.

Milkman, Ruth. "The New Labor Movement: Possibilities and Limits." *Contemporary Sociology* 27, no. 2 (1998): 125–29.

————, ed. *Organizing Immigrants: The Challenge for Unions and Workers in Contemporary California.* Ithaca, N.Y.: ILR Press, 2000.

Milkman, Ruth, and Kent Wong. "Organizing Immigrant Workers: Case Studies from Southern California." In *Rekindling the Movement: Labor's Quest for Relevance in the 21st Century,* edited by Lowell Turner, Harry Katz, and Richard Hurd, pp. 99–128. Ithaca, N.Y.: Cornell University Press, 2001.

Moody, Kim. *An Injury to All: The Decline of American Unionism.* New York: Verso, 1988.

————. *Workers in a Lean World: Unions in the International Economy.* New York: Verso, 1997.

Morris, Aldon. "Black Southern Student Sit-in Movement: An Analysis of Internal Organization." *American Sociological Review* 46 (1981): 744–67.

————. *The Origins of the Civil Rights Movement: Black Communities Organizing for Change.* New York: Free Press, 1984.

National Labor Relations Board. Case 6-CA-27453, *Complaint and Notice of Hearing.* 1996.

————. Cases 6-CA-27452 and 6-CA-27581, *Order Consolidating Cases, Consolidated Amended Complaint and Notice of Hearing and Order Rescheduling Hearing in Case 6-CA-27581.* 1996.

————. Cases 6-CA-27873 et al., *Decision and Statement of the Case.* 1997.

————. Cases 6-CA-28276 et al., *Decision and Statement of the Case.* 2000.

Needleman, Ruth. "Building Relationships for the Long Haul: Unions and Community Organizing Groups Working Together to Organize Low-Wage Workers." In *Organizing to Win: New Research on Union Strategies*, edited by Kate Bronfenbrenner, Sheldon Friedman, Richard W. Hurd, Rudolph A. Oswald, and Ronald L. Seeber, pp. 71–86. Ithaca, N.Y.: ILR Press, 1998.

Nissen, Bruce. "Utilizing the Membership to Organize the Unorganized." In *Organizing to Win: New Research on Union Strategies*, edited by Kate Bronfenbrenner, Sheldon Friedman, Richard W. Hurd, Rudolph A. Oswald, and Ronald L. Seeber, pp. 135–49. Ithaca, N.Y.: ILR Press, 1998.

———. "The Recent Past and Near Future of Private Sector Unionism in the U.S.: An Appraisal." *Journal of Labor Research* 24 (2003): 323–38.

Oberschall, Anthony. *Social Conflict and Social Movements*. Englewood Cliffs, N.J.: Prentice Hall, 1973.

———. "The Decline of the 1960s Social Movements." *Research in Social Movements, Conflicts and Change* 1 (1978): 257–89. Greenwich, Conn.: JAI Press.

O'Connor, James. *The Fiscal Crisis of the State*. New York: St. Martin's Press, 1973.

Offe, Claus, and Helmut Wiesenthal. "Two Logics of Collective Action: Theoretical Notes on Social Class and Organizational Form." *Political Power and Social Theory* 1 (1980): 67–115.

Olson, Mancur. *The Logic of Collective Action: Public Goods and the Theory of Groups*. Cambridge, Mass.: Harvard University Press, 1965.

Opp, Karl-Dieter, and Christiane Gern. "Dissident Groups, Personal Networks, and Spontaneous Cooperation: The East German Revolution of 1989." *American Sociological Review* 58 (1993): 659–80.

Parker, Mike, and Jane Slaughter. *Working Smart: A Union Guide to Participation Programs and Reengineering*. Detroit: Labor Notes Book, 1994.

Payne, Melanie. "Unions Gain in Public Sector as Private Membership Drops." *Sacramento Bee*, March 11, 2002.

Peters, Ronald, and Theresa Merrill. "Clergy and Religious Persons' Roles in Organizing at O'Hare Airport and St. Joseph Medical Center." In *Organizing to Win: New Research on Union Strategies*, edited by Kate Bronfenbrenner, Sheldon Friedman, Richard W. Hurd, Rudolph A. Oswald, and Ronald L. Seeber, pp. 164–77. Ithaca, N.Y.: ILR Press, 1998.

Peterson, Richard B., Thomas W. Lee, and Barbara Finnegan. "Strategies and Tactics in Union Organizing Campaigns." *Industrial Relations* 31 (1992): 371–81.

Piore, Michael. "Unions: A Reorientation to Survive." In *Labor Economics and*

Industrial Relations, edited by Clark Kerr and Paul Staudohar, pp. 512–41. Cambridge, Mass.: Harvard University Press, 1994.

Pittsburgh City Council. "Statement in Support of Megacorp Nursing Home Workers." March 16, 1996.

Piven, Frances Fox, and Richard A. Cloward. *Poor People's Movements: Why They Succeed, How They Fail.* New York: Random House, 1977.

Potter, Edward. "Love's Labor Lost? Changes in the U.S. Environment and Declining Private Sector Unionism." *Journal of Labor Research* 22 (2001): 321–34.

Puette, William J. *Through Jaundiced Eyes: How the Media Views Organized Labor.* Ithaca, N.Y.: ILR Press, 1992.

Rachleff, Peter. *Hard Times in the Heartland.* Boston: South End Press, 1993.

———. "Organizing Wall to Wall: The Independent Union of All Workers, 1933–37." In *"We Are All Leaders": The Alternative Unionism of the Early 1930s*, edited by Staughton Lynd, pp. 51–71. Urbana: University of Illinois Press, 1996.

Rathke, Wade. "Letting More Flowers Bloom under the Setting Sun." In *Which Direction for Organized Labor? Essays on Organizing, Outreach, and Internal Transformations*, edited by Bruce Nissen, pp. 75–94. Detroit: Wayne State University Press, 1999.

Reich, Robert. *The Work of Nations: Preparing Ourselves for 21st Century Capitalism.* New York: Knopf, 1991.

Rifkin, Jeremy. *The End of Work: The Decline of the Global Labor Force and the Dawn of the Post-Market Era.* New York: Putnam, 1995.

Robinson, Ian. "Neoliberal Restructuring and US Unions: Toward Social Movement Unionism?" *Critical Sociology* 26, no. 1 (2000): 109–38.

Rothstein, Richard. "Toward a More Perfect Union: New Labor's Hard Road." *American Prospect* 26 (1996): 47–53.

Rucht, Dieter. "Environmental Organizations in West Germany and France: Structure and Interorganizational Relations." *International Social Movement Research* 2 (1989): 61–94.

Russo, John, and Brian Corbin. "A System of Interpretation: Catholic Social Teaching and American Unionism," *Conflict* 11, no. 4 (1991): 237–66.

———. "Work, Organized Labor, and the Catholic Church: Boundaries and Opportunities for Community/Labor Coalitions." In *Which Direction for Organized Labor? Essays on Organizing, Outreach, and Internal Transformations*, edited by Bruce Nissen, pp. 95–112. Detroit: Wayne State University Press, 1999.

Sabel, Charles. "Bootstrapping Reform: Rebuilding Firms, the Welfare State, and Unions." *Politics and Society* 23, no. 1 (1995): 5–40.

Schlosser, Eric. *Fast Food Nation: The Dark Side of the All-American Meal.* Boston: Houghton Mifflin, 2001.

Sciacchitano, Katherine. "Finding the Community in the Union and the Union in the Community: The First-Contract Campaign at Steeltech." In *Organizing to Win: New Research on Union Strategies*, edited by Kate Bronfenbrenner, Sheldon Friedman, Richard W. Hurd, Rudolph A. Oswald, and Ronald L. Seeber, pp. 150–63. Ithaca, N.Y.: ILR Press, 1998.

Serrin, William. *Homestead: The Glory and Tragedy of an American Steel Town.* New York: Times Books, 1992.

Service Employees International Union. *Pennsylvania Dignity Campaign: Bargaining News Flash*, November 27, 1995.

———. "Support the Megacorp Bill." 1996.

———. *Megacorp Bulletin*, various dates, 1995–97.

———. *Caring Till It Hurts.* Washington, D.C.: Service Employees International Union, 1997.

Shaiken, Harley. "Advanced Manufacturing and Mexico: A New International Division of Labor?" *Latin American Research Review* 29, no. 2 (1994): 39–72.

Shaiken, Harley, Steve Lopez, and Isaac Mankita. "Two Routes to Team Production: Saturn and Chrysler Compared." *Industrial Relations* 36 (1997): 17–45.

Shailor, Barbara, and George Kourpias. "Developing and Enforcing International Labor Standards." In *A New Labor Movement for a New Century*, edited by Gregory Mantsios, pp. 277–85. New York: Monthly Review Press, 1998.

Shostak, Arthur. *Robust Unionism: Innovations in the Labor Movement.* Ithaca, N.Y.: ILR Press, 1991.

Smith, Christian. *Resisting Reagan: The U.S. Central America Peace Movement.* Chicago: University of Chicago Press, 1996.

Snow, David A., and Robert D. Benford. "Ideology, Frame Resonance, and Participant Mobilization." *International Social Movement Research* 1 (1988): 197–218.

Snow, David A., Louis A. Zurcher, Jr., and Sheldon Ekland-Olson. "Social Networks and Social Movements: A Microstructural Approach to Differential Recruitment." *American Sociological Review* 45 (1980): 787–801.

Southwestern Pennsylvania Economic Redevelopment Committee. *Pittsburgh Labor Market Study.* Pittsburgh: Southwestern Pennsylvania Economic Redevelopment Committee, 1995.

Staggenborg, Suzanne. "Coalition Work in the Pro-Choice Movement: Organizational and Environmental Opportunities and Obstacles." *Social Problems* 33 (1986): 374–90.

———. "The Consequences of Professionalization and Formalization in the Pro-Choice Movement." *American Sociological Review* 53 (1988): 585–606.

Stepan-Norris, Judith, and Maurice Zeitlin. "Union Democracy, Radical Leadership, and the Hegemony of Capital." *American Sociological Review* 60 (1995): 829–50.

Strauss, George. "Is the New Deal System Collapsing? With What Might It Be Replaced?" *Industrial Relations* 34 (1995): 329–49.

Tarrow, Sidney. "National Politics and Collective Action: Recent Theory and Research in Western Europe and the United States." *Annual Review of Sociology* 14 (1988): 421–40.

———. *Power in Movement: Social Movements, Collective Action, and Politics.* New York: Cambridge University Press, 1994.

Tilly, Charles. *From Mobilization to Revolution.* Reading, Mass.: Addison-Wesley, 1978.

Touraine, Alain. *Post-Industrial Society: Tomorrow's Social History. Classes, Conflicts, and Culture in the Programmed Society.* New York: Random House, 1971.

———. "An Introduction to the Study of Social Movements." *Social Research* 52 (1985): 749–87.

Turner, Lowell. "Rank and File Participation in Organizing at Home and Abroad." In *Organizing to Win: New Research on Union Strategies*, edited by Kate Bronfenbrenner, Sheldon Friedman, Richard W. Hurd, Rudolph A. Oswald, and Ronald L. Seeber, pp. 123–34. Ithaca, N.Y.: ILR Press, 1998.

Turner, Lowell, and Richard Hurd. "Building Social Movement Unionism: The Transformation of the American Labor Movement." In *Rekindling the Movement: Labor's Quest for Relevance in the 21st Century*, edited by Lowell Turner, Harry Katz, and Richard Hurd, pp. 9–26. Ithaca, N.Y.: Cornell University Press, 2001.

"UFCW, AFL-CIO Join in Wal-Mart Campaign." *Label Letter, Union Label and Service Trades Department, AFL-CIO* 25 (March/April 2000): 1.

U.S. Bureau of Labor Statistics. "Pittsburgh Area Jobs up 1.8 Percent since First Quarter 1998." 2000. Retrieved from ftp://ftp.bls.gov/pub/special.requests/philadelphia/cesqpit.txt.

———. "Current Employment Statistics/Local Area Unemployment Statistics, Not Seasonally Adjusted." 2000. Retrieved from ftp://ftp.bls.gov/pub/special.requests/philadelphia/fax_9529.txt.

———. "Metropolitan Area at a Glance." 2003. Retrieved from www.bls.gov/eag/eag.pa_pittsburgh.htm.

U.S. Bureau of the Census. "1990 Census of Population and Housing." Summary Tape File 3.

———. *County Business Patterns.* Washington, D.C.: U.S. Department of Commerce, various years.

Useem, Bert, and Mayer Zald. "From Pressure Group to Social Movement: Efforts to Promote the Use of Nuclear Power." *Social Problems* 30 (1982): 144–56.

Vigilante, Richard. *Strike: The Daily News War and the Future of American Labor.* New York: Simon and Schuster, 1994.

Voss, Kim, and Rachel Sherman. "Breaking the Iron Law of Oligarchy: Union Revitalization in the American Labor Movement." *American Journal of Sociology* 106 (2002): 303–49.

Waldinger, Roger, and Claudia Der-Martirosian. "Immigrant Workers and American Labor: Challenge . . . or Disaster?" In *Organizing Immigrants: The Challenge for Unions in Contemporary California*, edited by Ruth Milkman, pp. 49–80. Ithaca, N.Y.: ILR Press, 2000.

Waldinger, Roger, Chris Erickson, Ruth Milkman, Daniel J. B. Mitchell, Abel Valenguela, Kent Wong, and Maurice Zeitlin. "Helots No More: A Case Study of the Justice for Janitors Campaign in Los Angeles." In *Organizing to Win: New Research on Union Strategies*, edited by Kate Bronfenbrenner, Sheldon Friedman, Richard W. Hurd, Rudolph A. Oswald, and Ronald L. Seeber, pp. 102–20. Ithaca, N.Y.: ILR Press, 1998.

Weikle, Roger, Hoyt Wheeler, and John McClendon. "A Comparative Case Study of Union Success and Failure." In *Organizing to Win: New Research on Union Strategies*, edited by Kate Bronfenbrenner, Sheldon Friedman, Richard W. Hurd, Rudolph A. Oswald, and Ronald L. Seeber, pp. 197–212. Ithaca, N.Y.: ILR Press, 1998.

Weiler, Paul. "Promises to Keep: Securing Workers' Rights to Self-Organization under the NLRA." *Harvard Law Review* 96 (1983): 1769–1827.

———. "Striking a New Balance: Freedom of Contract and the Prospects for Union Representation." *Harvard Law Review* 98 (1984): 351–420.

———. *Governing the Workplace: The Future of Labor and Employment Law.* Cambridge, Mass.: Harvard University Press, 1990.

Weinbaum, Eva. "Organizing Labor in an Era of Contingent Work and Globalization." In *Which Direction for Organized Labor? Essays on Organizing, Out-*

reach, and Internal Transformations, edited by Bruce Nissen, pp. 37–58. Detroit: Wayne State University Press, 1999.

Wells, Miriam. "Immigration and Unionization in the San Francisco Hotel Industry." In *Organizing Immigrants: The Challenge for Unions in Contemporary California,* edited by Ruth Milkman, pp. 109–29. Ithaca, N.Y.: ILR Press, 2000.

Whittier, Nancy. *Feminist Generations: The Persistence of the Radical Women's Movement.* Philadelphia: Temple University Press, 1995.

Wial, Howard. "The Emerging Structure of Low-Wage Services." *Rutgers Law Review* 45 (1993): 671–738.

Williams, Jane. "Restructuring Labor's Identity: The Justice for Janitors Campaign in Washington, D.C." In *The Transformation of U.S. Unions: Voices, Visions, and Strategies from the Grassroots,* edited by Ray Tillman and Michael Cummings, pp. 203–17. Boulder, Colo.: Lynne Rienner, 1999.

Wood, Ellen M. "Labor, Class, and State in Global Capitalism." In *Rising from the Ashes? Labor in the Age of "Global" Capitalism,* edited by Ellen M. Wood, Peter Meiksins, and Michael Yates, pp. 3–16. New York: Monthly Review Press, 1998.

Wunderlich, Gooloo, Frank Sloan, and Carolyne Davice, eds. *Nursing Staff in Hospitals and Nursing Homes: Is It Adequate?* Washington, D.C.: National Academy Press, 1996.

Yates, Michael. *Power on the Job: The Legal Rights of Working People.* Boston: South End Press, 1994.

Zald, Mayer, and Roberta Ash. "Social Movement Organizations: Growth, Decay, and Change." *Social Forces* 44 (1966): 327–40.

Zald, Mayer, and John D. McCarthy. "Social Movement Industries: Competition and Cooperation among Social Movement Organizations." *Research in Social Movements, Conflict and Change* 3 (1980): 1–20.

Zald, Mayer, and Bert Useem. "Movement and Countermovement Interaction: Mobilization, Tactics, and State Involvement." In *Social Movements in an Organizational Society,* edited by Mayer Zald and John McCarthy, pp. 247–71. New Brunswick, N.J.: Transaction Books, 1987.

INDEX

Compositor:	BookMatters, Berkeley
Text:	10/15 Janson
Display:	Janson
Printer and Binder:	Sheridan Books, Inc.